Descartes
and the
Resilience
of Rhetoric

Varieties of Cartesian
Rhetorical Theory

Thomas M. Carr, Jr.

Southern Illinois University Press
Carbondale and Edwardsville

Library of Congress Cataloging-in-Publication Data

Carr, Thomas M., 1944–
   Descartes and the resilience of rhetoric : varieties of
Cartesian rhetorical theory / by Thomas M. Carr, Jr.
      p. cm.
   Bibliography: p.
   Includes index.
   1. Descartes, René, 1596–1650—Views on rhetoric. 2.
Rhetoric—Philosophy—History—17th century. 3. Rhetoric—
France—History—17th century. 4. Balzac, Jean-Louis Guez,
seigneur de, 1597–1654—Views on rhetoric. 5. Philosophy,
French—17th century.
   I. Title.
B1878.R47C37 1990
194—dc19   88-33376
ISBN 0–8093–1557–2   CIP

The paper used in this publication meets the minimum
requirements of American National Standard for
Information Sciences—Permanence of Paper for
Printed Library Materials, ANSI Z39.48-1984. ∞

Contents

Preface

This study originated far from Descartes in my efforts to understand what eighteenth-century writers meant when they invoked *le coeur et l'esprit* to account for persuasion. My inquiry into the role of the heart and the mind led back to how Cartesian psychology and physiology came to be adapted in seventeenth-century rhetorical thought.

In the case of France's two most illustrious philosophers of the seventeenth century, the approach I adopt is largely reconstructive. While both Descartes and Malebranche wrote short texts dealing specifically with the theory of eloquence, rhetoric was a topic on which neither commented extensively with all the rigor and method he was capable of bringing to an issue. My task involves situating their rather brief direct comments on rhetorical issues in the context of their vision of human nature.

In chapter 2, I show how Descartes considered the rhetorical tradition dating from antiquity irrelevant to his project of winning converts to his thought by comparing him to a fellow modernist, Jean-Louis Guez de Balzac, who sought to adapt the humanist tradition to the emerging culture of the *honnête homme*. In chapter 3, I analyze the rhetorical theory that can be generated from Descartes' notion of persuasion when it is combined with his psychophysiology of attention.

My discussion of Arnauld and Nicole in chapter 4 serves as a link between Descartes and subsequent Augustinians such as Malebranche and Lamy. Because of their concern for method, the Port-Royalists set as one of the principal goals of their *Logique de Port-Royal* the task of neutralizing the erroneous judgments induced by false eloquence. Such showy eloquence weakens the mind's capacity for attention by seducing it with the sense impressions that have bedazzled the mind since the Fall. However, their amalgam of Descartes and Augustine contains the seeds of a more positive view of eloquence. Their concepts of accessory ideas and of vivacity go beyond Descartes' sketchy linguistic comments to formulate a theory of the figures that Lamy exploits to full advantage.

In chapter 5, I examine Malebranche, who is best known for his denunciation of eloquence as a contagion. He exploits Cartesian psychophysiology to show how the imaginations of weak-minded individuals are infected by the appeal to the senses made by vigorous speakers. Imitation replaces judgment; the passions contaminate reason. However, this rhetoric of distraction, while better known, is only a part of Malebranche's account of persuasion. Combining Descartes and Augustine, he elaborates a notion of attention as mental prayer in which the senses and passions play a legitimate role. Furthermore, he invokes the concept of the Word made flesh in the Incarnation to justify an eloquence in which the corporal leads to the spiritual.

In chapter 6, I deal with Lamy, who produced the most comprehensive rhetorical treatise written by an advocate of the new philosophy, and whose text combines the humanist tradition with Cartesian science. Lamy uses Cartesian psychophysiology to define rhetoric broadly as the transmission of the speaker's thoughts and emotions in his widely influential *La Rhétorique ou l'art de parler,* which he constantly reworked between its initial publication in 1675 and his death in 1715. Within this art of speaking he reserves a space for eloquence with its own legitimate forms of proof and vivid style alongside geometric or philosophic discourse. His eloquence corresponds in many ways to Pascal's art of pleasing (*art d'agréer*), but whereas Pascal had despaired of fixing rules for winning over the fallen will, Lamy is confident that the new philosophy provides a knowledge of the heart sufficient to found a science of persuasion.

I am responsible for all translations from French and Latin. For modern commentators I cite the French text, although only the English translation is given. For seventeenth-century writers, the original French with modernized spelling follows the English translation. In the case of works by Descartes that were written in Latin but not translated by him or by some authorized representative (e.g., the *Regulae*), I append the original Latin text.

My thanks go to Emily Carr, Elaine Crawford, and Dale Hoyt who read portions of the manuscript.

I am especially indebted to two colleagues, Ralph Albanese, Jr.

and Dennis Bormann, for their encouragement and willingnesss to share their command of seventeenth- and eighteenth-century literature and rhetorical theory. Their critiques and thoughtful reading of the manuscript have been invaluable. I am grateful to the Rev. Roger J. Bunday for his willingness to listen to me discuss the project over the years and for his help with the translations from Latin. In Chul Shin also worked with me on the Latin translations. I also wish to acknowledge the financial support of the Research Council of the University of Nebraska-Lincoln at various stages of the project.

Descartes and the
Resilience of Rhetoric

1
Introduction

I thirsted for the broader rivers of
eloquence most ardently. But as
they make one crave more knowledge rather than quench one's
thirst, they could not satisfy me in
the least.

Latiora eloquentiae flumina cupi-
dissime sitiebam. Neque vero his,
quae scilicet sciendi sitim dant potius quam sedant, ullo modo satiatus.

Descartes, Dedication of his
thesis for his law degree

Descartes' earliest texts attest to his frustration with eloquence.
The recently discovered dedication of the theses he defended at
age twenty for his law degree at Poitiers in 1616 indicts the
rhetoric he had studied with the Jesuits for its failure to satisfy
his thirst for knowledge.

This distaste for formal rhetoric—one might even say Descartes' hostility toward it—is now a commonplace in the study
of the European rhetorical tradition. In fact, Cartesianism has
become a touchstone for those who seek to renew the ancient art
in various guises. Chaïm Perelman's efforts to revitalize argumentation as a "new rhetoric" were designed to overcome the
discredit Descartes' emphasis on self-evidence cast on the probable, the traditional domain of rhetoric.[1] Contemporary advocates
of Vico, who hope to reunite philosophy and rhetoric, amplify
Vico's contrast between the sterile geometric method of the
Cartesians and the creative power of the imagination that grasps
truth as metaphor rather than as clear and distinct ideas.[2] Decon-

structionists, whose origins have sometimes been traced back to Nietzsche's early lectures on rhetoric, have expressed discontent with pairings such as philosophy/rhetoric, in which the second term is devalued, and have pointed to the unstable status of the *cogito* as an exemplary case of how such oppositions can be dismantled.[3]

However, in spite of what Henri Gouhier has described as Descartes' aspiration toward a philosophy without rhetoric, a philosophy whose basis is a rational certainty immediately apparent to all,[4] any number of studies have shown that Descartes makes as skillful use of the rhetorician's stratagems as any orator.[5] Pierre-Alain Cahné has pointed out that many of Descartes' images, long thought to be similes providing rhetorical illustration, are in fact heuristic tools that give birth to concepts later presented in mathematical form.[6] To some extent they may be seen as satisfying Vico's desire to unite science and eloquence through metaphor. Similarly, Malebranche was early accused of using the imagination to write against the imagination. Thus, Cartesian rhetorical praxis is perhaps not so much at issue as Cartesian rhetorical theory.

Rhetoric, of course, is a protean discipline. Throughout this study my stress is on rhetoric as the notion of persuasion as seen by Descartes and a series of thinkers who drew heavily on him. I examine the implications for persuasion of their epistemological and psychological views rather than the varied strategies marshalled to win over readers, that is, their theory rather than their performance or the tension between the two.

I use the term *Cartesian rhetorical theory* as a shorthand notation for rhetorical theory among Cartesians, for a loose problematic of persuasion implicit in Descartes' thought. The resistance to Noam Chomsky's *Cartesian linguistics* is a reminder of the limits of positing, after the fact, the existence of such an archetype. The view of rhetoric of Descartes' admirers and disciples was never merely an extension of the problematic found in his writings since they brought to the question their own agendas and were subject to other influences.

My aim is an assessment of the contours of their theories, not a comprehensive history of Cartesian rhetoric. In the seventeenth century alone such a history might include writers such as

Gérauld de Cordemoy (whose 1668 *Discours physique de la parole* finds in Descartes' mind/body doctrine a metaphysical rationale for an eloquence that is civic in character) or the debate over the role of the imagination in religious oratory at the end of the century that involved, among others, Goibaud Dubois and Francois Lamy.

Nevertheless, it is helpful to keep in mind that the writers I have chosen—Descartes, the Port-Royalists Antoine Arnauld and Pierre Nicole, Nicolas Malebranche, and Bernard Lamy—were all major actors in the historical process that Hugh Davidson has described as the attrition of the rhetoric inherited from classical antiquity in seventeenth-century France.[7] In fact, in the Port-Royalists and Malebranche we find the convergence of the two major challenges that Davidson identifies to the Ciceronian view of rhetoric as the architectonic discipline of all verbal expression: the method of the new science stemming from Descartes and the Augustinian Counter-Reformation's subordination of literature to religious truth.

Davidson rightly notes the phoenixlike quality of rhetoric, its ability to reappear in new guises just when it appears to have been discounted. He points to the use by Fontenelle and by Voltaire of belletristic devices to vulgarize Cartesian and Newtonian astronomy. However, I stress that we need not wait for their scientific popularization or even for Bernard Lamy's more theoretical synthesis of traditional rhetoric, Descartes' psychophysiology, and Augustinian currents to find evidence of rhetoric's resilience. We can discover a theoretical justification for persuasive discourse even within the systems of such detractors of traditional rhetoric as Descartes or Malebranche, if we take as our point of departure the perennial questions surrounding persuasion itself rather than the particular solution to these problems that Ciceronian eloquence represents.

The problematic that shaped rhetorical thought for many seventeenth-century Cartesians—especially those with an Augustinian inclination such as the Port-Royalists, Malebranche, and Lamy—has three components, the heritage of Descartes himself, the concepts exemplified by the comments of Pascal, and a primarily linguistic element.

The first concerns the space left for rhetoric by the Cartesian philosophy of self-evidence. Descartes' method, modeled on geometry with its claim of universal validity and its stress on clear and distinct ideas, tends to assimilate all forms of discourse, including eloquence. What room is left for the use of vivid figures of speech when clear expression of thought is prized? Can appeals to the imagination or emotions in order to move an audience to action be reconciled with the primacy of pure thought? Is it necessary to take into account the individual characteristics of particular audiences if a universally valid method can compel consent? The renewal of rhetoric in the hands of the Renaissance humanists seems aborted by Descartes' new philosophy.

However, Descartes' method leaves room for rhetoric if it is considered not in terms of its outward form—the geometric chains of proof—but in terms of its vivifying core, the notion of attention. Attention enjoys a privileged status in Cartesian epistemology. It unites the mind's two chief faculties (the will and the understanding) as the will focuses the gaze of the mind's eye ever more sharply on ideas perceived in the understanding. The process of distinguishing clear and distinct ideas leads to the judgment of *évidence,* in which the unity of the mind's active and passive dimensions as a single thinking substance is affirmed. At the same time, attention is one bridge across the radical discontinuity of Cartesian metaphysics, the distinction between *res cogitans* and *res extensa,* for attention can be fostered or hindered by the sense perceptions and passions that stem from the mind's union with the body.

Attention had not been considered extensively in Greek and Roman rhetorical theory. It was usually discussed briefly in the section of treatises dealing with the *exordium;* Quintilian, for example, suggests that the orator strive to gain the attention of the audience along with its good will and readiness at the beginning of the speech.[8] Given attention's position at the center of Descartes' psychophysiology, however, it is hardly surprising that Cartesians increasingly came to invoke it when considering rhetorical problems. This is especially true of the writers I have selected for study. It appealed to their intellectualist bias while allowing them to consider persuasion in light of the dynamics of the mind/body dichotomy. Descartes' notion of attention provided a tool for the psychological analysis of persuasion that could be integrated easily into an Augustinian perspective, as seen in Malebranche, for whom attention is a form of natural prayer. Lamy eventually transposes this often rather abstract discussion of attention's role in persuasion to a more practical plane by showing how a wide range of figures and tropes function as devices for promoting attentiveness.

The second component of the problematic was set forth in its most forceful way in a text written after Descartes' death. In his celebrated "De l'Art de persuader," Pascal inquires why so often the demonstration of truth is not enough to win over opponents. Transposed into more Cartesian terms, in this text Pascal grapples with the difficulty of achieving and communicating the irresistible certainty of *évidence*. Pascal notes that the will, in the grips of concupiscence, turns its back on truths conflicting with its desire for pleasure. To avoid squarely envisaging their fallen state, humans invent all manner of *divertissements* to distract them from contemplating their emptiness and corruption. This refusal to attend to humanity's true state described by Pascal parallels on a religious plane Descartes' epistemological explanation of how we can refuse to consent to self-evidence by turning our attention away from it. However, just as Pascal never formulated the concept of attention with all the rigor Descartes brings to the point, Descartes himself would have preferred not to invoke theological dogmas like the Fall. Combining the psychology and epistemology found in the new philosophy with the acute awareness of concupiscence stemming from Augustine was left to Cartesians such as Arnauld, Malebranche, and Bernard Lamy, who were as much at home with Augustine as with Descartes.

The final component of the problematic of Cartesian rhetoric is linguistic: the search for an adequate medium to transmit the mental experience that results in persuasion. Descartes' own treatment of language stressing the representation of univocal ideas is meager at best and is hardly suited to account for the figures of speech. Lamy's analysis of eloquence in his *Art de parler* is the culmination of a process that begins with the Port-Royalists, by which the emphasis shifts from the clarity of the ideas being represented (Descartes' chief concern) to the vivacity of the process of representation itself.

2

Descartes and Guez de Balzac

Humanist Eloquence Spurned

> Putting aside Eloquence for Mathe-
> matics is like growing sick of a mis-
> tress of eighteen to fall in love with
> an old crone.
>
> Quitter l'Eloquence pour les Ma-
> thématiques, c'est être dégoûté
> d'une maîtresse de dix-huit ans et
> devenir amoureux d'une vieille.
>
> Balzac, letter
to M. de Tissandier

My goal in this chapter and the next is neither to examine how
Descartes' rhetoric fits into his philosophical concerns, as Henri
Gouhier has done, nor to examine the various persuasive strategies he uses to win adherents to his system along the lines of the
analyses of Peter France or Sylvie Romanowski. Instead, I am interested in the consequences of his thought, especially his epistemological and psychological views, for rhetorical theory—the task
allotted to rhetoric, its legitimacy, and its functioning. The question is not so much what kind of rhetoric Descartes employed, or
its role in his philosophy (although both these topics are relevant),
as much as how his approach to the issues that had traditionally
been the province of rhetoricians was determined by his notions
about human nature and the operation of the mind.

The Eloquence of *L'Honnête Homme*

A preliminary discussion of a contemporary and friend of
Descartes, Jean-Louis Guez de Balzac, who was a conscious

spokesman for the heritage of eloquence handed down from classical Rome, is instructive. This pairing of the writer known during his lifetime as *Unico eloquente* and the philosopher of self-evidence might seem paradoxical at first, but it focuses attention on the degree to which Descartes dismisses the ancient art.

The pursuit of eloquence was a hallmark of Renaissance humanism from its beginnings in Italy. The humanists' recovery of the rhetorical texts of the mature Cicero (*De oratore* and *Brutus*), of Quintilian, and of Aristotle's *Poetics*, their interest in moral philosophy as opposed to the metaphysics and theology of the scholastics, and their new civic model all combined to create among intellectuals an ideal of learning and experience expressed with the prestige of a carefully wrought style—an ideal of wisdom wed to eloquence.[1]

In sixteenth-century France, this synthesis took many forms as humanism grew in stature and maturity and as the political and social climate evolved from the optimism of François I's reign through the turbulence of the Wars of Religion. Trends such as the growing importance of rhetorical instruction in the new colleges, the quarrels between partisans of Attic and Asiatic styles, and the new emphasis on preaching in the post-Trentine Church formed the setting for the experiments of eloquence of such humanists as Budé, Pasquier, Montaigne, and Du Vair. The efforts of all such writers to create a secular French prose can be grouped under what Marc Fumaroli has labeled "the Gallican Republic of Letters of the magistrates," characterized by a love of learned citations along with a deep respect for judgment and good sense as the ultimate norm of eloquence.[2]

Perhaps more than any other writer, Balzac is responsible for shifting the arena of eloquence from the *parlements* and schools of the sixteenth-century humanists to the salons and court of the *honnêtes hommes* of the seventeenth century. The Malherbe of prose, Balzac epitomized the movement that took place during Louis XIII's reign away from the exuberance of Renaissance erudition to the more chaste prose of neoclassical literature under the Sun King, and although writers in the second half of the century were careful to avoid what they felt to be Balzac's stylistic excesses, they greatly profited from the more harmonious phrasing he had learned from Latin authors.[3]

For many years it was the fashion for critics to acknowledge Balzac's contribution to the formation of classical prose style while disparaging his eloquence as empty rhetoric: "Balzac . . . represents French prose undergoing before the public a double, a triple year of rhetorical studies"—Sainte-Beuve; "He is only a rhetor"—Lanson; "Balzac the Rhetor"—Bray.[4] Yet rhetoric for Balzac was much more than a matter of style. It went far deeper for him than polishing his metaphors and hyperboles or balancing his periods. Even if his own stylistic affinities are Senecan, he held a Ciceronian view of eloquence in which matters of state, moral questions, and even philosophic issues belong to the domain of eloquence. Indeed, the first editions of his *Lettres* in 1624 met with such an enthusiastic reception because his contemporaries saw in them a union of dignified, urbane expression and current political and moral issues. The letter for Balzac was the natural successor of the orations of Latin antiquity. In his eyes, all the precepts of Cicero and Quintilian found their modern expression in the epistle. His friend La Motte Aigron, writing a preface to the 1624 edition, hailed Balzac's letters as the culmination of rhetorical theory when he claimed that the epistle was the true subject of oratorical treatises.[5] Balzac had realized that with the advent of royal absolutism, political oratory had no future in France; likewise, given the increasing importance of the *honnête homme*, both in the salons and in court circles, his audience could not be one of learned specialists. In the letter he discovered a medium in which to realize the Horatian injunction to please and instruct with decorum, all the while maintaining an air of studied informality suitable for his new public. Successive editions of the *Lettres,* followed by the *Entretiens* (1657), and loose treatises like *Le Prince* (1631), and the *Socrate chrétien* (1652), continued this course within the middle range of style. His successors later in the seventeenth century may have found other genres equally congenial for their eloquence, but they did not forget their debt to him for laying the groundwork for pleasing this new audience. Marc Fumaroli, at the close of his massive study of French rhetoric of the sixteenth and early seventeenth centuries, salutes Balzac as the symbol of the reconciliation between the Renaissance Republic of Letters of the humanist jurists and scholars on the one hand, and the new court organizing itself around Richelieu that would determine the direction of French literature during the rest of the century.[6]

Fellow Modernists

It might seen strange at first that Descartes' most extensive text on rhetorical questions, a Latin letter written in 1628 to an unknown correspondent, is a warm defense of Balzac's 1624 *Lettres,* but the two men had much in common in terms of temperament and experience to draw them together. Both were born into provincial families that had only recently joined the ranks of minor nobility. Jean-Louis Guez de Balzac, born most probably in 1597, was the son of a man in the service of the Dukes of Epernon; Rene Descartes was born in 1596 to an official of the *parlement* of Rennes. Both were educated in the newly established Jesuit schools where Suarez's rhetorical manual, *De arte rhetorica,* was in use. Descartes studied at La Flèche, an academy under royal patronage, while Balzac attended the order's schools in Angoulême, Poitiers, and finally Paris. Both traveled widely during their youth. Balzac made several forays into Holland, where he was enrolled with Théophile de Viau at the University of Leyden, and later spent eighteen months in Italy as an agent of Cardinal de la Villette.[7] The stay in Rome seems to have marked him deeply with both a distaste for the corruption of the papal court and a vibrant admiration for the heritage of the late Republic and early Empire. Descartes also traveled in Holland and Italy and did a stint of military service in Germany in his quest to acquire knowledge in the book of the world rather than in libraries (1:577).[8]

Both were ambitious, conscious of their considerable talents, and avid for recognition. Descartes sought to replace the Aristotelian scholasticism of the universities and colleges with his own science and metaphysics, while Balzac's aspirations went beyond literary glory to the hope that his political eloquence could win him an active role in affairs of state.

Both were jealous of their independence, preferring to deal with their Parisian colleagues from afar. In his retreat in Holland Descartes found the freedom from inopportune demands that allowed him to pursue his meditations and experiments. His most evocative description of his solitude in the midst of the bustle of city life is offered in a 5 May 1631 letter sent to Balzac at his home near Angoulême:

> Everyday I go out strolling among the throngs of a great people with as much freedom and ease as you have in the paths of the parks of your estate, and I only heed the men I see with the attention that I would give the trees in your forest or the animals that graze among them.

> Je vais me promener tous les jours parmi la confusion d'un grand peuple, avec autant de liberté et de repos que vous sauriez faire dans vos allées, et je n'y considère pas autrement les hommes que j'y vois, que je ferais les arbres que se rencontrent en vos forêts, ou les animaux qui y paissent. (1:190)

Balzac's long years at his country seat outside of Angoulême were due in part to his weak health and in part to his disappointed political aspirations, but above all, they resulted from his stubbornly independent spirit. As Descartes noted in his apology for the *Lettres:* "If ever he undertakes to depict the vices of the Mighty, he is not prevented from speaking the truth by a servile fear of power" ("Si quando vitia Nobilium describenda suscipiat, non servili potentiae metu . . . a vero dicendo prohibetur" [1:36]). Unsuited for the life of a courtier, Balzac nevertheless wrote for the court, just as Descartes in Holland always kept in mind his audience in Paris.

Even more than such parallels in experience and temperament, which were shared by any number of provincial gentlemen of their generation, the two possessed intellectual affinities that mark their attitude toward eloquence. Both were rationalists, confident in the power of reason to distinguish truth from error. The first line of Descartes' *Discours de la méthode,* "Good sense is the best shared thing in the world" ("Le bon sens est la chose du monde la mieux partagée" [1:568]), may be better known than Balzac's statements to the same effect, but both believed that no one historical age or professional group could rightly claim a monopoly on reason. As Balzac says in *Entretien XVI:* "There exists such things as natural logic and wise men without learning. Reason by itself can accomplish great things without the aid of art or science" ("Il y a une logique naturelle, et des Sages ignorants. . . . La Raison peut faire toute seule de grandes choses, sans l'assistance de l'Art et de la Science" [2:394]).

In this regard, both are resolute modernists as well, anxious to speak to their age on its own terms. Both reject the notion that the road to truth must pass by the rediscovery and imitation of some lost wisdom of the ancients. Balzac had a healthy respect for the classical Greeks and Romans, criticizing scholars who reject them out of hand, but his ideal was emulation, not servile imitation. Descartes' attitude was more radical. While he had a tempered respect for poets such as Horace or moralists such as Seneca, he was confident that in the crucial disciplines of metaphysics and the natural sciences, the study of the ancients resulted only in confusion and error among his contemporaries.

Finally, this modernist attitude drew their attention to the problem of addressing a nonprofessional audience of *honnêtes hommes*. Both had scorn for the pedants and scholiasts of the university and colleges. Descartes' desire to win over as wide a public as possible led him to the use of many of the same techniques Balzac employed. His effort to free philosophy from technical jargon, to write in French on occasion, and to introduce autobiographical elements has been recognized as an attempt to find favor with the same public of *honnêtes hommes* Balzac had already won over.[9]

The Zeal for Truth: Descartes' Defense of Balzac's Eloquence

When what was to be Balzac's first installment of his *Lettres* appeared in 1624, the approbation was not universal. Polemics continued for some five years and included attacks from his former rhetoric teacher François Garasse and from Jean Goulu, the superior of the Feuillantine order. Balzac found himself charged with vanity, veiled obscenity, and mendacious use of hyperbole, among other accusations.[10] Two of the texts which appeared in his defense are especially relevant. The first, the *Apologie de Monsieur de Balzac* (1627) signed by François Ogier, contains statements of rhetorical principles that can be taken as Balzac's own since he is said to have inspired, or even written, it. The second text, Descartes' Latin letter of 1628, is especially significant because it contains his most extended discussion of rhetoric, and unlike his other references to the discipline, which occur in the context of his discussion of philosophical method, this one is written within the broad frame of rhetorical criticism, using traditional technical terminology and similes. [11]

Descartes organizes his letter around two complementary poles of eloquence—stylistic achievement and persuasive force, that is to say, the elocution and the arguments of a discourse. Under each category he lists a number of defective forms that contrast with Balzac's excellence in each area. Analysis of these brands of false eloquence allows us to mark off the limits that separate the goals and components of authentic rhetoric from its unworthy neighbors. Thus, after praising the purity, grace, and elegance of Balzac's language, which he will later identify with the usage of the court, Descartes enumerates four cases in which style can fail to support a writer's thought.

First, the ear can be satisfied by "a meticulous choice of words, carefully arranged, flowing copiously" ("verba lectissima, curioso ordine disposita, et liberali stilo profusa" [1:32]), but this stylistic abundance, which Morris Croll identified as influenced by Ciceronianism, cannot compensate for a lack of intellectual content or a flabby organization. On the other hand, the dry, semi-obscure style of the second group—Senecan, according to Croll[12]—can rebuff the reader, even if the discourse is well stocked with sensible, noble thoughts. "Others, on the contrary, with words that are replete with meaning, joined with an abundance of noble reflections often enchant more capable minds, but too often their concise, semi-obscure style wearies this audience" ("Si contra significantissimae dictiones, nobilium cognitationum abundantia, mentes capaciores interdum oblectent, easdem presso et subobscuro stilo saepius fatigant" [1:32]). A third group of writers tries to find a middle ground between this dry expression of solid content and the florid style that fails to mask an absence of thought; they try to observe "the true rule of discourse which is to express things simply" ("verum sermonis institutum in puris rebus exprimendis rigidius" [1:32]). Nonetheless, they miss the mark by falling into an austerity that does not please: "They have such an austerity that the discerning do not approve them" ("tam austeri sunt, ut a delicatis non amentur" [1:32]). Finally and worst of all, he faults authors who use all manner of conceits— wordplay, unusual vocabulary, striking poetical images—calculated to surprise and amaze: intellectual content is completely lacking, and they fail to please readers who possess even a slightly serious bent of mind.

The first and last of these cases show that style alone cannot compensate for an absence of content, while the second and third indicate that content alone is not enough if the style is arid or austere. Balzac, of course, is presented as attaining the happy equilibrium between style and content, "a happy concord of words and content" ("felici rerum cum sermone concordia" [1:33]), where expression neither detracts from, nor overpowers the writer's arguments: "[T]he abundance of the most elegant discourse does not dissipate the force of the arguments nor overwhelm them" ("[E]legantissimae orationis ubertas . . . vires argumentorum non dissipat, nec obruit" [1:33]). This last quotation shows that, for Descartes, the ideal harmony between style and message in no way implies equality between the two. Even in this discussion of the stylistic component of eloquence, the arguments themselves take priority over stylistic considerations.

When we turn to Descartes' analysis of the persuasive side of Balzac's eloquence, we see that this priority is affirmed even more decisively. His villains here are the political and forensic orators of Greece and Rome, for whom winning over their audience was more important than the truth or falsehood of the cause they were defending. He objects to them, first of all, because of their recourse to sophism, verbal tricks, and empty words rather than to the simple truth; above all, they used these artifices and deceits consciously in the service of unworthy ends, "as they took special pride in their skill in defending weaker causes" ("cum tamen praecipuam artis gloriam ponerent in deterioribus causis sustinendis" [1:35]). Their efforts were not in good faith because they had no scruples about arguing the worst of causes, and while they were skillful advocates, they earned for themselves only the reputation of dishonest men (1:34).

Authentic persuasion for Descartes is a matter of the speaker communicating a personal assurance of the truth to the audience. This was the case, he maintains, before eloquence was corrupted by the Greek demagogues. In that oratorical garden of Eden, language was transparent; it was the direct spontaneous expression of the sincerity of the soul.

> [I]n the primitive uncouth ages, before there were any quarrels in the world and when speech willingly followed the inclinations of a guileless mind, there was, in fact, in persons of greater intelligence a force of quasi god-like eloquence which poured forth from zeal for truth and an abundance of feeling.

> [P]rimis et incultis temporibus, antequam ulla fuissent adhuc mundo dissidia, et cum lingua candidae mentis affectus non invita sequebatur, erat quidem in maioribus ingeniis divina quaedam eloquentiae vis, quae ex zelo veritatis et sensus abundantia profluens. (1:34)

The same sincerity is the hallmark of Balzac, the paragon of modern eloquence, who cannot fail to convince "in every instance that he only demonstrates what he has previously persuaded himself of" ("potissimum quoties non alia probat, quam quae sibi prius ipse persuasit" [1:35]). He develops this praise of sincerity as an encomium of "this candor of a mind elevated above ordinary mortals" ("hunc candorem . . . ingenii supra vulgus positi" (1:37) possessed by Balzac, who was willing to speak openly of his own infirmities and of the vices of the powerful. The implication is that the heart of eloquence is not just the truth but "zeal for truth." What makes speakers truly eloquent is not simply that they communicate the truth, but that they communicate their sincere conviction that they speak the truth. For Descartes, this sincerity, a form of what rhetoricians label the ethical proof, when joined with the truth itself, is the only legitimate instrument of eloquent persuasion.

Divergent Views: Style and Sincerity

Whether Descartes' assessment of Balzac's achievement is accurate has been questioned by critics since Emile Krantz. J. Youssef, for example, suggests that Descartes' comparison of Balzac's writings to the healthy complexion of a young maiden who has no need for makeup applies more aptly to the later works of the mature Balzac than to the *Lettres* of 1624.[13] The critics' uneasiness with the portrait Descartes draws of Balzac is caused by a fundamental divergence between the attitudes toward rhetoric of the two friends, a divergence that Descartes could not address directly in his apology and that thus surfaces only to the extent that he transforms Balzac's eloquence to conform to his own ideal. The Balzac he praises is a Balzac revised and corrected along Cartesian norms. We can pursue this divergence and further eludicate the Cartesian ideal of eloquence as the ability of speakers to convey their conviction that they speak the truth—the "noble candor" ("generosa quaedam libertas" [1:35]) that Descartes attributes to Balzac—if we examine their views on a series of rhetorical issues. This confrontation reveals that despite numerous parallels, each man's thrust reflects opposing orientations to political and intellectual life.

This is not to say that there are not large areas of apparent agreement. For example, Balzac's writings, like Descartes' letter, contain many criticisms of faulty eloquence where style clashes with substance. Thus, just as Descartes had criticized works whose content was solid enough but whose style was overly dry, Balzac rejects philosophers who have written arid political treatises: "[T]heir ratiocination is usually so dry and emaciated that it appears that their goal was to instruct rather than to please; moreover, their style is so awkward and thorny that it seems that they only sought to teach those who are already learned" ("[L]eur ratiocination est d'ordinaire si sèche et si décharnée, qu'il paraît que leur intention a plutôt été d'instruire que d'agréer; et d'ailleurs leur style est si embarrassé et si épineux, qu'il semble qu'ils n'aient voulu enseigner que ceux qui sont doctes" [*Le Prince,* 1:190]). Nor does Balzac have any use for eloquence that attempts to conceal an absence of arguments under sonorous Ciceronian-sounding phrases. "There is such a thing as a maker of bouquets, a turner of periods—I do not dare to call it eloquence—that is all painted and gilded. . . . It is hollow, and empty of the essential things although it rings clear with pleasant tones" ("Il y a une Faiseuse de bouquets, et une Tourneuse de périodes, je ne l'ôse nommer Eloquence, qui est toute peinte et toute dorée. . . . Elle est creuse, et vide de choses essentielles bien qu'elle soit claire et résonnante de tons agréables" [*Paraphrase ou de la grande éloquence*, 1:277–78]). Both would thus agree that while stylistic flourishes cannot compensate for a lack of arguments, a jarring style detracts from an otherwise sound content.

Balzac also seems in agreement with Descartes in assigning priority to persuasion over style. Appealing to the example of the ancients, he assures Mlle de Gournay in a letter of 30 August 1624 that elocution is the lesser part of rhetoric.

> It is true that I devote much attention to elocution, and I know that grand subjects need the aid of words and that after having been properly conceived they must be aptly expressed. I am only saddened that people try to turn the least part of the rhetoric of the ancients into the whole of our own, and that in order to satisfy petty minds, it is necessary that our work resemble those burnt offerings for which the heart was removed, leaving only the tongue.

> Il est vrai que je donne beaucoup à l'élocution, et je sais que les grandes choses ont besoin de l'aide des paroles, et qu'après avoir été bien conçues, elles doivient être heureusement exprimées. Il me fâche seulement que la moindre partie de la Rhétorique des anciens on en veuille faire toute la nôtre, et que pour contenter les petits esprits, il faille que nos ouvrages ressemblent à ces victimes, à qui on ôtait le coeur, et on laissait seulement la langue de reste. (Bibas, 1:252)

Although his initial claim to eloquence lies primarily in his success as a stylist, the content of his writings is far from negligible, and thus he feels secure in rejecting those who would neglect persuasion and make elocution the whole of rhetoric. Style, his comparison here suggests, is but the tongue of eloquence; its heart is surely truth, and the communication of this message seems paramount.

Does this, however, reduce style to the role of a gratuitous ornament that has no relation to persuasion? On the contrary, Balzac ascribes to style a functional as well as a decorative role.

After having pursued truth all the way to the heavens it is now a matter of bringing her back to earth. She must be freed from the darkness of her solitary confinement in order to be exposed to the view of the populace. Here eloquence adorns and dresses her after reason has discovered and unveiled her.

> Après avoir poursuivi la Vérité jusque dans le Ciel, il est question de l'amener sur la Terre. Il la faut tirer de son secret et de ses ténèbres pour l'exposer à la vue des Peuples. Et c'est alors que l'Eloquence la pare et l'ajuste après que la Raison l'a découverte et l'a dévoilée. (*Entretiens XXIII*, 2:465)

If the eloquent writer decorates the truth, it is not merely for the sake of pleasing, but also to adjust reason's discoveries to the audience at hand, here "the populace." As a form of decoration, style is one means of adapting the message to the public and thus persuading that even philosophers neglect at their own peril. As his spokesman Ogier says in the *Apologie:* "If eloquence does not soften philosophy and does not transform its savage appearance, it becomes odious and unbearable" ("Si l'éloquence n'adoucit la Philosophie, et ne lui change son visage farouche, elle devient odieuse et insupportable").[14] Thus, even when paying homage to the priority of persuasion over elocution in eloquence, Balzac manages to celebrate his own forte as a stylist by stressing the role of style in the persuasive process.

Descartes is well aware of this notion of ornament as a form of audience adaptation, even if he protests that he does not have recourse to it. He writes of his works to Chanut: "I put them before the public without being adorned, with none of the ornaments that might draw the eyes of the people, so that those whose gaze stops only at the exterior will not see them and that they will be examined only by a few persons of sound mind" ("Je les ai fait sortir en public sans être parés, ni avoir aucun des ornements qui peuvent attirer les yeux du peuple, afin que ceux qui ne s'arrêtent qu'à l'extérieur ne les vissent pas, et qu'ils fussent seulement regardés par quelques personnes de bon esprit" [2 November 1646, 7:199]). Descartes professes an unwillingness as a philosopher to make such concessions to reach a popular readership as if such ornaments degrade the truth.

This difference in spirit between the two is further illustrated by Balzac's attitude toward the sincerity of the speaker, the conviction of truth that Descartes prized as essential to eloquence. We can find in Balzac similar statements about sincerity as a central element in persuasion (cp. *Le Prince*, 1:190), and he too condemns the ancient sophists (*Paraphrase*, 1:278). However, when it is opportune, he has no scruples about presenting himself as a sophist of sorts for whom rhetoric teaches the art of disguise and aims more at display than persuasion. "Rhetoric . . . can indeed still be practiced today on subjects that are far removed from run-of-the-mill opinions, and by means of delightful pretenses excite admiration in the minds of men instead of gaining their assent" ("La Rhétorique . . . peut bien encore aujourd'hui s'exercer sur des sujets qui sont éloignés des opinions communes, et par des feintes agréables, exciter plutôt de l'admiration en l'esprit des hommes, qu'y gagner de la créance" [Bibas, 2:29–30]).

To be sure, he appeals to this conception of rhetoric as artifice and display in a letter of reconciliation addressed to François Garasse, in which he attempts to retreat from a virulent denunciation of his former teacher for having corrupted both philosophy and rhetoric. Still, the very fact that Balzac does not hesitate to call into service the idea that eloquence is aimed at winning the admiration of the public rather than its assent is telling, for such a notion ultimately serves to justify a showy eloquence in which style and subtle argumentation are given precedence. It is certainly far from Descartes' insistence on conviction and sincerity as the hallmarks of the eloquent. While not denying the crucial role of persuasion in eloquence especially in its noblest forms, Balzac does not shrink from an element of play, from a refusal to take himself completely seriously, that is rare in Descartes. The striking hyperboles Balzac used in his letters must be evaluated in this context; as he puts it, "In a word, even the lives of wise men are not completely serious; their every word is not an oath, and all that they write is not their last will and testament" ("En un mot, la vie des sages mêmes n'est pas toute sérieuse, toutes leurs paroles ne sont pas des serments, et tout ce qu'ils écrivent n'est pas leur testament" [Bibas, 2:30]). A well-turned phrase, no matter what its content, was an occasion of pride for him, in ways it could not be for Descartes.

Rhetorical Training and Philosophy

Along with Balzac's sometimes excessive compliments, the rather cavalier attitude he at times expressed toward the value of rhetorical study can be attributed to this spirit of play. Both this tendency toward flattery and a conventional depreciation of rhetorical training are deftly illustrated by this praise directed at Louis XIII in the preface of *Le Prince:* " The life of the king has taught me more than all the precepts of rhetoricians, and I owe to the felicity of his reign all the merit of my book" ("La vie du Roi m'en a plus appris que tous les préceptes des Rhétoriciens; et je dois à la félicité de son Règne tout le mérite de mon ouvrage" [1:196]). Balzac here asserts the primacy of subject matter over command of the rules of rhetoric, a view which seems in harmony with Descartes' famous assessment in the *Discours* of the futility of rhetorical studies. This evaluation of poetry and eloquence occurs in the course of a review of the Jesuit curriculum based on the *Ratio studiorum* that Descartes had known at La Flèche where the fifth year of classes, called the year of rhetoric, was chiefly devoted to the explication of Cicero's speeches.

> I valued oratory and was fond of poetry; but I thought both were gifts of the mind rather than fruits of study. Those with the strongest reasoning who digest their ideas the best so as to make them clear and intelligible can always persuade the best what they propose, even if they speak only the dialect of lower Brittany and have never learned rhetoric.

> J'estimais fort l'éloquence, et j'étais amoureux de la poésie; mais je pensais que l'une et l'autre étaient des dons de l'esprit, plutôt que des fruits de l'étude. Ceux qui ont le raisonnement le plus fort, et qui digèrent le mieux leurs pensées, afin de les rendre claires et intelligibles, peuvent toujours le mieux persuader ce qu'ils proposent, encore qu'ils ne parlassent que bas breton, et qu'ils n'eussent jamais appris de rhétorique. (1:574)

Compared to Descartes' rejection of the art, Balzac's stance is only the modest self-depreciation that was not unusual among authors dedicating a work to the mighty. According to Descartes, the ability to reason vigorously, to reduce the meat of one's thought to clear and distinct ideas by ordering it properly, is all that is needed to persuade. The persuasive force of writers finds its source deep within their understanding of their subject, rather than being suggested from outside by rhetorical method. Persuasive force is first of all a product of a natural talent, a gift of the mind, an innate capacity for sound judgment. To persuade, one has only to display this judgment in action.

Since Isocrates rhetoricians had pointed to the importance of education in the trio of elements necessary to produce a distinguished orator, although they had usually ranked it in third place behind natural talent and practice. Descartes, however, goes farther. Formal rhetorical study is spurned as unnecessary; in fact, a period of training may be harmful, according to a remark found in his notebooks, where he implies that the study of rhetorical techniques threatens to disturb the spontaneity of this natural gift.[15] While Descartes is willing to allow that the rules found in rhetorical manuals have some value, alone they will only produce school exercises, not the speeches of Cicero.[16] But if study of the rules is of little use, practical experience can develop a natural gift for eloquence. Thus in the early *Studium Bonae Mentis,* Descartes classes rhetoric among the arts that require "besides the knowledge of the truth . . . a mental facility, or at least an acquaintance acquired through practice" ("outre la connaissance de la vérité . . . une facilité de l'esprit, ou du moins une habitude acquise par l'exercice").[17] Descartes' admiration for the eloquence of a Cicero or a Balzac is profound, but he is equally sure that neither rules nor training can substitute for innate talent and sound judgment.

When Balzac discusses the requirements of the model orator in his fifth discourse, the *Paraphrase, ou de la grande éloquence,* he too lists an innate gift for eloquence as the prerequisite, followed by sound judgment. He even uses an alimentary image, similar to Descartes' "digest the best their ideas" ("digèrent le mieux leurs pensées" [1:574]) of the *Discours de la méthode* to signal the importance of reflection and the proper ordering of one's thoughts in the orator's preparation for a speech: "Antiquity called that drawing one's speech from the gut, and having an eloquent soul" ("L'Antiquité appelait cela puiser ses discours dans l'estomac, et avoir l'âme Eloquente" [1:281]). However, Descartes' dismissal of eloquence and of the tradition of rhetorical training behind it could hardly have pleased the *Unico eloquente,* who had never hestitated to mention philosophy and eloquence in the same breath as related arts (cp. Bibas, 1:59). Jean Jehasse suggests, in fact, that relations between the two cooled considerably after the publication of the *Discours de la méthode* in 1637.[18] Moreover, in his *Paraphrase,* published in 1644, Balzac takes care to add a third element to his acknowledgment of the need for talent and judgment—the study of rhetorical principles. The form this recommendation takes is significant. Balzac is not interested in a manual of the art written for young students containing easily memorized recipes for eloquence; he has only scorn for "congenital grammarians" ("Grammairiens de race" [1:281]) and "the pedantry of compilers" ("la pédanterie de Compilateurs" [1:282]). Instead, he declares himself for the application of philosophic thought to eloquence. "[S]ound eloquence must take instruction from sound philosophy" ("[L]a bonne Eloquence doit recevoir instruction de la bonne Philosophie" [1:282]). But rather than his old friend Descartes, Balzac recommends as "sovereign Craftsman" the philosopher whom Descartes aspired to displace—Aristotle.

> The sovereign Craftsman will lay out for him the different avenues for laying seige to reason along with the strong and weak points of the human mind. With the method and craft that Aristotle will give him, he will learn the spots at which the soul can be conquered. He will learn how to excite or moderate the passions depending on whether it is necessary to incite or check the courage of his troops. He will subjugate the intellect by the force of reasoning and vanquish appetite by the violence of the figures.

> Ce souverain Artisan lui découvrira les différentes avenues du siège de la Raison, et le Fort et le Faible de l'esprit humain. Avec la méthode et les adresses qu'il lui donnera, les endroits par où l'âme est prenable lui seront connus. Les moyens d'y former des intelligences, ne lui manqueront

point. Il saura irriter et modérer les Passions selon qu'il
faudra pousser ou arrêter les Courages. Il s'assujettira l'Intellect par la force du raisonnement, et emportera l'Appétit
par la violence des figures. (1:282–83)

Whether the choice of Aristotle over Descartes was meant as a
slight directed at his old friend is not as important for us as
Balzac's defense of rhetorical studies and his aspiration toward
a philosophically grounded theory of rhetoric, one that would
explain the psychological principles behind persuasion rather
than merely provide pat formulas. His description of such a
philosophical rhetoric matches the approach found in Aristotle's
Rhetoric, an approach that shows the relation of rhetorical devices
like figures of speech or enthymemes to the operation of the
mind and the passions. Thus, for Balzac, just as eloquence can
serve philosophy by making its cold reasoning more appealing
through the application of pleasing stylistic features, philosophy
can furnish rhetorical theory the psychological and epistemological tools it needs to enhance the persuasive process. Balzac sees
eloquence and philosophy as companions who profit from each
other's company. For Descartes, on the contrary, they are strang-
ers pursuing separate paths. Philosophy has no need of eloquence to persuade, and given that rhetorical theory was at the
periphery of his interests, there was little chance that he would
heed Balzac's call to ground rhetoric in philosophy. The systematic application of the Cartesian system to rhetorical theory was
delayed until later in the century when disciples such as Bernard
Lamy took up the task.

Action versus Science

Furthermore, Balzac envisaged the noblest forms of persuasion, as had the Greeks and Latins, in terms of a call to action:
"an eloquence of state affairs and of service, born to command as
a sovereign, wholly efficacious and completely vigorous" ("une
éloquence d'affaires et de service; née au commandement et à la
souveraineté; toute efficace, et toute pleine de force" [*Paraphrase,*
1:279]). The glory of eloquence for him is its capacity to move
an audience to action; the arena may be political like that of

the statesmen he cites in the *Paraphrase* such as Pericles and Demosthenes in ancient times or Henri IV and Richelieu in his own day, or it may be religious as exemplified by the preachers he had heard in Rome. The effect is the same, "to conquer and reign" ("vaincre et régner" [1:284])—not a reign won by violence or physical force, but by the power of words alone. Language has so great a sway that when pronounced by a truly eloquent speaker, words become incorporated into the very substance of the listeners.

> They descend into the very center of the heart; they pierce to the core of the soul and mingle and mix there with the thoughts and other interior movements. They are no longer the words of the person who speaks or who writes. They are the sentiments of those who listen or who read. . . . [T]hey attach themselves inseparably to the foreign body who receives them, becoming part and parcel of this other person.

> Elles descendent jusqu'au fond du coeur; elles percent jusques au centre de l'âme et se vont mêler et remuer là-dedans avec les pensées et les autres mouvements intérieurs. Ce ne sont plus les paroles de celui qui parle, ou qui écrit. Ce sont les sentiments de ceux qui écoutent, ou qui lisent. . . . [E]lles s'attachent inséparablement au sujet étranger qui les reçoit, et deviennent partie et l'âme d'autrui. (1:283–84)

Words used persuasively become the cement of the state, binding together ruler and subjects. This civic character of eloquence in Balzac underlines the deep respect he maintained for the art.

Descartes also recognizes the role of eloquence as a political and social bond. In fact, in his 1628 letter defending Balzac, he exalts it as the force that made possible the emergence of civilization; eloquence is the original source of political power. "[I]t drew half savage men out of the forest, established laws, founded cities, and it had the power of at once persuading and ruling" ("[E]loquentiae vis . . . rudes homines ex sylvis eduxit, leges imposuit, urbes condidit, eademque habuit persuadendi potestatem simul et regnandi" [1:34]). However, this idyllic portrait represents a lost ideal, for he immediately adds a description of the fall of eloquence and its corruption at the hands of the

Greek and Roman lawyers and politicians: "It passed into the hands of base men who, despairing of winning the assent of the audience in open battle and with only truth as a weapon, had recourse to sophisms and empty verbal tricks" ("Transmisit enim ad vulgares homines, qui, cum aperto Marte et solius veritatis copiis auditorum animos vincere desperarent, confugiebant ad sophismata et inanes verborum insidias" [1:34]). Descartes goes on to suggest that Balzac has contributed to the rehabilitation of civic eloquence to its past glory, but on the whole, such political concerns do not fascinate him as they do Balzac. As we will see in more detail in the next chapter, he judges the act of persuasion in light of his own central concern, namely, the exercise of sound judgment. In the realm of knowledge, judgment manifests itself in the quest for *scientia*, the certainty he had experienced in mathematics. In the domain of action, Descartes is more concerned with questions of individual ethics than in political affairs that he was content to leave to princes.

The humanists' model of civic virtue and the effort to adapt the rhetorical tradition of the ancients to the court and salons of seventeenth-century France that give life to Balzac's notion of eloquence are absent from Descartes' thought. Descartes was resolved to speak directly to his contemporaries without the thought of the ancients or their eloquence as intermediaries. The truth of his system and his zeal for it would stand in the stead of any rhetorical devices.

However, Descartes was not always confident of his powers of persuasion. As he confesses to Mersenne in a 25 November 1630 letter, he was more convinced of the validity of his proof for God's existence than of any demonstration in geometry; yet, at the same time, he was unsure of his ability to bring others to this same conclusion: "I do not know if I will be able to bring everyone to understand it as I do" ("Je ne sais pas si je serais capable de la faire entendre à tout le monde, en la même façon que je l'entends"). He then goes on to express the same doubts as to whether his *Dioptrique* will win converts to his scientific principles: "I will test in the treatise on Dioptrics if I am able to explain my thoughts and persuade others of a truth after I have persuaded myself of it—something I am not at all sure of" ("J'éprouverai en la Dioptrique si je suis capable d'expliquer mes conceptions, et de persuader aux autres une vérité, après que je me la suis persuadée: ce que je ne pense nullement" [1:172]). His repeated attempts to cast his thought in differing guises—academic handbooks like the *Principes*, essays like the *Méditations*, or in dialogue form as in *La Recherche de la vérité*—testify to his realization that simply reiterating his message with clarity and method would not do. Where then was Descartes to turn? Certainly he would not seek aid in the techniques of persuasion as expounded by rhetoricians, given his opinion of rhetorical training expressed in the *Discours*. Instead, he makes the typical Cartesian move: he casts his gaze inward to his personal experience of *évidence* and to the difficulty of making his philosophy intelligible to others. Descartes' rhetorical theory is generated from within his own system. It is born from his notion of persuasion.

3
Descartes' Rhetoric of Generosity

> We seek out instead all the auxilia-
> ries that can maintain our thought
> in the state of attention.
>
> Omnia potius adjumenta perquiri-
> mus, quibus cogitatio nostra reti-
> neatur attenta.
>
> Descartes,
> *Regulae*

In the first part of the *Discours de la méthode* Descartes narrates the quest of a young man for assurance, both in the judgments of his intellectual life, and in the more practical moral affairs of existence: "I always had an intense desire to learn to distinguish truth from falsehood in order to see clearly in my actions and to walk with assurance in this life" ("J'avais toujours un extrême désir d'apprendre à distinguer le vrai d'avec le faux, pour voir clair en mes actions, et marcher avec assurance en cette vie" [1:577]). However, he found only disappointment in his studies. Instead of teaching him to distinguish truth from error, philosophy furnished only a welter of opinions that could be established as likely but not as certain; it was not a monument to truth, but to the vanity of philosophers and to their skill as dialecticians. Mathematics alone gave him some measure of satisfaction because of the certainty and self-evidence of its proofs, but he was later to realize that as a student he had scarcely recognized its potential application. When he turned from libraries to the great book of the world, his travels were hardly more reassuring; the diversity of customs among the peoples he visited paralleled the Babel of opinions among philosophers. Assurance, he discovered, was not to be found in the erudition of scholars any more than along the highways of his travels. Thus he decided to turn inward to reflection in search of a more successful method. "One day I also resolved to direct my study inward and to use all the strength of my mind to choose the paths that I should follow. I found this much more successful, it seems to me, than if I had never left my country or my books" ("Je pris un jour résolution d'étudier aussi en moi-même, et d'employer toutes les forces de mon esprit à choisir les chemins que je devais suivre. Ce qui me réussit beaucoup mieux, ce me semble, que si je ne me fusse jamais éloigné, ni de mon pays, ni de mes livres" ([1:578]).

The Rules of *Evidence:*
Rhetoric in Jeopardy

In the second part of the *Discours* Descartes relates how out of this period of intense meditation during the winter of 1619–20 came a vision of the unity of all knowledge and the ideal of a single method modeled on mathematics to solve problems in all disciplines. At the heart of this new method, summed up in its most famous and succinct form in the four rules of method, is the identification of truth with *évidence,* an intuition in which the mind makes immediate contact with reality in the form of ideas that are perceived both with clarity and distinction. The method's precepts are meant to insure that the intellect settles for nothing less than this self-evidence in its pursuit of truth.

The first rule stands as a call to vigilance against slothful judgments taken in haste or based on received and untested opinion; only self-evidence will do. The second, requiring a division of problems into their most simple components, is calculated to make it easier for the mind to attain the clear and distinct ideas that are the sign of truth by eliminating all that is not immediately relevant. Once the problem has been broken down into its parts, the third rule is to form chains of clear and distinct ideas beginning with the most simple, in geometric fashion so that the mind can assemble complicated demonstrations that proceed from self-evident point to self-evident point. But since *évidence* is known as an immediate intuition, and the mind cannot maintain its focus adequately on all the discrete links of self-evident truth comprising such chains, Descartes' fourth rule requires frequent reviews to assure that no element is allowed undue entry or omitted from the demonstration.

At first glance, it might seem that such a method aimed at the production of knowledge should not apply directly to rhetoric, which Descartes recognized to be more concerned with communication (1:130). Yet as a universal method, the rules for achieving self-evidence tend to extend themselves into all endeavors, reducing the specificity of individual disciplines and submitting them all to the same standard. When self-evidence becomes the sole criterion of truth, the legitimacy of many traditional rhetorical practices is called into question. Immediately suspect are forms of proof long recommended by rhetoricians based on appeals to the emotions of the audience or to the character of the speaker. Even the intellectual proofs are jeopardized because Descartes' insistence on *évidence* is aimed in great measure against the probable. To be sure, his intended target was not the orator's use of probable arguments, but the dialectic of the scholastic philosophers of his day.[1] He detected in their disputes and debates a willingness to settle for probability; rather than require certainty, the scholastics made room in their proofs for arguments based on what was merely likely. Thus even if Descartes would grant that some measure of truth was attained through their exercises, he found it so mixed with error and probability that it was virtually useless (1:82; 1:585). Rhetoric is perforce implicated in this attack against dialectic, whose tools are the "contortions of the schoolmen's probable syllogisms" ("scholasticorum . . . probabilium syllogismorum tormenta" [1:81–82; A.-T., 10:363]), because rhetoric also traditionally dealt in probabilities, both in the proofs it used and in its subject matter.[2] The three branches of eloquence identified by Aristotle—deliberative, forensic, and epideictic—all use arguments based on commonly accepted opinions; necessary truths were only found in pure mathematics, metaphysics and the first principles of physics, according to Aristotle. Rhetoric thus deals with contingent situations that cannot be resolved in terms of necessary, universal principles.

The reign of *évidence* also seems to negate another longstanding concern of rhetoric—adapting a message to a particular audience. If common sense, the capacity to judge soundly and to distinguish truth from error, is as widely distributed as Descartes claims in the opening line of the *Discours* (1:568), and *évidence* manifests itself directly to the mind as an intuition of clear and distinct ideas, does not truth have a universal character recognizable by all in identical fashion? This view is behind Descartes' frequent assertions that anyone who properly understands his teachings will be convinced of their truthfulness. For example, he writes Regius in July 1645, "I consider them to be certain and evident enough to remove all occasion for discussion from those who have truly understood them" ("[S]ed tam certas evidentesque esse consido, ut illis a quibus recte intelligantur, omnen disputandi occasionem sint sublaturae" [4:262–63; A. T., 4.248]). Is rhetoric to be replaced by an impersonal speaker addressing a universal audience and using a format that apes geometry?

Two considerations indicate that not only is a rhetoric of philosophical discourse implicit in his notion of *évidence*, but an accommodation with rhetoric in the realm of human conduct, as exemplified by Balzac's eloquence, is possible as well.

A Rhetoric of Philosophy: From Self-Persuasion to the Persuasion of Others

Even at the moment when Descartes is alone with his newly experienced *évidence*, a point that is most properly prerhetorical because it does not involve communicating this truth to others, an intervening psychological factor authorizes the appearance of rhetoric on the scene. Henri Gouhier has pointed out several texts in which Descartes admits that on occasion he had attained *assensio* without *persuasio*. His intellect had apparently been satisfied that *évidence* had been achieved, thus his *assensio;* but he had not experienced the assurance, the *persuasio* that he prized so much. According to Gouhier, "an irresistible *assensio* coexisted with a hesistant *persuasio*."[3] At the close of his reply to the sixth objections against the *Méditations*, Descartes describes just this situation in regard to a crucial doctrine in his system.

When I had for the first time concluded by virtue of the arguments contained in my Meditations that the human

mind is truly distinct from the body, and that it is even easier
to know than the body—along with several other things that
are treated there—I felt in truth obliged to acquiesce by the
fact that I had seen nothing in them that was not consequent
and not drawn from evident principles according to the
rules of logic. However, I confess that I was not wholly
persuaded for all that, and the same thing happened to
me as to astronomers who, after having been convinced by
powerful reasons that the sun is several times larger than the
whole earth, nevertheless, cannot prevent themselves from
judging that it is smaller when they cast their eyes on it.

Lorsque j'eus la première fois conclu, en suite des raisons
qui sont contenues dans mes Méditations, que l'esprit hu-
main est réellement distingué du corps, et qu'il est même
plus aisé à connaître que lui, et plusieurs autres choses dont
il est là traité, je me sentais à la vérité obligé d'y acquiescer,
par ce que je ne remarquais rien en elles qui ne fût bien
suivi, et qui ne fût tiré de principes très évidents suivant les
règles de la logique. Toutefois je confesse que je ne fus pas
pour cela pleinement persuadé, et qu'il m'arriva presque la
même chose qu'aux astronomes, qui, après avoir été convaincu par de puissantes raisons que le soleil est plusieurs
fois plus grand que toute la terre, ne sauraient pourtant
s'empêcher de juger qu'il est plus petit, lorsqu'ils jettent les
yeux sur lui. (2:882–83)

Persuasio, according to Gouhier, is a state of certainty coupled
with security: "this state of certitude which attaches us to our
opinions and allows us to dispense with calling into question what
we believe, whether rightly or wrongly, to be the truth."[4] An
initial *persuasio* finds its source in our feelings, our habits, even
in the unexamined inclinations of our minds; conviction, on the
other hand, is won by the force of explicit proofs that compel
consent. However, this rational *assensio,* once established in the
mind, can engender a more solid *persuasio* born of self-evidence.[5]

How does Descartes account for this delay between the moment when intellectual assent is achieved and the experience of
the assurance that ideally should coincide with it? In the *Sixièmes
Réponses* he attributes it to the lingering influence of prolonged
childhood, that is, to the prejudices he had acquired in his youth,

but never examined philosophically. "I found that the chief reason was that, from my youth, I had arrived at numerous judgments concerning the properties of nature . . . and that I had ever since held on to the same opinions that I had previously formed concerning them" ("[J]e trouvai que la principale raison était que, dès ma jeunesse, j'avais fait plusieurs jugements touchant les choses naturelles . . . et que j'avais toujours retenu depuis les mêmes opinions que j'avais autrefois formées de ces choses-là" [2:884]). The consequences for rhetoric are significant. As Gouhier concludes, if even within the philosopher a stubborn resistance to *persuasio* is possible, when the philosopher turns outward will not a similar resistance be likely in others; "will it not be necessary to envisage an art of argumentation that will provoke a *persuasio* that will go hand in hand with the art of demonstration that provokes the *assensio?*"[6] When the philosopher of self-evidence becomes a professor of philosophy, rhetorical strategies will be required to overcome the same effects of prolonged childhood in the audience as had earlier been experienced by the philosopher. At the very least, a rhetoric of philosophical discourse will be required.

Rhetoric and the Affairs of Life

The self-evidence inspired by mathematics might have been his ideal, but Descartes recognized that neither this model of certainty, nor the deductive procedures of mathematics could be extended beyond metaphysics to all endeavors.[7] Even in the physical sciences, experiments must confirm hypotheses proposed by deduction, and at the end of the *Principes,* he admits that in the physical sciences one must often be satisfied with moral certitude that is sufficient to govern action; in these disciplines the metaphysical certitude of *scientia* which is grounded in self-evidence and guaranteed by the existence of a God who does not deceive is not always possible (3:521–24).

More important, *évidence* itself is impossible in the domain of human action. As he put it in a 1641 letter, "One would assuredly wish for as much certitude in the things concerning the direction of life as is needed to acquire science; however, it is very easy to demonstrate that such a great certitude is not to be sought nor hoped for in these matters" ("Optanda quidem esset tanta certitudo in iis quae pertinent ad vitam regendam, quanta ad scientiam acquirendam desideratur; sed tantam tamen non esse ibi quaerendam nec expectandam, perfacile demonstratur" [August 1641, 5:38–39; A.-T., 3:422; cp. April/May 1638, 2:236]).

The perfect certitude of *évidence* required for *scientia* cannot be achieved in practical affairs where moral certitude "sufficient for the conduct of ordinary life" ("sufficiente pour régler nos moeurs" [3:522]) will do. As the complete title of the *Discours* indicates—*Discours de la méthode pour bien conduire sa raison et chercher la vérité dans les sciences*—his method that excludes recourse to the probable is designed to guide reason and seek truth in the sciences. In the conduct of one's life, Descartes allows for the probable and for *vraisemblance*, as seen in the rules of his "provisional code of morality" ("morale par provision" [1:592]) in the third part of the *Discours*. In his first precept he recommends obeying the laws, customs, and religion of one's childhood country in the absence of self-evident moral principles. Descartes suggests that among such received opinions it is wisest to select the most moderate as probably the best (1:594). The second precept, a counsel to follow resolutely a course of action once chosen, is even more emphatic in its appeal to the probable. The exigencies of time do not allow sorting out the truth from among the mass of competing views on behavior or unraveling the complexities of each contingent situation.

> And as the actions of life often do not allow for any delay, it is a very certain truth that when we cannot discern the truest opinions we must follow the most probable ones, and even when we do not find more probability in some than in others, we must nonetheless adopt some and regard them afterwards not as doubtful in so far as they pertain to practical matters, but as most true and certain because reason, which leads us to adopt them, is itself true and certain.

> Et, ainsi, les actions de la vie ne souffrant souvent aucun délai, c'est une vérité très certaine que lorsqu'il n'est pas en notre pouvoir de discerner les plus vraies opinions, nous devons suivre les plus probables; et même qu'encore que

nous ne remarquions point davantage de probabilité aux unes qu'aux autres, nous devons néanmoins nous déterminer à quelques-unes, et les considérer après, non plus comme douteuses, en tant qu'elles se rapportent à la pratique, mais comme très vraies et très certaines, à cause que la raison qui nous y a fait déterminer se trouve telle. (1:595)

Descartes did not abandon this acceptance of the probable when the precepts of the *Discours* took more definitive form in his 1645 letters on ethics to the princess Elizabeth (cp. 15 September 1645, 6:303). The perfect moral system is beyond the reach of humans because only God has the complete knowledge necessary to establish a definitive ethics.[8] We must strive towards it, but in practice, we are required only to resolve to act on the basis of the best possible reason available (cp. 20 November 1647, 7:363). In moral questions frequent recourse to conjecture is permitted (2:821).

If Descartes does not use this distinction between the moral certitude allowed in practical affairs and the *évidence* of science to legitimize rhetoric, in the way that Aristotle distinguished between the probabilities of rhetoric and the necessary truths of science, it is because for Descartes the aspiration toward self-evidence applies in both instances. He hesitates to formalize two standards of proof, one for dialectics and rhetoric, and another for philosophy, as Aristotle had allowed. Just the same, once the best possible course of action has been settled upon, a sort of deliberative rhetoric seems appropriate in confirming one's resolve and encouraging others to adopt it.

In fact, Descartes' insistence on the *persuasio* discussed in the previous section is relevant. The implications of this assurance of truth extend beyond a rhetoric of philosophy to the broader forms of eloquence exemplified by Balzac. A parallel exists between the conviction of truth sought by Descartes the philosopher as a complement to the *assensio* of self-evidence and the "zeal for the truth" he had singled out in his letter on Balzac along with good sense as the source of primitive authentic eloquence. We have seen that Balzac, the paragon of modern eloquence, was most successful, according to Descartes, in persuading others precisely when he had first persuaded himself. What is uniquely persuasive about the eloquent is not just that they speak the truth, but that at the same time they communicate their own *persuasio* that they are truthful, a persuasion akin to that Descartes required in philosophy. In terms of traditional rhetorical invention, one might say that the intellectual proofs grounded in self-evidence are reinforced by ethical ones based on the speaker's character. Thus, when practical persuasion is the goal, the assurance that all has been done to seek the best possible solution bolsters the speaker's arguments in cases where only the most probable opinion can be ascertained rather than self-evidence, just as firmness of resolve compensates for lack of certainty when action must be taken.

Disposition as Audience Adaptation

The proper ordering of thought was all important to Descartes. When he asserts in his critique of eloquence in the *Discours* that those who "digest their ideas the best so as to make them clear and intelligible can always best persuade what they propose" (1:574), "digest" is the equivalent of "to put in order," as the Latin translation, *ordine disponunt* (A.-T., 6:543) indicates. I have already noted that the third rule of the *Discours* prescribes a progression from the simple to the more complicated in the search for truth. Descartes' comments on his *Méditations* demonstrate how this precept was elaborated into a method of exposition. In discussing this work with Mersenne, he points out that he goes "from easier matters to more difficult ones" ("a facilioribus ad difficiliora"), that is, he used "the order of arguments" ("l'ordre des raisons"), not "the order of topics" ("l'ordre des matières"):

> I make what deductions I can, sometimes on one topic, sometimes on another; in my opinion, this is the true path for finding and explaining the truth. And as for the order of topics, it is only good for people whose arguments are disjointed and who can say as much about one difficulty as about another.

> [J]'en déduis ce que je puis, tantôt pour une matière, tantôt pour une autre; ce qui est, à mon avis, le vrai chemin pour trouver et expliquer la vérité. Et pour l'ordre des matières,

il n'est bon que pour ceux dont toutes les raisons sont détachées, et qui peuvent dire autant d'une difficulté que d'une
autre. (24 December 1640, 4:240)

The order of topics is rejected as unwieldy because it attempts to
be exhaustive, to set down in a single place everything concerning
a subject. The replies to the second queries to the *Méditations*
develop further the same distinction, using slightly different
terminology. There Descartes distinguishes two forms of demonstration: analysis and synthesis (2:581–82). The first has the advantage of recreating the thought process by which the truth to
be communicated was discovered, so that as the audience follows
the demonstration it becomes a co-inventor alongside the philosopher:

> Analysis displays the true road by which a topic has been
> discovered using method and shows how the effects depend
> on the causes so that if the reader wishes to follow it and
> examine carefully all that it contains, he will not understand
> the subject as demonstrated any less perfectly, and it will be
> no less his own property than if he had discovered it himself.

> L'analyse montre la vraie voie par laquelle une chose a été
> méthodiquement inventée, et fait voir comment les effets
> dépendent des causes; en sorte que, si le lecteur la veut
> suivre, et jeter les yeux soigneusement sur tout ce qu'elle
> contient, il n'entendra pas moins parfaitement la chose ainsi
> démontrée, et ne la rendra pas moins sienne, que si lui-
> même l'avait inventée. (2:582)

Synthesis, on the other hand, follows the model of Euclidean
geometric proof with axioms, definitions, and theorems so that
the reader is forced to recognize that the conclusions of an argument follow inevitably from its premises. The advantage of synthesis is that it compels the reader's consent; but on the other
hand, it is less satisfying than analysis because the rigid demonstration of synthetic proof conceals the method by which the
conclusion was first reached. As a sample, Descartes offers proofs
of God's existence arranged in geometric fashion (1:586), but it

is clear that his heart is not in the exercise. He prefers analysis, the form he insists he used in the *Méditations* themselves.[9]

Descartes' reflections on the potential of these two modes of exposition confirm his rhetorical sensitivity to the need to take into account both the character of the audience and the message to be presented. Synthesis, as the more compelling form, is destined for those whose attention is faltering and whose prejudices are persistent. Only the most robust intellects can follow Descartes along the path of analysis, and even for them, he suggests that several readings of his text are in order. Likewise, in his discussion of synthesis, he shows that the same manner of proof is not suitable for all subject matter. Synthesis, in fact, is more appropriate for geometry, where the primary notions are universally accepted because they conform to the experience of the senses, than it is for metaphysics, whose primary notions, although clear and distinct, conflict with prejudices stemming from the senses of prolonged childhood (2:584). Since the compelling force of synthesis depends on the clarity of the premises from which the conclusions are deduced, such a method is useful only in disciplines where the first principles are rather obvious. This explains why he chose analysis for his *Méditations,* the first systematic treatment of his metaphysical system whose key principles are in conflict with the commonsensical prejudices of prolonged childhood. Self-evidence may be a direct intuition, whether the truths involved are geometric axioms or metaphysical principles, but the method used to provoke it in others must be shaped by the nature of the message as well as by the intelligence of the audience.

Descartes approaches his potential readers as intellectual weaklings. He has no quarrel with the traditional rhetorical notion that any message must be adapted to its audience, but this in no way implies a respect for his readers' intelligence or their opinions. Rather it requires making allowances for their frailty and prejudice. He must cope with the uninitiated who come to his philosophy holding views about sensible reality that seem to be authorized by common sense, but which stem from false judgments. Even more troubling is the fact that the very nature of the mind makes it difficult to overcome these errors. Descartes might protest modestly in the first part of the *Discours* that all human beings are equally endowed with reason and that he does not dare prescribe a method that everyone must follow. Nonetheless, by the sixth part of the *Discours*, it is clear that he believes not only that he has discovered and has begun to apply the proper method, but also that he is justified in turning his back on the previous history of philosophy.

Audience adaptation is not a mutual pursuit of the truth for Descartes; it is an invitation to the disciples to follow along the course the master has already charted. Even when analysis, which retraces the mind's path to *évidence*, is the mode of exposition rather than the more cumbersome synthesis, with its rigid chains of axioms and definitions, the conclusion is known in advance with certainty, at least by the guide. As he says at the beginning of *La Recherche de la vérité*, the weight of the many obstacles to the discovery of truth in adults dominated by prejudice is so great that, barring the possession of exceptional natural talent, only the instructions of some sage can point to the true road leading to the heights occupied by knowledge (2:1105–6).

The Epistemological Foundations of a Rhetoric of Attention

It would be tempting to attribute the need for rhetoric exclusively to the body. After all, the prejudices of childhood result from its union with the mind. However, while the body may multiply the difficulties inherent in achieving *évidence*, recourse to rhetoric is implicit in Descartes' notion of the operation of the mind.

How is it that we so often fall short of the clear and distinct ideas that are the mark of truth? Descartes refuses to blame either God or a fallen human nature for error; instead, he holds responsible the misuse of the mind's two chief faculties, a misuse that stems from their unequal strength.

> From what source then do my errors spring? From the single fact that although the will's scope is wider and more extended than the understanding, I do not restrain it within the same limits, but I extend it as well to topics I do not understand; and since the will is itself indifferent about

them, it goes astray readily and chooses evil for good, and error for truth.

> D'où est-ce donc que naissent mes erreurs? C'est à savoir de cela seul que, la volonté étant beaucoup plus ample et plus étendue que l'entendement, je ne la contiens pas dans les mêmes limites, mais que je l'étends aussi aux choses que je n'entends pas; auxquelles étant de soi indifférente, elle s'égare fort aisément, et choisit le mal pour le bien, ou le faux pour le vrai. (2:463)

The understanding or *entendement* is the passive dimension of the mind, its faculty of perception; it receives and registers all ideas, whether they be the sense data reported by the body, the images formed by the imagination, or the purely intellectual ideas devoid of any mental picture. The will or *volonté* is the mind's active power, its capacity to make decisions of all kinds, both intellectual and moral. Thus, while the understanding apprehends and conceives, the will affirms, denies, or doubts. Its role is crucial in arriving at truth because it alone possesses the power to judge, thanks to its freedom by which human beings carry the image and likeness of God (2:461). Ideally, it should accept as true only ideas that present themselves to the understanding with the irresistible clarity and distinctness of self-evidence. Yet because the will's reach is infinite while the capacity of the understanding is more restricted, the will frequently gives its consent too readily, without the compulsion of *évidence;* instead, it accepts the probable or even mere conjecture. Error is thus ultimately seen as an abuse of the will's freedom to judge, that is, the will's ability to assent or deny, which is the supreme exercise of human liberty. Sound judgment is the key to intellectual life for Descartes, just as the resolve to follow one's best judgments is the essence of virtue in the moral domain.

The will, therefore, must protect itself against error while seeking out the truth. On the defensive side, it must withhold consent; it must struggle patiently to keep the judgment in suspension until *évidence* has been reached. Precipitation is the foe. Descartes warns against hasty judgments and preconceived notions in the first rule of the *Discours* because the prejudices of

prolonged childhood that present such obstacles to his philosophy are the accumulated residue of hasty judgments made before
the will was mature. Cartesian hyperbolic doubt directed against
these prejudices is a radical, albeit more active, form of the
suspension of judgment that guards against precipitation.
Concomitant to this refusal to judge with haste, a vigorous
consideration of the question at hand is required. Descartes labels
this patient mental concentration commanded by the will attention.[10] If the intuition of *évidence* is a kind of intellectual sight
for Descartes, the direction of this vision is attention. It is "an
examination by the mind" ("une inspection de l'esprit" [2:426]),
the *acies mentis*, the fine point of the mind. The ninth rule of the
Regulae develops the parallel with sight by comparing the act of
attention to the meticulous work of craftsmen trained to concentrate their vision on one minute detail after another.

> Craftsmen who do precision work and who are accustomed
> to directing their gaze attentively on each point acquire with
> practice the power of discerning perfectly the smallest and
> most subtle things; in the same manner, those who never
> dissipate their thought on several objects at the same time
> and who concentrate it entirely on the consideration of the
> smallest and most accessible things acquire perspicacity.

> Sed Artifices illi, qui in minutis operibus exercentur, et ocu-
> lorum aciem ad singula puncta attente dirigere consuever-
> unt, usu capacitatem acquirunt res quantumlibet exiguas et
> subtiles perfecte distinguendi; ita etiam illi, qui variis simul
> objectis cogitationem nunquam distrahunt, sed ad simplicis-
> sima quaeque et facillima consideranda totam semper occu-
> pant, fiunt perspicaces. (A.-T., 10:401)

Descartes' attention is a highly selective process, with the result
that all but its object fades into the unconscious.

In fact, the clarity and distinctness of self-evidence are functions of attention. Clarity denotes a vivacity due to the intensity
of presence that takes possession of the mind's attention. Article
45 of the *Principes* defines it in terms of attention: "I call clear
that which is present and manifest to an attentive mind; in the
same way we speak of seeing clearly objects when they are present

and highly stimulating so that our eyes are inclined to gaze at them" ("J'appelle claire celle qui est présente et manifeste à un esprit attentif; de même que nous disons voir clairement les objets lorsque étant présents ils agissent assez fort, et que nos yeux sont disposés à les regarder" [3:117]). Yet clarity in itself is no guarantee of *évidence,* for sense perceptions are often vivid and yet confused. Descartes cites as example the fact that while a pain can be clear and distinct in itself, often it loses its distinctness when the false judgment that the pain is located in the wounded part of the body (rather than in the mind) is added to the experience of the pain (3:118). A further effort of attention is required to separate the painful sensation from the false judgment concerning its location, that is, to arrive at an idea that is both clear and distinct. A notion is distinct when it is "so precise and different from all others that it only includes in itself what appears manifest to a person who considers it properly" ("tellement précise et différente de toutes les autres, qu'elle ne comprend en soi que ce qui paraît manifestement à celui qui la considère comme il faut" [3:117–18]). Fortunately, as an idea becomes detached from other ideas thus increasing its presence as a distinct notion, its clarity is also heightened, allowing the mind to maintain its attention more easily.

Time is attention's adversary. Because of the mind's limited capacity, the will can concentrate only on a single point at any given moment. "One cannot be very attentive to several things at the same time" ("On ne peut être fort attentif à plusieurs choses en même temps" [1:462]). Thus, in order to focus on a single point while disregarding all that is extraneous, considerable effort must be marshalled. Attention to self-evidence is described in the fifth Meditation as a great application of the mind (2:477) requiring strength of will. In contrast to sensations, whose vivid presence overwhelms the attention mechanically, the clarity of clear and distinct ideas is the result of a laborious concentration that focuses on each aspect of a problem until it has been broken down into its constituent parts.

The attraction of *évidence* is all but irresistible and compels consent, but this consent lasts only as long as the mind continues to experience the clarity and distinctness of the idea, that is, only as long as attention is sustained. Thus, time remains its enemy.

When the faltering attention is distracted by some other topic, the memory of *évidence* previously achieved may not be strong enough to maintain the will's consent (2 May 1644, 6:144). Perhaps even more importantly, in an affirmation of the will's freedom, we can turn our attention away from *évidence*. We can escape its compelling force by directing our gaze away from its clarity, voluntarily choosing error over truth (9 February 1645, 6:196–97).

Attention as the Core of Method and Ethics

Thus it is not surprising that a method for eliminating all irrelevant aspects of a problem and focusing on its simplest components is at the heart of the Cartesian program. In fact, the four rules of the *Discours*, which Jean Laporte calls "habits of attention," furnish just such a method for maintaining and fortifying the attention necessary to distinguish clear and distinct ideas.[11] This method is not a fixed set of formulas, conveniently numbered steps, to be applied mechanically to a problem. Commentators who complain that Descartes' four rules of method are banal and unexceptional miss the point; the precepts are less a series of procedures than an appreciation of the psychology of attention, reminders of how to purify and direct it. Thus, suspension of consent is required because of the difficulty of maintaining attention long enough to arrive at *évidence*. Distinct ideas are the product of attention's ability to focus on ever more minute details as required by the second rule, and the frequent reviews prescribed in the last rule are needed to compensate for the fleeting nature of *évidence*. His precepts are not recipes that, when correctly applied, guarantee correct conclusions; for Descartes, truth can be known only by means of a direct intuition, a personal contact with clear and distinct ideas.

Descartes rejects the syllogism of the scholastics for having fallen short of this standard. The syllogism is unable to guarantee the truth of its conclusions because its practitioners substitute blind faith in the forms of argument for attention. Lulled by confidence in these forms of reasoning, they neglect their arguments' content and allow error to slip into their premises (1:129). His own method is designed to make this impossible by fostering attention to the subject at hand while proceeding from one self-evident intuition to the next. A syllogism is only as good as its premises, yet too often logicians are so attentive to the mode of their argument that they neglect its grounds (1:158–59). Such improperly formulated syllogisms do not guarantee truth, but lead to eloquent yet futile debates that settle nothing (1:81). Thus at its best, the syllogism is a method of exposition, not discovery, for Descartes. It does not yield new truth, but only renders explicit conclusions already implicit in its major premise. "[D]ialectic as it is commonly understood is perfectly useless to those who wish to explore the truth of things but can only be used occasionally to set forth more easily to others arguments that are already known; for this reason it should be transferred from philosophy to rhetoric" ("[V]ulgarem dialecticam omnino esse inutilem rerum veritatem investigare cupientibus, sed prodesse tantummodo interdum posse ad rationes iam cognitas facilius aliis exponendas, ac proinde illam ex philosophia ad rhetoricam esse transferendam" [1:130; A.-T., 10:406]). The syllogism is a figure of rhetoric and an inefficient one at that.

Attention is at the heart of the paradox that underlies Descartes' rhetoric. On the one hand, rhetoric is not the original quest for truth, but a reenactment. Yet, if truth is to fulfill its ethical function, it must be discovered, not absorbed passively.[12] Attention serves as the common denominator between the initial search of the philosopher and its staged rhetorical version. The self-evidence to which attention leads is always experienced as a revelation, whether it is achieved through the solitary quest of the philosopher or under the guidance of a mentor. It is not a fact to be learned by rote, but is an intuition whose discovery is a privileged moment in the life of the individual.

Attention's ethical ramifications make it as revelant in practical affairs as in the pursuit of knowledge. Even as an instrument of science, Jean-Marc Gabaude calls it an intellectual virtue because of the effort of purification it imposes.[13] As a guide to action it is also a moral virtue. For Descartes, right action follows closely on right judgment; to judge well is to act well. Given attention's role as a prelude to judgment, it is indispensable in the moral life. Moreover, continued attention to moral principles after an initial judgment has been made is necessary if the will's resolve to act virtuously is to be maintained. Attention must become a habit through "a long and frequent meditation" ("une longue et fréquente méditation" [15 September 1645, 6:303]).

If a pure and attentive intellect (1:87) is the prerequisite for the philosopher's discovery of truth and for the right judgments on which virtue depends, successful communication requires fostering the same mental state in the audience. For those who refuse the philosopher all attention, nothing can be done. "I cannot open the eyes of readers or force them to pay attention to the things one must consider in order to know clearly the truth" ("Je ne puis pas ouvrir les yeux des lecteurs, ni les forcer d'avoir de l'attention aux choses qu'il faut considérer pour connaître clairement la vérité" [21 January 1641, 4:253]). However, for those who make the first step, his rhetoric is one of attention. Hence the constant appeals throughout his writings to the *attentus lector* that Geneviève Rodis-Lewis has noted.[14]

Yet this rhetoric of attention consists of far more than exhortations to attentiveness. It is a rhetoric that preserves the mind from precipitate judgment, strengthens its concentration, and compensates for its weakness. Descartes never was concerned to elaborate the *elocutio* of this rhetoric—the specific linguistic devices that heighten attention. But given his constant interest in psychology, we are able to trace the main lines of its *inventio*— how the mind and body interact to produce the attention to a speaker's proofs necessary to persuade.

The Psychophysiology of the Rhetoric of Attention

The most fundamental of all self-evident intuitions, "I think, therefore, I am" ("je pense, donc je suis" [1:604]), provides the basis for the crucial distinction in Descartes' system between *res cogitans* and *res extensa*. He exists most properly as a thinker, with a clear and distinct idea of the nature of thought that can be defined without reference to anything pertaining to the body. Extension enters nowhere into this awareness of himself as a thinker that he could know even if he possessed no body. Descartes' radical separation of thinking and material substance is one of his proudest metaphysical achievements since it freed each realm to be studied according to its particular specificity.

Metaphysics could pursue pure thought untrammeled by the imagination or senses, and the physical world could be examined without the intrusion of spiritualistic explanations. The body is but a machine, ruled by the same laws of mechanics that govern the rest of the extended world; the soul is identical to the thinking mind, and not the animating force of the body as scholastic philosophy taught.

Yet no sooner had Descartes separated thought from extension than he had to come to grips with the unique union of these two modes in humanity. Although utterly dissimilar, these two substances do not merely coexist, they form a single entity in a union he calls substantial. "I am not only lodged in my body like a pilot in his ship, but, in addition, I am so tightly conjoined and so greatly blended and intermingled that I form a single unit with my body" ("Je ne suis pas seulement logé dans mon corps, ainsi qu'un pilote en son navire, mais, outre cela, que je lui suis conjoint très étroitement et tellement confondu et mêlé, que je compose un seul tout avec lui" [2:492]). Only by taking into account the body's role in the life of the intellect can we understand how the pure and attentive mind, the precondition for the assimilation of the Cartesian message, can function.

The actual locus of this interaction of mind and body is the pineal gland suspended in the passage between the anterior and posterior cavities of the brain. Although the soul is united to the whole body, this gland is its principal seat (3:978), where the soul exercises its functions more immediately and particularly than elsewhere, because the gland is ideally situated to activate the animal spirits or to be activated by them (3:977). These animal spirits are extremely mobile and vaporous particles of the blood which circulate swiftly throughout a network of nerves linking the brain to every part of the body. Spirits from the bloodstream flow into the brain's cavities through pores in the surface of the gland. Here the animal spirits transfer messages from other parts of the body to the mind; and conversely, the mind can set in motion the spirits in the gland in such a way that they cause the muscles to move the body or stimulate the memory of sense perceptions (3:980).

Of course, it is one thing to claim to locate the site of such interaction and even to describe the functioning of the gland and quite another to account metaphysically for how two such radically different substances as mind and matter interact. Descartes' failure on this score is indicated by his disciples' haste to replace his emphasis on the pineal gland with some alternate explanation, as is found in Malebranche's occasionalism or the pre-established harmony of Leibnitz. Nonetheless, so great was the fascination that Descartes' psychophysiology held for seventeenth-century audiences that an account is useful at this point because in its general lines it underpins the psychology of the Port-Royalists, Malebranche, and Lamy. Details that appear to the twentieth-century reader as quaint pseudoscience filled his contemporaries with enthusiasm for what they took to be rigorous observation.[15]

The Limitations and Dangers of the Senses

According to Descartes' account in *L'Homme*, data about objects in the material world are transmitted as sense perceptions to the brain through the nerves. The brain itself can be envisaged as a network of tubes and passageways that are extremely pliant, like wax or lead (1:443), surrounding a central cavity in which the pineal gland is suspended. The nerves are tiny conduits running from a sense organ to minuscule pores located on the interior surface of the cerebral cavity. These pores are controlled by a slender fiber that runs within each nerve. When the sense organ is activated, the fibers in the nerves contract, thus opening the pores on the surface of the brain cavity. Animal spirits pour out of the gland hanging at the cavity's center and are attracted to the openings of the nerve pores. The exact nature of these openings—their location and size—determines the direction and velocity of the animal spirits flowing from the gland. The precise character of each sense impression as experienced by the mind corresponds to the nature of this flow of spirits out of the pineal gland across the cavity and into the pores at the nerve endings (1:449–51). Once the animal spirits enter the nerves they proceed back to members of the body where they activitate the muscles in response to the sense impression.

The imagination is closely related to this direct perception by the senses. Descartes explains it in mechanistic terms as a form of corporal memory by which the mind represents as a sense image some absent object from the realm of extended substance. When animal spirits rush through the malleable passageways of cerebral matter during the process of sense perception, they leave imprints that might be called the signatures of the sense perceptions which originally activated them (1:451–52). A subsequent flow of spirits over these traces will reactivate the images that left the initial imprints. Such mental pictures can be created by the aleatory flow of animal spirits as in reveries or dreams. More important for rhetorical purposes, they can also be summoned up voluntarily if the will sets in motion a flow of spirits, and indeed, it is this process which most properly constitutes the imagination.

Sense knowledge bears primary responsibility for the state of prolonged childhood that stubbornly resists the Cartesian message, making the *assensio* to self-evidence and the *persuasio* that should accompany it difficult to achieve. This is not to say that the senses are by definition unreliable or deceitful. Although they can, on occasion, supply misinformation, on the whole they are accurate, within the limits of their proper function. They exist to inform us of the relation of our bodies to objects in the exterior world and the harm or good such objects can cause. Only rarely are they able to provide any knowledge about the nature of exterior objects (3:148). Error stems from asking more of the senses than they can supply. Since the will is stronger than the understanding where the data from the senses is lodged, it jumps to hasty conclusions without sufficient reflection. This precipitation is almost inevitable in childhood when the mind's powers are undeveloped in comparison to the body which overwhelms the young understanding with intense sense perceptions. The result is all manner of commonsensical erroneous judgments—that the earth is flat, that our bodies are easier to know than our minds, that nothing can exist without a body, that the stars are small, and so on. Such errors formed in childhood become fixed as tenacious prejudices so that even when they have been demonstrated to be false, once the reason is stronger, we remain under their influence (3:139–41). *Persuasio* comes with difficulty, and we are always in danger of falling back into some false preconceived idea (3:141). This is the ingrained, unexamined irrational belief that the rhetoric of attention must be designed to overcome.

Beyond the difficulty of effacing the vestiges of prejudice accumulated in the distant past of childhood, the senses still represent a present danger, whether as the direct testimony of the senses, or second hand, in the form of the imagination. The mental pictures that the senses provide to the understanding are too easily mistaken for the clear and distinct ideas of the pure understanding, the faculty of the understanding that needs no such mental images. "Our senses do not reveal to us the nature of anything at all, but only our reason when it intervenes" ("Ce ne sont point nos sens qui nous font découvrir la nature de quoi que ce soit, mais seulement notre raison lorsqu'elle y intervient" [3:142]). In the sixth meditation Descartes illustrates the superiority of the pure understanding over the imagination that depends on the body's senses. A triangle can be represented mentally by both the pure understanding, which conceives it as a three-sided figure, and by the imagination that visualizes it. However, the imagination, the eyes of the mind (2:481), is of limited use in representing a chiliagon. While the understanding can easily conceive the notion of a thousand-sided figure, the imagination cannot form a mental picture of one with any precision.

Worse perhaps than the limitations of sense knowledge is its seductive appeal. In *L'Homme* Descartes describes a mechanical attention to sense impressions (1:462) that exercises an attraction much stronger than the one produced by the clear ideas in the pure understanding. While the pure understanding operates without any intervention of animal spirits, the spirits leave profound traces in the brain when the sense impressions are processed. The mind finds it easier to concentrate on these sense ideas reinforced by the flow of animal spirits than to pass on to the clear and distinct ideas of the pure understanding. "Our soul . . . does not apply itself to anything with so much fatigue as to purely intelligible topics that are present neither to the senses nor the imagination" ("Notre âme . . . ne s'applique à rien avec tant de peine qu'aux choses purement intelligibles, qui ne sont présentes ni aux sens ni à l'imagination" [3:142])

The Imagination in a Rhetoric of Attention

No aspect of Descartes' rhetoric is more problematic than the use of images appealing to the imagination. The inconsistencies between his early and mature discussions of the issue and the tension between his theory and practice bring to surface the limits of the notion of rhetoric as a reenactment. The senses and imagination need not be banished entirely from a rhetoric of attention. Caution must be exercised in their use because of their power of seduction, but sense knowledge in itself can be reliable. Errors based on sense perceptions are the result of faulty judgments when the will attempts to extract from the senses more information than they can provide, rather than because of the failure of the senses themselves. Thus, Descartes' constant preoccupation is to demarcate the limits of the senses and the imagination, while showing at the same time how they can be used in concert with the pure understanding. The thrust of his radical separation of thought and extension is to show that progress in the sciences, whether metaphysical or physical, can come only from reserving for each domain its proper principles of explanation.

A letter to the princess Elizabeth succinctly delineates the contribution of the imagination to knowledge of the three primitive finite notions that encompass all reality—extension, mind, and their union as man.

> The soul is only conceived by the pure understanding; the body, that is to say, extension, figures, and motion, can also be known by the understanding alone, but much better by the understanding aided by the imagination; and finally, the things which belong to the union of body and soul are only known obscurely by the understanding alone; but they are known very clearly by the senses.

> L'âme ne se conçoit que par l'entendement pur; le corps, c'est-à-dire, l'extension, les figures et les mouvements, se peuvent aussi connaître par l'entendement seul, mais beaucoup mieux par l'entendement aidé de l'imagination; et enfin, les choses qui appartiennent à l'union de l'âme et du corps, ne se connaissent qu'obscurément par l'entendement

seul, ni même par l'entendement aidé de l'imagination; mais elles se connaissent très clairement par les sens. (28 June 1643, 5:322–23)

The imagination belongs most properly to the second of these categories. Thus, he chides Gassendi in the Fifth Replies to the *Méditations* for trying to introduce the imagination into the explanation of the mind/body union that is most properly experienced by the sensations (2:836). Likewise, the imagination is useless in understanding the soul because by its nature it cannot be represented by a corporal image (July 1641, 4:378). In fact, in the realm of metaphysics, the imagination which can be of particular aid in mathematics causes more harm than good (13 November 1639, 3:262).

This position marks a turnabout from the one recorded in his early *Olympica*. There the physical world holds a key for understanding spiritual reality:

> Just as the imagination uses figures to conceive physical bodies, so the intellect uses certain bodies perceived by the senses such as wind and light to give form to spiritual things. Whence it follows that when we philosophize in a higher fashion, we can elevate the mind, by means of knowledge, to the heights. . . . Things that can be perceived by the senses permit us to conceive Olympian matters: wind signifies spirit, extended motion signifies life, light signifies knowledge; heat signifies love; instantaneous activity, creation.

> Ut imaginatio utitur figuris ad corpora concipienda, ita intellectus utitur quibusdam corporibus sensibilibus ad spiritualia figuranda, ut vento, lumine: unde altius philosophantes mentem cognitione possumus in sublime tollere. . . . Sensibilia apta concipiendis Olympicis: ventus spiritum significat; motus cum tempore vitam, lumen cognitionem, calor amorem, activitas instantanea creationem. (1:61–62; A.-T., 10:217–19)

However, as Gouhier points out, when Descartes wrote these fragments around 1620 he possessed neither the foundations of his physics, nor his metaphysics. The discontinuity he was to posit between extended and thinking substance would discredit the symbolism of the *Olympica* by destroying the analogy between matter and spirit on which it is based.[16]

Still, much of his youthful confidence in such symbolism lingers in his mature rhetorical practice, even if condemned in theory. Images stud his writings, including those dealing with the objects of pure thought. For example, he reconciles divine prescience and human freedom to Elizabeth with an elaborate parabole of a king who orders two enemies to the same spot knowing their inclination toward dueling (January 1646, 7:2). Even in the *Méditations,* written for the most erudite of audiences, he explains that God's existence is as inseparable from his essence as the notion of valley from that of mountain. The fact that such images are invariably presented as similes, where the introductory *comme* indicates that they are only illustrative devices rather than metaphors implying a closer identity between the two elements compared, does not obviate the fact that rhetoric here is no longer a reenactment.[17] Assuming that Descartes reached these abstract notions without reference to the senses, he seems unable to share his vision with others without making a detour back to the sensible world.

The imagination is most appropriate in the domain of extended substance, yet even here, and in a more telling way, Descartes' use of simile conflicts with rhetoric as a reenactment. In mathematics the imagination can aid the mind in the form of the simplified notations he introduced into algebra; geometers find certain figures and diagrams useful, but as the example of the chiliagon in the sixth meditation shows, such mental pictures are not absolutely necessary, or even always possible. In fact, we see the limitations of the imagination as an aid to the understanding perhaps most clearly in geometric figures where the visual element is reduced to an absolute minimum. As Geneviève Rodis-Lewis shows, the imagination is a resting point, a way station for the pure understanding, not the ultimate destination, and the geometer who is content to investigate only those figures that can be visualized will never advance beyond the rudiments of the science.[18]

In his scientific works Descartes allows for the use of comparisons and analogies that exploit more fully the visual appeal of

the imagination than do the line drawings of the geometer. Phenomena too small to be perceived directly by the senses can be
studied in terms of those that are large enough to be observed
because the difference is merely one of proportion (12 September 1638, 3:67). Likewise, the products of human craftsmen can
be used to explain the works of nature since both are governed
by the same laws of mechanics (3:520). The human clockmaker
works according to the same physical laws that God established
in creating the universe. While it is true that the visual appeal of
such comparisons conflicts to a certain extent with Descartes'
aspiration to replace the sensible with mathematical proofs, the
analogy depends for its validity on the mathematical character
of the underlying laws, rather than on the purely visual elements.

The problem lies in the rhetorical status of these comparisons.
For Descartes, they are not merely illustrative devices that allow
him to clarify certain difficult points for readers unable to follow
a more abstract explanation. They are also heuristic instruments
by which he himself proceeds from the known into regions that
he is unable to observe directly. In itself this use of comparisons
appealing to the imagination seems appropriate in a rhetoric
requiring the audience to reenact the journey of the master. The
same analogies he used as a tool of discovery will aid the readers.
However, as Pierre-Alain Cahné has shown, Descartes usually
disguises the fact that the metaphor is a method of investigation,
not just proof or exposition. The comparisons with objects in
the everyday world that abound in his scientific writings appear
merely to illustrate or clarify concepts that were first discovered
through the application of his geometric method. Yet Cahné
demonstrates that the comparison, not his famous method, is
Descartes' chief heuristic device when dealing with the physical
world. "The creative image sometimes occurs in the course of the
exposition well after the formulation in mechanistic, systematic
language that the image made possible so that the *ratio docendi*
camouflages the *ratio inveniendi*."[19] Seen in this optic, the scientific
similes no longer aid the reader in reenacting Descartes' discoveries. The similes exchange places with the rules of method;
method becomes the agent of exposition hiding the fact that the
accompanying comparisons are not only illustrations, but also
the tool by which Descartes arrived at his conclusions. Impersonal

synthetic exposition replaces analysis. The reader's experience of *évidence* may be just as firm when synthesis is employed, but the appreciation of how the *évidence* was attained is faulty.

The Passions in a Rhetoric of Attention

The psychophysiology of the passions, which Descartes treats in detail in *Les Passions de l'âme* (1649), resembles that of sense perception in many ways, for like the senses the passions are a form of confused thought (1 February 1647, 7:255). The chief difference is that the passions affect the will rather than the understanding. They are caused automatically without the direct intervention of the will by the prolonged movement of animal spirits pouring out of the pineal gland in the brain upon the occasion of some sense image in the understanding. The distinctive "flavor" that characterizes each emotion is determined by secretions added to the blood stream by the internal organs—the stomach, spleen, the liver, and so on—that remain when the blood is distilled into animal spirits (3:964). Their effects are seen in Descartes' illustration of the fear excited by the sight of some strange beast. The animal spirits spread throughout the nervous system, but particularly to the heart where the passion is most strongly registered. Involuntary muscle responses can result, as when a person flees some dreadful sight before ever making a conscious decision to do so. Thus, like the senses, the passions exist for the good of the body and the mind/body union. They move the body to act mechanically in its interest on the basis of information provided by the senses. Their role is to second the judgment of the will inciting it to action and encouraging it to persevere on behalf of the body's welfare (3:998). They are harmful only when they stray from this legitimate function by excess either by giving undue resonance to thoughts that might be proper in themselves, or worse, to ones that should best be avoided (3:1009).

Much of the danger posed by the passions, especially the strong ones, results from the increased agitation of the blood and animal spirits that accompany them. The resulting commotion is too intense for the attention to ignore, no matter how much the will struggles to block out the passion. Unfortunately, the passions are not content with the subordinate role of reinforcing the judgments of the will. The automatic responses they set in motion in the body can replace the deliberate reflection of the mind. Moreover, their nature is to exaggerate and to push the will to act with more impulsion than calm judgment might allow. "They almost always make things seem much grander and more important that they are—whether good things or evil ones—so that they incite us to seek out the former and to flee the latter with more ardor and care than is appropriate" ("Elles font paraître presque toujours, tant les biens que les maux qu'elles représentent, beaucoup plus grands et plus importants qu'ils ne sont, en sorte qu'elles nous incitent à rechercher les uns et fuir les autres avec plus d'ardeur et plus de soin qu'il n'est convenable" [3:1054]).

Yet the passions have a useful role to play in both the intellectual and moral life, and by extension, they can serve in a rhetoric of attention geared to leading the audience toward truth and exciting the desire to act upon it. While the primary function of the passions is to promote the good of the body, they need not be excluded from the pursuit of truth since attention is among the actions of the will which they fortify. Descartes particularly recommends an initial dose of *admiration,* by which he means surprise and wonder rather than approval or esteem. He not only includes admiration among his six primitive passions in which all the others find their source (3:1006), he labels it the first of all the passions (3:999). This admiration is "a sudden surprise of the soul which brings it to consider with attention objects that seem rare and extraordinary to it" ("une subite surprise de l'âme, qui fait qu'elle se porte à considérer avec attention les objets qui lui semblent rares et extraordinaires" [3:1006]). Unlike the other passions which excite the body to action, admiration is chiefly intellectual. It is not aroused because an object seems useful or harmful to the body, but merely unusual; in addition, the flow of animal spirits it causes remains localized in the brain rather than spreading to the heart and nervous system as is the case of the other passions (3:1006). It thus has the power to assist in initially fixing the attention and strengthening the memory. So important is this passion, that those who lack a natural disposition to it are usually among the ignorant (3:1010). Yet as with all the passions, an excess of admiration can prove dangerous, leading either to immobile contemplation or to a frantic search for new curiosities. Thus, while we should profit from the inclination toward the sciences afforded by admiration, Descartes would prefer that as we mature intellectually, the will be trained to do without this aid from the body. An extra effort on the part of the will, he maintains, can always compensate for its absence by promoting a special state of reflection and attention (3:1011).

While admiration functions as the most important passion in scientific or philosophic endeavors where the pursuit of truth is the goal, the multitude of other passions he describes plays a significant role in the moral realm of human action. The will may have no direct control over the passions, but Descartes insists that knowledge of the mechanism by which they can be calmed or excited constitutes a crucial component of practical ethics (3:1101–2). It also has application for a rhetoric aimed at persuading an audience to adopt a certain line of action. He notes that the will cannot turn the passions on or off by simple command, any more than it can order the pupil of the eye to close or enlarge. Nonetheless, just as the size of the pupil can be controlled by directing the vision at an object that is distant or near, the will can act on the passions indirectly by conjuring in the imagination images that are normally associated with certain emotional responses (3:987). An awareness of this mechanism allows mastery of our passions in the moral arena; for example, he recommends to Elizabeth a strategy for avoiding sadness by turning the imagination away from a consideration of her afflictions (May/June 1645, 6:237–39). The implications of this mechanism for persuasive discourse are apparent if we transpose to the context of a speech Descartes' description of how courage can be excited:

> An act of the will is not enough to excite in oneself boldness and remove fear. Rather one must consider diligently the arguments, objects, and examples that persuade one that the danger is not great, that there is always more safety in defense than in flight and similar considerations.

> Pour exciter en soi la hardiesse et ôter la peur, il ne suffit pas d'en avoir la volonté, mais il faut s'appliquer à considérer les raisons, les objets ou les exemples qui persuadent que le

péril n'est pas grand; qu'il y a toujours plus de sûreté en la
défense qu'en la fuite . . . et choses semblables. (3:988)

The will thus uses a roundabout method to stimulate itself; it
invokes the imagination to excite the passions, which in turn
reinforce the desires of the will.

Descartes' advice here, of course, only parallels a longstanding
recommendation of rhetoricians. Quintilian, for example, had
noted that speakers are most effective in stirring the emotions of
an audience when they first feel the emotions themselves, and
that they could provoke such emotions by painting vivid mental
pictures.[20] Rather than suggest any particular rhetorical devices,
Descartes' contribution is to describe the psychophysiological
mechanism underlying the strategies to which the orator has
recourse. Thus, a second dimension is added to the imagination's
functions in persuasion. We had previously seen how it could aid
the understanding in the form of comparisons and analogies;
here it acts on the will through the passions.

The corporal passions can be further strengthened by a second
class of emotions which depend directly on the will and which
are experienced by the mind alone, without the participation of
the animal spirits.[21] The difference between these intellectual
emotions and the corporal passions which the mind experiences
because of its union with the body is somewhat similar to the
difference between the sense ideas perceived in the imagination
and pure thought detached of all sensible impressions. Unlike
the physical passions resulting from the intense circulation of
animal spirits that are the automatic reaction to some sense perception, these intellectual emotions are caused by a judgment of
the will without any intervention of the body. However, they are
seldom experienced alone, even though the body plays no role
in their production, because they are usually accompanied by a
physical response that occurs first in the imagination and is then
followed by some corporal passion (3:505–6). Thus intellectual
joy is most often accompanied by corporal joy, intellectual sadness with corporal sadness.

Because they are constituted by intense acts of volition (3:975),
the intellectual emotions are more solid and lasting than the
passions that depend on the circulation of animal spirits. Indeed,

they are at the core of moral life. The highest natural pleasure humans can experience, the internal satisfaction that comes from doing all one can to judge and act wisely, is their most important manifestation (3:1064). Persuasion that succeeds in reaching the will, thus finds its effect greatly amplified by these intellectual emotions that heighten the resolve to act and reinforce it with additional corporal passions.

Générosité and the Ethical Proof

The most fundamental passion in Descartes' rhetoric is not excited in the audiences by appeals to the imagination; it is the zeal for truth that Descartes attributes in his defense of Balzac to the ideal orator before the corruption of eloquence at the hands of Greek and Roman demagogues. This zeal is the source of the frankness that Descartes praises so highly in Balzac. In general terms, such a passion for truth is to a rhetor embarked in the communication process what the assurance experienced in self-evidence is to the philosopher in its discovery. Descartes does not treat this passion explicitly in *Les passions de l'âme*, but it can be analyzed in terms of the six principal passions in his system (admiration, love, hate, joy, sorrow, and desire) out of which all the others are composed.

Indeed, three of these primitive passions are involved. This zeal combines love of truth with the desire to communicate it, a desire born of *générosité*, which is itself the most perfect form of admiration. The link to admiration is significant given its privileged position as the most intellectual of the Cartesian passions and its key role in Descartes' ethical thought. To practice *générosité*, when it fully informs the will, is to follow perfectly the path of virtue. It is "the key to all the other virtues and a general remedy against all the disorders of the passions" ("la clef de toutes les autres vertus et un remède général contre tous les dérèglements des passions" [3:1074]). The nobility of spirit associated with *générosité* was an important concept in the gentleman's moral code of this period; it is frequently invoked, for example, by Corneille's heroes. Descartes takes pains to separate the notion from false pride and to emphasize that *générosité* is above all the product of an accurate judgment of one's worth, a just esteem of one's merit. Accidents such as wealth, physical beauty, or honors of the sort that so many of his aristocratic contemporaries were inordinately proud are not the essence of true *générosité*. The only worthy object of this self-inspection is one's use of free will. Free will, after all, according to Descartes, is the most god-like characteristic of humans, and only its use or misuse merits praise or blame. At the same time, *générosité* is the firm resolution to execute what one has determined to be the best course of action. This resolve to act according to one's best judgments is what transforms *générosité* into a virtue, making it the full exercise of the freedom that is the essence of human nature (3:1067).

It is, then, no accident that Descartes praised Balzac's frankness as his "generosa quaedam libertas" (1:35), combining two of the principal themes in his ethical thought, freedom and *générosité*. First of all, this frankness is a form of freedom, for what better use can be made of one's free will than to assert openly the truth affirmed in the act of judgment. In doing so, the will celebrates the product of its most prized capacity, that is, its power to judge. At the same time, the truly generous souls who have accurately assessed their own worth are magnanimous in their dealings with others, esteeming nothing greater than to benefit their fellows (3:1069; cp. 3:1088). Their frankness impels them to communicate openly their judgments. They will share their discoveries with others, much as Descartes declares in the sixth part of the *Discours* that he felt compelled to bring his physics to the attention of the public as soon as he recognized its potential practical benefits (1:634).

When this generous exercise of freedom, the zeal for truth, informs a discourse, it becomes a powerful aid to attention. It is certainly the most fitting form of the ethical proof for a philosopher who prized self-evidence above all. Descartes had complained to Mersenne of those who refused to take the first step toward truth: "I cannot give intelligence to men or make people who refuse to step inside see what is at the far end of a study" ("Je ne puis pas donner de l'esprit aux hommes, ni faire voir ce qui est au fond d'un cabinet, à des gens qui ne veulent pas entrer dedans pour regarder" [21 January 1641, 4:254]). A display of the speaker's love and desire for truth can awaken an initial admiration, an interest in those who are otherwise indifferent or hostile. A similar passion for truth, once aroused in the public, will serve as the foundation for an attention that can be heightened by additional strategies.

Anything less than this zeal for truth is an affront against *générosité*. Prudence may dictate that on occasion one not divulge all one thinks, but to undertake willingly to argue a cause that is foreign to one's sentiments is the act of an abject person without integrity (July 1645, 6:271). He claims as his personal rule of action a simplicity and frankness where "the chief wile is not to seek recourse to wiles" ("la principale finesse est de ne vouloir point du tout user de finesse" [January 1645, 7:5]). This moral dimension assures him a final test for evaluating persuasive discourse. A frank and sincere *générosité* informs authentic eloquence, while false eloquence tends toward obfuscation, futile quibbling, if not outright deception. Thus it is not surprising to find a strong dose of moral superiority in most of Descartes' comments on his opponents' rhetoric. If the disputes and debates so popular among his scholastic rivals do not produce truth, faulty method is not the sole cause; such controversies are often motivated, he would maintain, by vanity and false pride, the opposites of *générosité*. They are animated by the longing to appear brilliant and to triumph over their enemies, not by the quest for truth.

False versus Authentic Eloquence

Descartes never undertook as extensive a refutation of what he held to be false eloquence as Malebranche later provided in his attack against Tertullian, Seneca, and Montaigne in *La Recherche de la vérité*. Nonetheless, we can see the basis of his objections to such defective eloquence in the *Cinquièmes Réponses*, where Descartes stigmatizes Gassendi for having recourse to all the artifices of an orator (2:787), and for using the tricks of rhetoric (2:790) to avoid dealing with his arguments. He depicts Gassendi as being locked in the thralls of the prejudices and hasty judgments of prolonged childhood before the mind has corrected the errors induced by the body. As if to emphasize the body's hold on Gassendi's intellect, Descartes playfully addresses him throughout as "O Flesh" ("ô caro") using what he admits to be a not unpleasant rhetorical figure (2:793). Gassendi's arguments themselves are tagged as worthless because he is guilty of confusing the realm of the body and that of the mind: "You wish to submit to the examination of the imagination topics which by their nature are not subject to its jurisdiction" ("quae ex natura sua sub imaginationem non cadunt, ad eius tamen examen velis revocare" [2:836–37; A.-T., 7:104]). The only reader he convinces is one who clings more to a multitude of words than to the force of proofs (2:794). Gassendi's prolixity cannot mask his absence of judgment. Ultimately for Descartes, Gassendi is little better than the sophists Descartes condemned in his letter defending Balzac; Gassendi is described as lacking the same philosophic honesty (2:790) that Descartes singled out there as the hallmark of the truly eloquent.

Such false eloquence is reprehensible because it functions almost entirely at the level of the body. In psychophysiological terms, the commotion of animal spirits in the brain can be so vigorous as to short-circuit the operation of the understanding and the will. The colors of rhetoric Descartes refers to in his condemnation of Gassendi's eloquence (2:790) create images in the imagination so vivid that they seem more present, more real than the self-evidence of clear and distinct ideas. They excite the passions, which in turn deflect the will's attention, distracting it from the quest for truth, just as they can produce an agitation so strong as to overrule any resolution of the will to act. The corporal machine literally overcomes the mind.

Descartes had reason to extend his distrust of what he understood to be Gassendi's body-centered eloquence to the range of humanist-inspired rhetoric of the early seventeenth century. For example, François Ogier's encomium of the power of eloquence over its hearers found in his *Apologie de Monsieur de Balzac* (which Descartes must certainly have read in preparing his own defense of the *Unico eloquente*) emphasizes the grip the material component of the orator's words has on the bodies of the members of the audience.

> Even if one does not intend to retain the words with precision, they are nevertheless so well and so aptly placed that thanks to this order and admirable arrangement they enter

the most unfortunate memories without resistance and attach themselves so strongly to our imagination that they become like parts of our being. . . . It is this secret power of speech that acts on the body of the listeners so that the entire man is vanquished and that his second part is not exempt from the jurisdiction of eloquence. This is what the ancient rhetoricians called the *mystery of their art*, what persuades our hearing before reason has persuaded our intellect.

[E]ncore qu'on n'ait pas dessein d'en retenir précisément les paroles, elles sont néanmoins si bien et si justement placées, qu'avec cet ordre et cet arrangement admirable, elles entrent sans résistance dans les plus malheureuses mémoires, et s'attachent si fortement à notre imagination, qu'elles deviennent comme parties de nous-mêmes. . . . C'est cette vertu secrète de l'Oraison, qui agit sur le corps des Auditeurs, afin que l'homme soit vaincu tout entier, et que sa seconde partie ne s'exempte pas de la jurisdiction de l'éloquence. C'est ce que les anciens Rhétoriciens ont appelé *le mystère de leur art*, ce qui persuade notre ouïe, avant que la raison ait persuadé notre intelligence.[22]

Descartes could not help but mistrust an eloquence that aimed frankly at the body before the mind with the result that the speaker's words become incorporated into the very being of the listeners. From a Cartesian perspective, Ogier is oblivious to the prudence born from a sound appreciation of the mind/body union. He is willing to settle for a *persuasio* born of the senses, not the more solid one that is engendered by self-evidence.

In contrast to the false eloquence exemplified by Gassendi, where the body holds sway, authentic eloquence gives primacy to the mind. It must aim at producing judgments in the will affirming the *évidence* grasped by the understanding. It is a reenactment of the process by which the mind discovers truth, guided by the master who made the original quest and who takes into account the fraility of the party he leads. Its constant preoccupation must be strengthening and extending the power of attention, the will's power to sift through appearances and probability to the clear and distinct ideas whose presence to the mind as self-evidence is the ultimate sign of truth. It is an aggressive rhetoric

that targets the deeply rooted prejudices of prolonged childhood—the received ideas which are so persistent because they
seem authorized by common sense. This authentic eloquence is
all the more effective in that it is grounded in an analysis of the
mind/body union. It is well equipped to combat the prejudices
of childhood because it is grounded in an understanding of their
origin; it is poised to harness the imagination and the passions
because it takes into account their mechanism. The psychological
assurance of persuasion it produces is united with self-evidence.

Yet since the mind is our principal and better part, Descartes'
rhetoric uses the affective and imaginative strategies the body
furnishes with due caution, lest the body's powerful attraction
usurp the mind's proper dominion. Above all, his rhetoric is
infused with *générosité*. As ethical proof, the presence of the zeal
for truth in the speaker is the most potent of all aids to attention
in fostering the presence of *évidence* in the mind of the listener.
But even more important, this *générosité* is the guarantee of moral
purpose and the safeguard against sophistry.

4

Port-Royal and Eloquence

Rhetoric at the Margins

As for rhetoric . . . the assistance it provides in finding the proper wording and embellishments was not so considerable. The mind furnishes sufficient ideas, usage provides the wording, and as for figures and ornaments, there are always too many.

En ce qui regarde la Rhétorique . . . le secours qu'on en pouvait tirer pour trouver des expressions, et des embellissements, n'était pas si considérable. L'esprit fournit assez de pensées, l'usage donne les expressions; et pour les figures et les ornements, on n'en a toujours que trop.

Arnauld and Nicole,
Logique de Port-Royal

Invoking both a Cartesian preference for clear and distinct ideas and a moralist's urge to limit the consequences of the Fall, the authors of *La Logique, ou l'art de penser,* the text known as the *Logique de Port-Royal* (1662), pride themselves on having all but eliminated eloquence:

[A]s for rhetoric . . . almost all of it consists in turning away from certain bad manners of writing and speaking, and above all from an artificial style typical of rhetoricians composed of false hyperbolic ideas and strained figures, which is the greatest of all the vices.

[E]n ce qui regarde la Rhétorique . . . tout consiste presque à s'éloigner de certaines mauvaises manières d'écrire et de parler, et surtout d'un style artificiel et rhétoricien composé de pensées fausses et hyperboliques et de figures forcées, qui est le plus grand de tous les vices.[1]

Almost everything useful that the study of rhetoric can furnish is negative: how to avoid unacceptable patterns of discourse, especially the pitfalls of a hyperbolic style reminiscent of Balzac's. The irony, of course, is that Antoine Arnauld and Pierre Nicole cannot confine rhetoric's positive value to the tiny space represented by "almost." Their effort to subordinate rhetoric to other disciplines—whether logic as analyzed by Hugh Davidson,[2] or semiotics according to the more recent study of Sara Melzer[3]— proves vain. For Louis Marin, the only perfect eloquence according to Arnauld and Nicole's criteria is realized in the eucharistic formulas which they analyze in the course of their defense of the Catholic doctrine of transubstantiation.[4] Nonetheless, I will show that they allow for more accessible forms of eloquence. Indeed, in spite of the fact that they exclude rhetorical theory and push the rhetorical to the margins of logic and linguistics, the grudging concessions they make to traditional rhetoric for the sake of sermons can be extended to legitimize a more wide-ranging eloquence than they admit.

Polemics and Pedagogy
as Prologue to Theory

Much more so than Descartes, whose efforts at persuasion were limited to promoting his philosophical views in learned circles or giving moral advice to a select group of correspondents, Arnauld and Nicole arrived at their *Logique de Port-Royal* with more practical rhetorical experience, both as polemicists on behalf of Jansenism and as educators in Port-Royal's "little schools." Antoine Arnauld was nurtured in a rhetorical environment.[5] He was born in 1612 in a clan of Parisian magistrates Balzac called "the eloquent family," in which three generations had earned the title of the French Cicero.[6] His earliest recorded text is a Latin poem celebrating the civic eloquence of Balzac's *Le Prince* (42:414–16). When Antoine, the youngest of twenty children, wrote this poem in 1631, his family had already moved into the orbit of the austere Saint-Cyran. Arnauld quickly became the most vigorous champion of Jansenism, a distinction that early earned him harrassment and later exile to Belgium, where he died in 1694. By 1660, when the treatises that concern us were written, he had been engaged in long years of controversy over his *Fréquente Communion* (1643) and had participated in the elaboration of Pascal's *Lettres provinciales* (1656–57) against the Jesuits, for which he and Nicole furnished background papers and advice. Some thirteen years Arnauld's junior, Nicole was called on to aid Arnauld around 1655 because of his theological training and fluid Latin style, thus beginning a long collaboration.[7] Interspersed in the polemical texts of these years we find remarks on persuasion and style that were later given theoretical formulation in the *Logique de Port-Royal*. For example, in the *Réponse à la lettre d'une personne de condition* (1654), Arnauld defends the impassioned, biting tone of the church fathers against the claim that only a calm, rational approach is appropriate to religious disputes (27:21, 41).

The pedagogical impulse was nurtured in the little schools of Port-Royal. Nicole taught rhetoric and philosophy in these classes organized between 1646 and 1660 by the *solitaires* who gravitated around the abbey, and Arnauld served as an advisor. Arnauld's *Règlement des études dans les lettres humaines*, while perhaps not written for the *petites écoles*, provides an indication of the spirit in which the humanities were taught there. The aim of rhetorical training is not to teach students to write compositions or to deliver speeches in Latin, a skill for which doctors, magistrates, priests, and merchants have little need (41:85–86). A reading knowledge of Latin will suffice for most (41:87). Instead, study of the classical authors should lead to an analytic temper of mind requisite in the Church, the courts, and councils of state (41:88). "By filling their head with beautiful models, their judgment will be formed" ("En leur remplissant la tête de beaux modèles, ils se formeront le jugement" [41:97]). Arnauld thus claims that the study of the humanities and rhetoric, when properly pursued, can contribute to the same apprenticeship in sound judgment that logic and geometry provide.

A trio of texts extended the influence of the Port-Royal schools after their forced closing by the authorities in 1660 through numerous editions and translations that remained popular well into the eighteenth century: *La Grammaire générale et raisonnée* (1660), *La Logique, ou l'art de penser* (1662), and *Les Nouveaux Eléments de géométrie* (1667). All three were conceived around 1660, and all bear the imprint of Arnauld's rigorous analysis. The *Logique de Port-Royal* is generally acknowledged as the centerpiece since its account of the mind's four operations—conceiving, judging, reasoning, and ordering—informs the others. Thus the *Grammaire générale*, written with Claude Lancelot, analyzes language in terms of these intellectual operations with an emphasis on judgment.[8] The *Nouveaux Eléments de géométrie* uses the synthetic form of demonstration discussed in the fourth part of the *Logique de Port-Royal* to reorder the proofs of Euclid in a more natural sequence.[9] Their geometry textbook has generally been overlooked by commentators on Port-Royal's rhetorical theory despite its important preface by Nicole that removes moral and practical concerns from the sphere of geometric method.

Attention versus Eloquence

Port-Royal was not particularly favorable to philosophy in general, or to Descartes in particular. In fact, Arnauld, who was attracted by the distinction between the pure intellect and sense perception in Cartesian epistemology, stands out as an exception in his attachment to the new philosophy, for even Nicole harbored reservations.[10] As early as 1641, in the *Quatrièmes Objections* to the *Méditations,* Arnauld had noted the convergence of Descartes' philosophy with that of Augustine. Indeed, the explicit discussion of eloquence in terms of Cartesian attention that is inaugurated in the *Logique de Port-Royal* is a product of Nicole and Arnauld's allegiance to Descartes' psychophysiology coupled with their Augustinian stress on concupiscence. At each step, Cartesian elements are re-oriented by a theological imperative. In the first chapter of the *Logique de Port-Royal* the superiority of pure thought over sense ideas, which Arnauld had noted with approval in the *Quatrièmes Objections* (2:642), is repeated, using Descartes' example of the difficulty of imagining a thousand-sided figure (*Logique*, 40). The distinction between the two kinds of ideas takes on a religious color absent in Descartes when Arnauld and Nicole cite Augustine's teaching that, since the Fall, humans find it more pleasurable to attend to the product of the senses represented by corporal images than to pure ideas (*Logique*, 40). The false judgments induced by the attention's attraction to the sensible thus find their ultimate source in original sin. Seen in this light, when like Descartes, they attribute most errors of judgment to precipitation and lack of attention (*Logique*, 17), it is not surprising that Arnauld and Nicole do not point so much to the will's disproportionate strength vis-à-vis the understanding as to moral failure. "The little love that men have for the truth results in them not taking the trouble most of the time to distinguish what is true from what is false" ("Le peu d'amour que les hommes ont pour la vérité, fait qu'ils ne se mettent pas en peine la plupart du temps de distinguer ce qui est vrai de ce qui est faux" [*Logique*, 17]). Proper scientific procedure is only the immediate goal of their logic; it is but a propaedeutic for the moral judgment that determines a person's salvation.

For Arnauld and Nicole, Descartes' state of prolonged childhood, when prejudice dominates the mind, should be attributed to original corruption. Children's attention is naturally attracted to outward sensible appearances, a condition that many adults never outgrow. As Nicole states in the preface of the *Nouveaux Eléments de géométrie*, "Their whole application is always directed toward pleasing manners. . . . They only use their mind to study what delights and the art of pleasing, as well as the things that flatter concupiscence and the senses" ("Toute leur application est toujours aux manières agréables. . . . Ils ne se servent de leur esprit que pour étudier l'agrément et l'art de plaire, pour les choses qui flattent la concupiscence et les sens" [42:6]).

The will that directs attention is tugged by concupiscence toward the sensual pleasure produced by material objects (*Logique*, 78). The result is a failure to attend to the distinction between the true source of happiness that is God, and the pleasing sensations obtained from objects. This weakness of attention in fallen mankind represented by the attraction of the sensible explains susceptibility to the errors of judgment induced by false eloquence. In their present condition most humans do not have sufficient attention to attain difficult truths. Indeed, many are content to attend to the most accessible ones and clamor for an eloquent presentation: "[T]here are even minds that can only apply themselves to understanding truths that are of easy access and clothed in the ornaments of eloquence" ("[I]l y a même des esprits qui ne se peuvent appliquer à comprendre que les vérités faciles et revêtues des ornements de l'éloquence" [*Logique*, 22]).

The dichotomy implicit here in the identification of eloquence with ornamentation is indicative of the negative approach to eloquence throughout the *Logique de Port-Royal*. Interior truth is contrasted to appearances, the substance or *fond* to the accompanying *manières* (*Logique*, 288), and *res* to *verba* (*Logique*, 276). In every case, Arnauld and Nicole assume that the mind's attention is more attracted to the ideas perceived by the senses that characterize the second member than to the pure ones of the first. "The air of the speech usually enters the mind before its arguments" ("L'air du discours entre ordinairement dans l'esprit avant les raisons" [*Logique*, 288]). The false judgments thus engendered when the attention is seduced by sense pleasures are typical of false eloquence. Conversely, ineffective eloquence on behalf of truth results from orators forgetting that an audience is likely to reject even sound reasoning if the outward manner offends.

The need to fortify attention is highlighted in the mission of preventing false judgments, which Arnauld and Nicole assign to logic (*Logique*, 21): "[T]he sole means of defending oneself from them is to bring an exacting attention to our judgments and thoughts" ("[L]'unique moyen de s'en garantir est d'apporter une attention exacte à nos jugements et à nos pensées" [*Logique*, 19]). Thus, analysis, the principal method for the discovery of truth, is defined in terms of attention. "Analysis consists chiefly in the attention one pays to what is known in the question one wishes to resolve" ("C'est dans l'attention que l'on fait à ce qui est de connu dans la question que l'on veut résoudre, que consiste principalement l'analyse" [*Logique*, 303]). Analysis is more a question of sound judgment and an alert mind than the application of particular rules (*Logique*, 305). Furthermore, in the name of attention, Arnauld and Nicole reject as useless the method of invention based on the commonplaces taught by both logicians and rhetoricians, just as Descartes had rejected the syllogism as a means of discovery. Artificial methods such as the topics give birth only to amplifications, not to the solid proofs that "attentive consideration of the subject" ("la considération attentive de son sujet" [*Logique*, 234; cp. 235]) alone can produce. Moreover, synthesis, the preferred mode of exposition for Arnauld and Nicole, replaces rhetoric as a method of communication. Logic offers the hope of collapsing the distinction between *fond* and *manières* so that the mind can make direct contact with content alone. The only ornaments Arnauld and Nicole accept in theory are the ideas themselves. "[V]ivid and natural reasons . . . are the true ornaments of every kind of discourse" ("[L]es raisons vives et naturelles . . . sont les vrais ornements de toute sorte de discours" [*Logique*, 235]).

The truth alone, discovered by analysis and demonstrated by synthesis, should make rhetoric superfluous. But at every step, Arnauld and Nicole make concessions to rhetoric without, however, considering all the consequences. Whether it is a question of the subject matter itself, the speaker's relation to the subject, or the relation between speaker and audience, a legitimate space for eloquence alongside logic appears.

The Return of the Rhetorical

In regard to subject matter, Arnauld and Nicole do not explicitly recognize the rights of eloquence to a specific territory, although their desire to limit the scope of Descartes' rule of *évidence* does provide a legitimization of the probable that Bernard Lamy will later exploit. Like Descartes in the *Regulae*, they label *science* the vivid and penetrating certitude of clear and distinct ideas produced by a long and exact attention (*Logique*, 292). Science aims not just at convincing the mind, but enlightening it by providing the intellectual satisfaction that results from an understanding of the principles underlying phenomena (*Logique*, 328). The demonstrations conducted according to the method of logic have as their goal this conviction of science (*Logique*, 291). Nonetheless, the *Logique de Port-Royal* notes that in many metaphysical questions treated by philosphers, one can only hope to arrive at clear ideas. Other metaphysical ones, such as those regarding the power of God, are inaccessible because they are beyond the limits of the human mind or because we have no principles to guide us (*Logique*, 295). Arnauld and Nicole do not assign such problematic topics to eloquence, but rather counsel prudence and advise that if they are treated at all, they serve to humble the mind by reminding it of its weakness (*Logique*, 298).

The Port-Royalists then proceed to a second class where science is impossible—questions of fact like past events or future contingencies. Arguments appealing to the probable and *vraisemblance* are at issue in both aspects that must be considered when dealing with historical data: the internal circumstances concerning the possibility of an event occuring, and the external ones based on the reliability of human witnesses (*Logique*, 340). Since it would be ridiculous to expect to arrive at a necessary truth concerning such contingencies (*Logique*, 339), it is enough to weigh the probabilities involved. In this regard, they cite Descartes' distinction between metaphysical and the moral certitude, noting that often in the affairs of life, we must be content with the most probable (*Logique*, 340; cp. 348). Here, however, Arnauld and Nicole are not so much interested in appealing to the legitimacy of the probable in order to authorize rhetoric as they are anxious to establish the reasonableness of historical proofs in their Christian apologetics. Although Descartes had devoted even less attention to history than to rhetoric, his exclusion of erudition and the probable from true science tended to call into question the historical disciplines just as it did eloquence. As their examples dealing with the credibility of miracles show, the Port-Royalists are determined to safeguard sacred history from the attacks of historical pyrrhonists by showing how recourse to the probable can be justified when dealing with the past.[11]

They accept the probable as well in dealing with future contingencies (*Logique*, 351). Such problematic eventualities had been one of the staple subjects of classical deliberative eloquence. However, Arnauld and Nicole attempt to narrow the gap between them and *évidence* by turning to a loose mathematics of probabilities inspired by Pascal's work with probability theory (*Logique*, 353–54). Ian Hacking identifies this argument as the first in-

stance of the use of the term "probability" in the modern sense of "susceptible of numerical measurement."[12]
Only in Nicole's preface to the *Nouveaux Eléments de géométrie* is the probable distinguished from self-evidence in a way that is useful to eloquence. There he notes that the geometric model of methodical demonstration leading to self-evident conclusions cannot be applied across the board. "This custom of rejecting everything which is not entirely clear can lead to a considerable failing which is to wish to practice this exactitude with every kind of topic" ("Cette coutume même de rejeter tout ce qui n'est pas entièrement clair, peut engager dans un défaut très considérable, qui est de vouloir pratiquer cette exactitude en toute sorte de matières" [42:8]). The chains of proofs formed by a succession of propositions one finds in geometry cannot be duplicated in every instance. The exceptions he cites are precisely the areas reserved traditionally for eloquence:

> Most moral and human topics are among this number; and there are even religious truths that are proved much better by the light of several principles that give each other mutual aid and support than by proofs that resemble those of geometric demonstrations.

> La plupart des matières morales et humaines sont de ce nombre; et il y a même des vérités de la Religion, qui se prouvent beaucoup mieux par la lumière de plusieurs principes, qui s'entr'aident et se soutiennent les uns les autres, que par des raisonnements semblables aux démonstrations géométriques. (42:8)

Here probabilites and *vraisemblance* must suffice, but a convergence of such proofs carries conviction. "There are different degrees of proof: some from which one draws conclusions that are certain; others from which one draws apparent conclusions; and from several apparent ones joined together, one sometimes draws a certain conclusion to which all reasonable minds must submit" ("Il y a différents dégrés de preuves. Il y en a dont on conclut la certitude, et d'autres dont on conclut l'apparence; et de plusieurs apparences jointes ensemble, on conclut quelquefois une certitude à laquelle tous les esprits raisonnables se doivent rendre" [42:9]). Thus, even if rhetoric is not invoked, this area is explicitly withdrawn from the geometric proof that is the model of their logic. I show in chapter 6 that Bernard Lamy adapts Nicole's analysis to distinguish between the realms of eloquence and mathematics in his *Art de parler*.

On the other hand, when Arnauld and Nicole consider the speaker's stance toward the subject, they use the occasion for an attack against their scholastic enemies whose arid style is unfavorably contrasted to the eloquence of the fathers of the church. Appeals to the emotions generated by rhetorical means are openly allowed under certain circumstances. The *Logique de Port Royal* adopts as a given Descartes' psychophysiology, with its explanation of the sensations and emotions in terms of animal spirits. However, Descartes' worries about the dangers of the passions are inevitably heightened by their conviction that these affective movements second a will that has been disordered by the Fall. Thus, they discuss at length in the chapter "Sophisms of pride, self-interest, and passion" ("Des sophismes d'amour-propre, d'intérêt, et de passion" [*Logique*, 261–74]) how the passions, reinforcing this "disorder of the will" ("dérèglement de la volonté" [*Logique*, 261]), persuade us to accept false judgments.

Yet in other than purely speculative matters, Arnauld and Nicole hold that reason itself requires accompanying movements. "[W]hen the topic one treats is such that one should be reasonably touched by it, to speak of it in a dry, cold manner without stirring is a failing because it is a failing not to be touched by what should touch" ("[L]orsque la matière que l'on traite est telle qu'elle nous doit raisonnablement toucher, c'est un défaut d'en parler d'une manière sèche, froide, et sans mouvement, parce que c'est un défaut de n'être pas touché de ce que l'on doit" (*Logique*, 97). In such cases the will not only must judge the truth or error of the ideas and arguments presented by the understanding, but also must react more intimately by establishing a personal stance toward it. Such judgments as love, hate, and respect can legitimately be seconded by a movement of the corporal passions. Arnauld and Nicole explicitly single out religious truth that should be loved and revered, not just neutrally affirmed. However, the range of non-speculative topics entering into this category is much more extensive, corresponding in fact to the traditional subject matter of rhetoric. Logic involves only part of the mind's capacity. Here Arnauld and Nicole recognize the need to engage more than the pure understanding and the will's power to discriminate between truth and error. By authorizing further movements of the will such as love and respect as well as accompanying passions, they implicitly make room for the use of the emotions when dealing with all questions of value, not just the theological ones they privilege.

Finally, the ideal of a message that presents itself directly without passing through the filter of a speaker also proves too narrow. Arnauld and Nicole note that the perfect orator may strive to obey the spirit, if not the letter, of Pascal's injunction that "an *honnête homme* must avoid naming himself" ("un honnête homme devait éviter de se nommer") out of fear that a display of the speaker's ego will irritate the listeners' own feelings of self-importance (*Logique*, 266–67). Similarly, the orator's vanity, presumption, or ill-temper may prevent the public from attending to the message itself (*Logique*, 288). However, as Arnauld and Nicole must immediately concede, the orator's presence cannot always be so easily eliminated. Some topics must be settled on the basis of the authority of witnesses rather than reason and require that the audience be able to judge the speaker's reliability (*Logique*, 283). Character would seem to be inseparable from proof in these cases.

Morever, even when the orator's character can be classified as a manner distinct from the proof itself, Pascalian self-effacement is only half the advice given by the *Logique de Port-Royal*. Speakers should certainly avoid all *manières* that might shock an audience, but they likewise should seek out ones that favorably dispose their public. "It is fitting that those who wish to persuade others of some truth they have recognized apply themselves to clothing it with the favorable manners that will win approval and to avoiding the shocking ones that are only capable of driving people away" ("Il est juste aussi que ceux qui désirent persuader les autres de quelque vérité qu'ils ont reconnue, s'étudient à la revêtir des manières favorables qui sont propres à la faire approuver, et à éviter les manières odieuses qui ne sont capables que d'en éloigner les hommes" [*Logique*, 287–88]). These include such personal traits as modesty, moderation, and prudence (*Logique*, 289). Thus the neutral manner of impersonal presentation, however appealing in principle, is not an absolute rule.

The Language of Eloquence:
Beyond Descartes

When we turn from *res* to *verba*, from invention to elocution, we find a corresponding return of the rhetorical. To be sure, their point of departure is a notion of language similar to Descartes' that sees words as simple counters for ideas and sees elocution as stylistic flourish departing from ordinary usage that only hinders the reception of a message. However, Arnauld and Nicole arrive at a position that allows for the use of figures of speech. Their preference might be for communcation that bypasses the linguistic sign, but nonetheless, language plays a much greater role in their theory than in Descartes'. Port-Royal's linguistics, unlike Descartes', specifically provides room for eloquence.

Language was an even more peripheral issue for Descartes than persuasion, and one has only to remember the storm of protest from historians of linguisitics against Noam Chomsky's *Cartesian Linguistics* to realize that linguistic questions were not at the center of his preoccupations.[13] As W. Keith Percival has noted, "unlike most of the other major philosophers of the seventeenth century, Descartes was relatively uninterested in language,"[14] and André Robinet in his *Le Langage à l'âge classique* entitles his chapter on Descartes "Descartes' Oversight of Language"[15] When Descartes does treat language, it is almost always simply by way of illustrating some topic he considered more basic in his system, not to elucidate the nature of language itself.

This is true to a large extent of the three points about language made by Descartes that serve as a springboard for Arnauld and Nicole's reflections on eloquence. First, the priority of language over thought is evoked during Descartes' discussion of language as a sign that humans, unlike animals, possess thought. Individuals may have immediate access to their own nature as thinking beings, but their only assurance that other bodies possess thought as well is deduced from the observation that these bodies are able to communicate thoughts through language. "Speech is the unique sign and the only sure mark of thought hidden and enclosed in the body" ("Haec enim loquela unicum est cogitationis in corpore latentis signum certum" [5 February 1649 A.-T., 5:278]). Second, the arbitrary relation between the signified and the signifier in the linguisitic sign is mentioned in *Le Monde* to illustrate the dissimilarity between our sensations and the objects that produce them (1:315–16). Finally, the ideal of a universal language where each word would represent a single idea, first mentioned in a 1629 letter to Mersenne, is proposed as a means of eliminating equivocal meanings that lead to false judgments (20 November 1629, 1:90–93). In the *Principes*, Descartes lists this imprecision that language introduces into both thought and communication as one of the principal causes of error, along with prolonged childhood and the weakness of attention (3:139–43). If Descartes does not treat language in its own right, this is largely because he takes it for granted. To be sure, it is an imperfect instrument of communication, introducing misunderstandings and fostering imprecise ideas, but on the whole, one senses that he sees it as adequate. His confidence in the vigor of the mind reassures him about any insufficiencies of language, since in his view thought itself does not depend on language and *évidence* can be obtained without recourse to it.

As Augustinians, Arnauld and Nicole can only concur with Descartes' assumption that thought exists independently of language. Likewise, their insistence that the role of language in conceiving thoughts must be clarified before judgment and reasoning can be discussed is in many ways a gloss on Descartes' comment in the *Principes* on the difficulty of separating language from thought. Speech, he affirms there, may arise initially out of the need for minds to find a material medium for the communication of their ideas, but it nevertheless begins to insinuate itself into the thinking process (3:143). As the Port-Royalists put it:

> If the reflections that we make on our thoughts never concerned anyone but ourselves, it would suffice to examine them in themselves without clothing them in any words or any other signs; but because we can only make our thoughts known to each other by accompanying them with exterior

signs and because even this habit is so ingrained that when we think alone things only present themselves to our minds with the words in which we are accustomed to clothing them when speaking to others. It thus is necessary for logic to consider ideas joined to words and words joined to ideas.

Si les réflexions que nous faisons sur nos pensées n'avaient jamais regardé que nous-mêmes, il aurait suffi de les considérer en elles-mêmes, sans les revêtir d'aucunes paroles, ni d'aucuns autres signes: mais parce que nous ne pouvons faire entendre nos pensées les uns aux autres, qu'en les accompagnant de signes extérieurs: et que même cette accoutumance est si forte, que quand nous pensons seuls, les choses ne se présentent à notre esprit qu'avec les mots dont nous avons accoutumé de les revêtir en parlant aux autres; il est nécessaire dans la Logique de considérer les idées jointes aux mots, et les mots joints aux idées. (*Logique*, 38)

Accessory Ideas and Attention

Descartes' remarks center on reducing the ambiguity of various terms used by philosophers, and thus he was concerned chiefly with the fit between an idea and the word used to represent it. In terms of the analysis of the parts of speech in the *Grammaire générale,* his discussion deals primarily with nouns and adjectives whose function is to represent ideas in the understanding. Since the *Logique de Port-Royal* is concerned with mental operations involved in formulating logical propositions, it adopts the *Grammaire*'s identification of verbs with affirmations and judgments and of conjunctions with shorthand signs for various other mental functions.

The innovation for rhetoric of the *Logique de Port-Royal,* however, is to indicate a linguistic means for representing forms of mental activity not required by logic—the passions. The *Grammaire* pointed only to interjections as marking movements of the mind.[16] In the *Logique de Port-Royal* figures of speech are described as communicating emotions as well as a specific concept. "[F]igured locutions signify the movement and the passion of the person speaking in addition to the principal notion, and thus they imprint both ideas in the mind, while plain expression only

points to the naked truth" ("[L]es expressions figurées signifient
outre la chose principale, le mouvement et la passion de celui qui
parle, et impriment ainsi l'un et l'autre idée dans l'esprit, au
lieu que l'expression simple ne marque que la vérité toute nue"
[*Logique*, 96]). Language thus possesses an adequate instrument
to convey the vigor that characterizes the passions.

Arnauld and Nicole's example shows how the twisted word
order of a verse from the *Aeneid* represents both the abstract idea
of an emotion and its "image" as the passion shapes the flow of
words.

> If this half verse of Vergil: *Usque adeone mori miserum esti!*
> was expressed simply and without figures in this way: *Non
> est usque adeo mori miserum* without doubt it would have much
> less force. . . . Because it expresses not only the thought that
> death is not as great an evil as one thinks, but in addition it
> represents the idea of a man who steels himself against death
> and who envisages it without terror—an image much more
> vivid than the same thought to which it is attached. Thus it
> is not strange that the idea strikes with more force because
> the mind learns through the image of truth, but it is scarcely
> touched except by the image of movements.

> Si ce demi vers de Virgile: *Usque adeone mori miserum est!* était
> exprimé simplement et sans figure de cette sorte: *Non est
> usque adeo mori miserum:* il est sans doute qu'il aurait beaucoup
> moins de force. . . . Car elle n'exprime pas seulement cette
> pensée, que la mort n'est pas un si grand mal que l'on croit;
> mais elle représente de plus l'idée d'un homme qui se raidit
> contre la mort, et qui l'envisage sans effroi: image beaucoup
> plus vive que n'est la pensée même à laquelle elle est jointe.
> Ainsi il n'est pas étrange qu'elle frappe davantage, parce que
> l'âme s'instruit par les images des vérités mais elle ne s'émeut
> guère que par l'image des mouvements. (*Logique*, 96)

Not only does the understanding register the concept that death
is less to be feared than often believed, the will is touched as well
by the movements of passion.

Since rhetoric is treated only incidentally in the *Logique de Port-
Royal*, this discussion of the figures occurs in the midst of their

treatment of definitions, a topic they consider more central to logic. Like Descartes, they deplore the ambiguity occasioned by the multiple meanings of words and suggest as one remedy a new language in which meanings would be precise and fixed (*Logique*, 86). However, in the absence of such a univocal language, they propose their theory of principal and accessory ideas as a means of resolving the disputes over the meanings usage attaches to words (*Logique*, 94). Confusion arises in common usage because of a failure of attention.

Men often do not pay attention to the complete meaning of words, that is to say, words often have more meaning than they seem, and when one wishes to explain their meaning, one does not represent the whole impression that they make on the mind. . . . Thus it often occurs that in addition to the principal idea that one regards as the proper meaning of a word, the word excites several other ideas that one might call accessory to which one does not pay heed, even though the mind receives their impression.

Les hommes ne font pas souvent attention à toute la signification des mots, c'est-à-dire que les mots signifient souvent plus qu'il ne semble, et que lorsqu'on en veut expliquer la signification, on ne représente pas toute l'impression qu'ils font dans l'esprit. . . . Or il arrive souvent qu'un mot outre l'idée principale que l'on regarde comme la signification propre de ce mot, excite plusieurs autres idées qu'on peut appeler accessoires, auxquelles on ne prend pas garde, quoique l'esprit en reçoive l'impression. (*Logique*, 94)

These accessory ideas can assume several forms. They are most often connotations attached by usage to words and recognized by all speakers of a language, as the notion of scorn associated with the accusation that someone has lied (*Logique*, 95). In other cases they are not always part of the normal baggage of a word but added to the principal idea by the speaker. For example, body language, or intonation add a layer of meaning to the words they accompany (*Logique*, 95). Similarly, as in the example of the hyperbaton used by Virgil, a figure of speech can supply the accessory meaning. Careful speakers attend to both levels of meaning. They know the connotations that convention attaches to the words they use (Arnauld and Nicole suggest that dictionaries list the accessory meanings as an aid in this regard), as well as the meaning generally implied by a tone of voice or the effect of a particular figure (*Logique*, 95).

Because of the mind's limited power of attention, it normally concentrates only on the primary ideas. The accessory ones are present, but only at the threshold of attention. Nonetheless, they carry meaning, coloring the principal one, just as blurred objects at the edge of one's field of vision form a background for the object on which one focuses. As logicians, Arnauld and Nicole are concerned to show that by retrieving these secondary meanings numerous misunderstandings can be resolved; attending to the connotations that accessory ideas add is the first step to subjecting them to rigorous analysis.

Eloquence as an Accessory Idea

In effect, Arnauld and Nicole relegate eloquence to this marginal area bordering on the subconscious that is potentially accessible to the inspection of attention, but generally left unexamined. Logic requires subjecting these undisclosed meanings to scrutiny, moving them temporarily to the center of attention. Eloquence, on the other hand, leaves in the background the additional meanings contributed by rhetorical figures to the plain statement of an idea.

In fact, Arnauld and Nicole's distinction between the accessory idea supplied by the figure and the principal one that would subsist without it can be extended to a speech's *fond* and its *manières*. Just as the accessory meaning of the figure of speech should be subordinate to the principal meaning, these *manières*, composed of an amalgam of such elements as body language, figured speech, and tone of voice, should merely reinforce the speaker's thesis. Their operation is thus somewhat surreptitious. How can such a peripheral phenomenon render an idea more forceful and vivid? All the examples Arnauld and Nicole cite involve some subjective reaction of the speaker, for example, an emotional response, or a moral judgment like indignation or shame. The effect is to engage the will, and this energy, even if diffuse, invigorates the principal idea.

False eloquence reverses the rightful hierarchy of attention: the accessory elements take precedence, deflecting the attention from consideration of the primary message. Dazzled by the peripheral, the mind overlooks the error that constitutes the discourse's thesis, resulting in erroneous judgments.

In the worst cases, the attention is not attracted from the principal ideas to secondary meanings, but merely to the material component of the linguistic sign. Applying to eloquence Descartes' complaint that too often "men attend to words instead of to the subject matter" ("les hommes donnent leur attention aux paroles plutot qu'aux choses" [3:143]), Arnauld and Nicole deplore the tendency to attend more to sounds than to the ideas they represent, "because the purety of language and the harmony of the figures in eloquence are at most what the color scheme is in painting, that is, the most lowly and material part" ("car la pureté du langage, le nombre des figures, sont tout au plus dans l'éloquence ce que le coloris est dans la peinture, c'est-à-dire, que ce n'en est que la partie la plus basse et la plus materielle" [*Logique*, 276]). Orators shape their acoustic raw material with more focus on the rhythm and harmony of the sounds than on ideas (*Logique*, 277). Given the general attraction of attention toward the sensible, this concern for verbal ornament can result only in "some twisting of the truth" ("quelque contorsion à la vérité" [*Logique*, 277]). "This prospect turns them away from their subject and weakens the vigor of their thoughts . . . the mind not being capable of this double application, and one harming the other" ("Cette vue les détourne des choses, et affaiblit la vigueur de leurs pensées . . . l'esprit n'étant pas capable de cette double application, et l'un nuisant à l'autre" [*Logique*, 276]). The shift of the attention's focus from the arguments is so imperceptible that the listeners, and even the speaker, are often not aware that it has occurred.

> These faulty arguments are often imperceptible to those who make them and deceive them before anyone else; they become dazed by the sound of their own words; the sparkle of their figures dazzles them, and the magnificence of certain

words attracts them without their noticing it to ideas scarcely so solid that they would reject them without a doubt if they reflected on them a little.

Ces mauvais raisonnements sont souvent imperceptibles à ceux qui les font, et les trompent les premiers; ils s'étourdissent par le son de leurs paroles, l'éclat de leurs figures les éblouit, et la magnificence de certains mots les attire, sans qu'ils s'en apperçoivent, à des pensées si peu solides, qu'ils les rejetteraient sans doute, s'ils y faisaient quelque réflexion. (*Logique*, 278)

Vivid Representation

The ideal, however, is an eloquence in which the attention is directed not at the words but at the mental states they represent. Arnauld and Nicole affirm their preference in a formula that parallels Descartes' expression of confidence in the *Discours de la méthode* that sound reasoning properly ordered will persuade, even if the orator speaks the dialect of lower Brittany:

The chief thing consists in powerfully conceiving the subject matter and expressing it so that one conveys to the mind of the listeners a vivid and luminous image that not only presents the subject in naked form but the movements with which it is conceived; this can be found in people who are not very exact in their choice of words and not very skilled in harmonious phrasing.

La principale consiste à concevoir fortement les choses, et à les exprimer en sorte qu'on en porte dans l'esprit des auditeurs une image vive et lumineuse, qui ne présente pas seulement ces choses toutes nues, mais aussi les mouvements avec lesquels on les conçoit; et c'est ce qui se peut rencontrer en des personnes peu exactes dans la langue, et peu justes dans le nombre. (*Logique*, 276)

Avoiding grammatical errors and jarring rhythms is less important than the ability to communicate a vivid image of the ideas themselves and the accompanying emotions. We see here how Arnauld and Nicole have expanded Descartes' recipe for eloquence in the *Discours*. Movements of the passions should second the intellectual concepts, and vivacity is demanded besides well digested ideas. Perhaps as important as the fact that the Port-Royalists require an emotional charge is the shift in emphasis they accomplish from the clear and distinct ideas alone, which had been enough for Descartes, to the representation of these ideas, which must be vivid. To be sure, the ideas and emotional movements that win persuasion are at issue, but how this mental experience is represented becomes the crux of eloquence.

Descartes and Pascal

It is instructive at this point to situate Arnauld and Nicole in terms of the rhetorical theory of Pascal, whom the *Logique de Port-Royal* describes as knowing "as much about true rhetoric as anyone ever knew" ("qui savait autant de véritable Rhétorique que personne en ait jamais su" [*Logique*, 267]). One need not follow Sara Melzer's Nietzschean interpretation of a Pascal caught in an aporia of faith and uncertainty, fallen from truth into a language that is opaque,[17] to find rhetorical questions closer to his central preoccupations than they are for Descartes. Descartes after all was chiefly concerned with winning converts to his metaphysics and scientific theories. On the other hand, two enterprises gave Pascal a more acute awareness that persuasion requires adapting one's message to a particular audience: his defense in the *Provinciales* of the moral integrity which Port-Royal incarnated for him, and his project of converting unbelievers that has come down to us as the *Pensées*. Thus, even if, along with Hugh Davidson, we align him with Plato, for whom rhetoric depends on truth discovered by methods that are outside of rhetoric[18] (a lineage to which Descartes also belongs), Pascal has a broader view of persuasion than Descartes.

An assessment, especially a brief one, of Pascal's notion of persuasion is no easy matter. While he gave more attention to rhetorical issues than Descartes, Pascal's premature death left to scholars the task of harmonizing the theory found in "De l'Esprit géométrique," which explicitly does not apply to religious questions, with the conversion-oriented rhetoric of the *Pensées*. The first, as its title suggests, requires univocal definitions as the basis of tightly reasoned proofs, while the second allows for paradox, digression, and figures of speech. Moreover, although commentators have established the coherence of Pascal's view of human psychology, due to his failure to employ a consistent technical vocabulary, his description of the three orders of body, mind, and spirit that he posits in the *Pensées* lacks the clarity of Descartes' dualist psychophysiology. The difficulty that critics have had in arriving at an appreciation of the role of the heart is the most notorious example.[19]

Pascal never embraced with enthusiasm Descartes' criterion of *évidence* and came to see limitations in his ideal of demonstrations formed by chains of self-evident ideas. While Descartes recognized the difficulty of applying this standard to questions of ethics and practical conduct, he did not elaborate an alternative approach. Pascal, on the other hand, acknowledged the geometric style of reasoning as a model. In "De l'Esprit géométrique" he describes the true method of demonstration as consisting of two points: "[F]irst, not to use any term whose meaning has not been previously clearly explained; and second, never to advance any proposition that is not proven by truths already known" ("[L]'une, de n'employer aucun terme dont on n'eût auparavant expliqué nettement le sens; l'autre, de n'avancer jamais aucune proposition qu'on ne démontrât par des vérités déjà connues").[20] However, he was not inclined to identify a single starting point for metaphysical or scientific proofs such as the Cartesian *cogito*. Rather, he envisaged a multitude of discontinuous principles which serve as points of departure for demonstrations. These might be commonly held notions such as time or space, the results of experiments in the physical sciences, the desires of individuals in human affairs, or the values and opinions of various groups. With such principles serving as premises, proofs conceived along geometric lines could be elaborated, but given the heterogenous nature of the principles, no overarching unity can be established.[21]

This stress on the diversity of principles also explains why Pascal includes both an art of convincing and a more potent art of pleasing within his "De l'Art de persuader." The will's desires and the pleasures that satisfy them (which serve as starting points for demonstrations in the *art d'agréer*) are more powerful than the various notions lodged in the understanding that serve as the basis of the *art de convaincre*.[22] Persuasion that purports to address itself to the understanding alone and that fails to take into account the principles of the will is maimed.

Furthermore, his discussion in the *Pensées* of the intuitive and geometric minds (*esprit de finesse* and *esprit de géométrie*) uses the distinction between initial principles to suggest that the demonstrations themselves might not always follow the linear geometric model. In geometry the basic principles are out of the ordinary, but easy enough to grasp once perceived because of their concreteness.[23] On the other hand, in the practical affairs of life, the principles are familiar to all, but so numerous and so subtle that a special talent for intuiting them all at once is required.[24] Moreover, because, in matters of *finesse*, the starting principles are extremely numerous, intuitive minds do not normally set out their arguments in the linear form of geometers, but proceed to a conclusion in a single operation. It may be that such demonstrations can be reduced to a series of linear proofs after the fact, but in practice this is most difficult.[25]

Finally, outside the sciences, the certainty of *évidence* is problematic for Pascal. Even in philosophy, reason alone cannot arrive at undisputed propositions. The competing theses of the sceptics and dogmatists are partial expressions of truth at best that must be complemented by the opposing view. "There is no rule, it is said, that does not have an exception, nor any truth so general that it does not have a side which is deficient" ("Il n'y a point, dit-on, de règle qui n'ait quelque exception ni de vérité si générale qui n'ait quelque face par où elle manque").[26] This belief that the mind's capacity to grasp truth is severely limited results in his "continual shifting from pro to con" ("le renversement continuel du pour au contre"),[27] a method of exposition in which a succession of points of view are revealed to be inadequate.

Moreover, religious truths can only be known by means of inspiration and find expression in figurative language where multiple levels of meaning are superimposed. Thus, the linear chains of self-evident ideas, as valid as they might be in mathematics, are irrelevant in the domains that are the most urgent. Descartes is "useless and uncertain" ("inutile et incertain")[28] because the Cartesian proofs proceeding from the *cogito* lead to a deistic

God at best, not the Christ of Scripture. Proofs of the truth of Christianity must advance in an indirect fashion, making frequent use of digression and repetition. Such a model of disposition was employed by Jesus, by Paul, and by Augustine: "This order consists chiefly in digression upon each point that is related to the conclusion so as to keep it [the conclusion] always in view" ("Cet ordre consiste principalement à la digression sur chaque point qui a rapport à la fin, pour la montrer toujours").[29] In terms of Pascal's three orders of reality—the physical world, the mind, and the spirit—the linear proofs of geometry are addressed to the mind's understanding while digression belongs to the highest order, that of charity, where the heart is the faculty of perception.

As a manual of logic, the *Logique de Port-Royal* is naturally concerned with the middle order, that of the mind, where reasoned demonstration prevails, but Arnauld and Nicole's synthesis of Cartesian and Pascalian elements does not even refer to the possibility of Pascal's third order. To be sure, they acknowledge their debt to "De l'Esprit géométrique." Indeed, much of the fourth part on method is an amplification of Pascal's requirement to "define all terms, prove all propositions" ("à définir tous les termes et à prouver toutes les propositions").[30] However, "De l'Esprit géométrique" is already closer in many ways to the spirit of Descartes' *Regulae* than to the *Pensées*, and the Port-Royalists' additions reinforce the Cartesian orientation. For example, the rules they give for identifying propositions so obvious that they can serve as starting principles are inspired by Descartes' equation of clear and distinct ideas with self-evidence (*Logique*, 317–20). Exposition in the *Logique de Port-Royal* is conceived as setting out proofs in linear chains.

On the other hand, Nicole's comments in the preface of the *Nouveaux Eléments de géométrie* on the inadequacy of the geometric method in questions of ethics and human affairs have parallels with Pascal's *esprit de finesse*. Nicole notes that the great number of proofs and circumstances that serve as principles in such cases must be grasped in a single glance. The convergence of mutually supporting principles he describes is similar to Pascal's description of the operation of the intuitive mind. Nicole, however, goes farther than Pascal when he attributes a greater certainty to such proofs in matters of religion than a geometric demonstration might have, or when he allows that several apparent truths joined together can provide a certainty to which all reasonable persons must acquiesce.[31] Here, in fact, we discover why Arnauld and Nicole make less room for rhetoric than Pascal. More confident than Pascal in the mind's power to know and to demonstrate truths, even those of religion, they have less need for persuasion.[32] Certainly, like Pascal, they acknowledge that no conversion is possible without grace and that reason alone is not sufficient, but they still hold that useful truths about God can be attained independently of faith. Because they value logic more than Pascal, they prize rhetoric less. Indeed, the Pascalian rhetoric they admire so greatly is that of the *Provinciales*, which comes closer to the spirit of geometric proof, not that of the *Pensées*, to which they were profoundly ambivalent.[33]

The Rhetorical without Rhetoric

Arnauld and Nicole's desire for an impersonal eloquence of *évidence* where the only ornament is truth itself thus gives way to modes of proof whose contours resemble the traditional intellectual, emotional, and ethical ones. Logic's imperialist claims in the intellectual area are humbled by the admission in the *Nouveaux Eléments de géométrie* that the strict mathematical model is not applicable in precisely the domain which Arnauld and Nicole hold to be the most urgent—that of moral judgment bearing on action. The paradox, however, is that although Arnauld and Nicole point to an area outside of logic, an area that might be called rhetorical, they hesitate to consider it in terms of rhetoric. Rather than either deny its existence or formulate a theory to account for it, they assign it to the margins of logic and grammar. In part, this is due to their identification of rhetorical theory with the rules and nomenclature forced on young students. They cite Augustine on the irrelevancy of such precepts in fostering eloquence: "One finds, he says, that the rules of eloquence are observed in the speeches of eloquent persons although they do not think about them when making them, whether they know them or not" ("On trouve, dit-il, que les règles de l'éloquence sont observées dans les discours des personnes éloquentes, quoiqu'ils n'y pensent pas en les faisant, soit qu'ils les sachent, soit qu'ils les ignorent" [*Logique*, 234]). When Arnauld and Nicole do consent to give rules themselves—and they promise to supply the essence of rhetorical doctrine so that readers can generate the rest on their own (*Logique*, 29)—their advice is invariably negative. For example, "the greatest precept of rhetoric" ("le plus grand précepte de la Rhétorique") is revealed to be avoiding shocking manners that might awaken the aversion of an audience (*Logique*, 288).

At their most positive, they supply, as we have just seen, not a theory, or even rules, but a description of ideal eloquence transmitting the image of both ideas and movements. It is no accident that this description is mentioned in connection with preaching, just as their first reference to the propriety of affective displays invokes the fathers of the church. Arnauld and Nicole are unwilling to stake out the limits of this domain beyond logic, where the naked truth alone is not enough. Instead of investigating further such problematic areas of moral contingencies where *évidence* is impossible, they settle on the safe ground of dogma where faith, not reason, guarantees truth. Instead of discussing the full range of the passions' involvement in action, they mention only the love and respect for God. This allows them to acknowledge the existence of the rhetorical, yet without accounting fully for it in theory.

What Pierre Kuentz has called Port-Royal's *bivium*[34] comprised of the *Logique de Port-Royal* and the *Grammaire générale* is doubly inadequate. The generous dose of ethical issues the *Logique de Port-Royal* includes in its "motley" ("bigarure" [*Logique*, 28]) is insufficient to ground rhetoric. It does provide ample warning of how concupiscence must be neutralized if false moral judgments are to be avoided, but offers little advice for applying logic to make sound ones, even though this is where self-evidence is impossible and where a convergence of probabilities and circumstantial arguments must determine action. Likewise, their treatment of the emotions is perfunctory. The only role allowed them is that of supporting the ideas of the orator. Any emotions that stray beyond this subordinate status are not only unnatural, but akin to convulsions (*Logique*, 96). No effort, for example, is made to follow up on Descartes' suggestions about the passions' potential for strengthening attention. Such psychological analysis had traditionally been found in treatises on rhetoric or morals. But since Arnauld and Nicole claim to have supplied the essence of the former (*Logique*, 29) and demur on the latter as too lengthy a task (*Logique*, 260), the reader is left with a truncated psychology that does not fully account for the rhetorical.[35]

Given language's dependence on thought for Port-Royal, the *Logique de Port-Royal*'s focus on those mental operations required for logic results in a linguistic analysis that is barely adequate for the eloquence it describes. The *Grammaire générale* had treated only four figures—syllepsis, ellipsis, pleonasm and hyperbaton—all figures of thought involving the order of words. It had not delved into their effects other than to mention that, although these figures are grammatical irregularities, they may sometimes be numbered among the beauties and perfections of language.[36] Only in the *Logique de Port-Royal* is the figures' potential for conveying emotion presented, and there it occurs as part of the discussion of accessory meanings, itself a parenthesis in the discussion of definitions. The example given, Virgil's hyperbaton, is again a figure of thought. Little attempt is made to analyze tropes such as metaphor or metonymy that involve more complex shifts of meaning, except in the context of their defense of the Catholic interpretation of the eucharist.

Even if eloquence remains at the margins of linguistics and logic for Arnauld and Nicole, they still treat it more conspicuously than Descartes, who dwells more on the psychology of persuasion than on how persuasion is effected through language. By applying their theory of accessory ideas to the figures, they account for the communication of passion, as well as ideas, through language. The linguistic sign can represent all mental experience—thought in its most general meaning for Descartes—and not only ideas or arguments that combine and manipulate concepts. Thus, if eloquence is an accessory idea at the periphery of logic and grammar for the *Logique de Port-Royal*, Arnauld and Nicole have at least begun the process of subjecting it to the scrutiny of attention.

5

Malebranche's Rhetoric
of the Incarnation

> The gift of speech is the greatest
> talent, the language of the imagina-
> tion is the surest of instruments, and
> a memory well-stocked with incom-
> prehensible terms will always make
> its appearance with more brilliance,
> whatever the Cartesians say.
>
> Le don de la parole est le plus grand
> des talents, le langage d'imagination
> est le plus sûr des moyens et une
> mémoire remplie de termes incom-
> préhensibles paraîtra toujours avec
> éclat, quoique les Cartésiens en puis-
> sent dire.
>
> Malebranche,
> *Eclaircissement XII*

The Oratorian Nicolas Malebranche immediately established his reputation for hostility toward rhetoric in his first published work. The second book of *La Recherche de la vérité* (1674) indicts the imagination as a source of error. As examples of "the contagious communication of strong imaginations" ("la communication contagieuse des imaginations fortes"),[1] the power of speakers with vivid imaginations to persuade an uncritical audience, he cites Tertullian, Seneca, and Montaigne. These three authors represent strikingly divergent styles of eloquence, but all enjoyed popularity in the seventeenth century for their treatment of moral and religious questions. Tertullian was popular among preachers, Seneca epitomized the neo-stoic revival, and Montaigne did much to shape the ideal of the *honnête homme*. On the basis of these attacks Bernard Tocanne declares that "in Malebranche all the arguments brought into play by the opponents of rhetoric at the end of the century are pressed into service," and Peter France labels the Oratorian "a philosopher who had no love for rhetoric."[2]

Descartes and Augustine as *Moniteurs*

The Cartesian impetus for this critique of eloquence in *La Recherche* is readily apparent. Malebranche makes use of the mechanistic psychophysiology that stems from Descartes to accuse Tertullian, Seneca, and Montaigne of winning over their readers with a mirage of style appealing to the imagination rather than to the *évidence* of reason. In a sense, this attack on glittering but empty eloquence has its roots in Malebranche's famous chance encounter ten years earlier in a Parisian bookshop with Claude Clerselier's 1664 edition of Descartes' physiological treatise *L'Homme*. As J. Lelong, an early biographer, puts it:

> [A]lthough this posthumous work was one of the least important of this great philosopher, the method of reasoning and the mechanical principles that he perceived there while leafing through it pleased him so much that he bought the book and read it with so much pleasure that he found himself obliged from time to time to interrupt this reading because he was seized by palpitations of the heart.

> [Q]uoique cet ouvrage posthume fût un des moindres de ce grand philosophe, la méthode de raisonner, et la mécanique qu'il y aperçut en le feuilletant lui plurent si fort qu'il acheta le livre, et le lut avec tant de plaisir qu'il se trouvait de temps en temps obligé d'interrompre cette lecture à cause du battement de coeur qui lui prenait.[3]

Both elements of the Cartesian system mentioned by Lelong which seemed to have impressed him initially—the method and the mechanistic physiology—figure prominently in his condemnation ten years later of false eloquence. Even more significant is that the revelation of Descartes opened up new perspectives on philosophy, science, and theology to the twenty-six year old Malebranche. The pious, young Oratorian seems to have undergone his earlier training in scholastic theology and philosophy at the Collège de la Marche and the Sorbonne with relative indifference. All this was changed by the discovery of Descartes.

Viewed from the perspective of his mature thought, it is not surprising that a dry physiological text would awaken a philosophical vocation in Malebranche. Inquiry into the natural world held great appeal for him until his death in 1715. Scientific questions and experiments played a central role in the program of studies he laid out for himself from 1664 to 1669 when he reeducated himself along Cartesian lines before he began to write *La Recherche*. This interest in scientific debates culminated in his collaboration at the Academy of Sciences to which he was elected in 1699 and where his paper of the same year on the properties of light was the first explanation of color in terms of wave lengths. So deep, in fact, is this scientific impulse that Ferdinand Alquié sees in Malebranche's thought the attempt to extend the method and laws of physics to the religious and metaphysical domains: "He is led to seek the explication of religious mysteries in proofs of a physicist."[4]

Henri Gouhier, nonetheless, has shown that Malebranche found much more than an introduction to Cartesian science in the 1664 edition of *L'Homme*.[5] Descartes' system was beginning to encounter stiff opposition in theological circles in the early 1660s. Because of this climate, Clerselier surrounded Descartes' physiological treatise with other texts by himself, Louis La Forge, and Florent Schuyl that were designed to demonstrate the utility of the new philosophy to the faith. La Forge and Schuyl highlight a number of themes that could only reinforce the appeal of the scientific text for the devout Malebranche, schooled in the spirituality of Bérulle's Oratory, where Augustine was the master of theology. The introduction contrasts the solidity of Descartes' achievement with the verbalism of the scholastic followers of Aristotle and stresses the utter dependence of all creatures on the Creator for both their continued existence and our knowledge of them. In addition, Clerselier and Schuyl present the radical distinction of matter and mind as proof of the spirituality and immortality of the soul and of God's existence. Finally, a long quotation from *De Trinitate* illustrates the harmony between Descartes' metaphysics and Augustine.

The originality of Malebranche's system is marked by just such a symbiosis of the modern philosophy of Descartes and of the thought of the foremost doctor of the Latin Church interpreted in the light of Bérulle's stress on the Incarnation. Just the same, when we consider a brief list of the components of this system which conditions his rhetorical theory, it is clear that he did much more than assemble various Cartesian and Augustinian doctrines. As he claims in the preface to *La Recherche*, they were *moniteurs* for him, not *maîtres;* they are guides who prompt him toward the truth, not his masters or its final repository (1:23). In his early works, *La Recherche* (1674–75) and the *Conversations chrétiennes* (1677), his debt to Descartes is readily apparent. Descartes' method and rule of *évidence* provided the rationalist methodology; Cartesian mind/body dualism is at the heart of his metaphysics, and Cartesian science, whose physiology is particularly relevant to his rhetorical theory, provides the foundation and program of his scientific investigations. Even when he found himself in opposition to Descartes on this or that point, as was more and more frequently the case, he continued to think of himself as a disciple. He might reject an increasing number of Cartesian doctrines—innate ideas, created truths, a clear and distinct idea of the mind, and so on—still, Malebranche justified any departure from Cartesianism by an appeal to Descartes' spirit and method: "I admit nevertheless that I owe to Descartes or to his manner of philosophizing the opinions I oppose to him along with the boldness with which I correct him" ("J'avoue cependant que je dois à M. Descartes ou à sa manière de philosopher les sentiments que j'oppose aux siens, et la hardiesse de le reprendre" [2:449]). Even when there is apparent agreement, Malebranche rarely gives quite the same meaning to a term as Descartes.

According to André Robinet, if Malebranche had died in 1678 before the publication of the *Eclaircissements*, and above all the *Traité de la nature et de la grace* (1680), he would have been no more than "a novel post-Cartesian."[6] When we turn to this latter work, which marks the birth of his mature thought, we find further evidence that his synthesis is a distinctly personal system rather than an compound of Cartesian and Augustinian doc-

trines. To be sure, his concept of occasionalism and of the ineffi-
cacy of secondary causes owes much to Augustine's theocentrism,
as well as to debates among Cartesians. Likewise, his notion of
the mind's union with God is inspired by the Augustinian Interior
Master and the illumination of the mind by God. The emergence
of a number of other doctrines to form a coherent system characterizes the originality of the *Traité:* his notion of moral order
founded on the hierarchy of attributes, the concept that all creation is ruled by a few simple, unvarying laws, and the view of
the Incarnation as the principal design of God in creating the
universe. All these doctrines coalesce to form a world view in
which both the natural domain and the domain of grace are
governed by the same simple occasionalist laws.[7] Precisely because the *Traité* marks Malebranche's emergence as an original
thinker, it also marks the beginning of a polemic with the more
orthodox Cartesian Antoine Arnauld. Arnauld defended Descartes' position that ideas are modifications of the mind against
Malebranche's vision in God; as a theologian, he attacked Malebranche's efforts to rationalize the mysteries of the distribution
and the operation of grace. According to Arnauld, the Oratorian
departed from Augustine's teaching and attributed human motivation to God while purporting to speak in the name of the
simplicity of reason.

The Apostolate of Reason

For twentieth-century readers, this interpenetration of faith
and reason is the most astonishing aspect of Malebranche's originality. We are perhaps more at home with the approach of Descartes for whom there was no conflict between faith and reason
and who preferred to leave questions that ultimately must be
settled on the authority of faith to theologians. He was more
interested in scientific and philosophical questions that could be
settled by reason alone, or, in an intermediate area—issues such
as the existence of God or the distinction of mind and body—
that are accessible to reason as well as to faith and where reason
can serve as a preface to theology. He envisaged his philosophy
as serving religion, yet he refused to fuse the two.[8]

The Oratorian could not conceive of separating the truths of reason and of dogma as sharply as Descartes.[9] Much as Augustine inscribed a *philosophia christiana* within his theology without ever claiming to write as a philosopher, Malebranche takes theological doctrines for granted in his philosophy. One might characterize the role of theology in Malebranche's system in the same way Etienne Gilson described the place of philosophy in Augustine's thought: "[I]t is everywhere and nowhere."[10] Philosophy for Malebranche is Christian philosophy directed at salvation. "Religion is the true philosophy" ("La religion, c'est la vraie philosophie" [11:34]). On the one hand, he accomplishes this by expanding Descartes' mixed category of truths accessible to reason and to faith to include questions like original sin and the necessity of grace. In such cases dogma confirms solutions obtained through the use of reason.[11] At the same time, he treats all questions—moral, theological, as well as scientific—with the single geometric method of Descartes the physicist with the result that the distribution of grace is governed by the same laws that operate in the world of mechanics.[12] Malebranche sees the truths of both faith and *évidence* as varieties of a single truth. Faith provides certainty based on authority, while the certainty of reason originates in the light of self-evidence (1:62). Faith is a short cut to truth, needed because of the limits on the intellect, but it will some day be replaced with the superior light of *évidence*. "Evidence, understanding, is preferable to faith. Because faith will pass, but understanding will subsist eternally" ("L'évidence, l'intelligence est préférable à la foi. Car la foi passera mais l'intelligence subsistera éternellement" [11:34]).

Finally, we can appreciate the mixture of theology and philosophy in Malebranche in which Cartesian physics is invoked to explain the transmission of original sin, or in which Adam's Fall is the key epistemological event, if we remember that theology for the Oratorian is identified with apologetics. As Gouhier has pointed out, Malebranche's own apostolate is to the philosophers, in particular to the Cartesians: "His will be an apologetics of reason."[13]

Malebranche's vocation as an apostle of reason is essential for understanding the dynamics of his rhetorical system. Cartesian antecedents, transformed and given new urgency by Malebranche's theocentric preoccupations, underlie both his denunciation of false eloquence and his vision of authentic persuasion. Cartesian psychophysiology provides the basis for what I call the *rhetoric of distraction* which perpetuates the Fall of Adam. Malebranche's deepened understanding of Descartes' notion of attention, made possible by his doctrine of the mind's union with the Divine Reason, allowed him to envisage a *rhetoric of attention* whose ultimate model is the Incarnation, and where the sensible and the intelligible, grace and nature, complement each other. The key components of both the attack against the rhetoric of distraction and the analysis of the rhetoric of attention are present in early texts such as *La Recherche* and the *Conversations chrétiennes*. However, the role of grace, which supplements the rhetoric of attention, becomes more clearly defined in the *Traité de la nature et de la grâce* and later writings. Furthermore, in dialogues like the *Converstions chrétiennes,* but especially in the mature *Méditations chrétiennes* (1683) and *Entretiens sur la métaphysique et sur la religion* (1688), one can see this restored rhetoric in operation. These works, which envisage persuasion taking place under ideal conditions, contain both theoretical discussions of the communication process and practical advice on how to convert even the most obdurate. Finally, this redeemed rhetoric of attention is only a prelude to the *rhetoric of praise* of the saved in heaven.

The Psychophysiological Level: Satan's Rhetoric of Distraction

Malebranche's indictment of false eloquence can be analyzed on three levels. First, on the level of individual psychophysiology the commotion of animal spirits in the brain dulls the attention which the mind requires to attain truth. Second, in the social dimension humans are transformed into mindless machines persuading each other mechanically through their bodies. Finally, on the level of expression, which forms part of the *manières* analyzed by Arnauld and Nicole, the speaker's words or delivery—the air, tone, or spoken words—form a complex medium which bypasses the pure understanding.

It is no accident that Malebranche includes an account of our first parents' sin within his attack on Seneca (1:352–53), for it is the prototype of all false eloquence. The Fall exemplifies the psychophysiological mechanism of false eloquence, and the consequences of original sin shed light on the susceptibility of Adam's posterity to such seduction both as individuals and members of society.

Before the Fall, Adam's mind was joined both to God and to his body. His understanding was united to God in whom he perceived the light of *évidence;* his will was likewise linked to God, who had endowed it with an innate attraction toward the good in general, which ultimately must be identified with God himself. Adam was free, that is, able to direct his will's inclination to the good in general toward particular objects that seemed to possess this goodness. Because of his union with the body, Adam experienced sensations and passions, but they could be contained within their legitimate function of informing him of potential benefits and dangers to the body so that they did not interfere with the life of the mind. Adam enjoyed the ability to control his senses and passions by stopping them on command once they had sounded their warning so that he could direct his undivided attention to God (1:75). The mind, as a spiritual entity, was made to know God, not matter. Adam freely chose his duty to God because of his clear perception of his relation to his Creator (3:46).

Nevertheless, Adam fell, and his sin was one of distraction (3:76). Satan induced him to turn away his attention from his clear knowledge of his duty to God by attracting him to some sensible pleasure. Malebranche lists a variety of possible temptations: the beauty and sweetness of the forbidden fruit, a presumptuous joy in his own natural perfection, and a tenderness for his wife (1:75). The discussion of the Fall contained within the critique of Seneca is especially interesting because it emphasizes how the serpent's rhetoric exploited the most fundamental of the will's inclinations—its desire to achieve union with God. By promising Adam and Eve that they would become like gods, Satan deflected this movement toward God into a selfish love of their own grandeur and independence (1:352). Absorbed in the sensual pleasure of his own glory, Adam was distracted from his view of his true source of happiness.

The first book of *La Recherche,* where Malebranche shows the role sense perceptions can play in inducing intellectual and moral error, provides the psychophysiological basis for Satan's success as well as for all false eloquence. On the one hand, sensations like heat or cold, taste, color, and pain or pleasure are only modifications of the mind. Because they exist solely in the mind of each individual, they are entirely subjective. They vary in intensity from person to person and cannot be measured with precision. Thus they are unable to furnish the foundation of any scientific knowledge of the objects that are their occasional causes. Only pure ideas perceived uniformly by all humans can provide certain knowledge. Just the same, such sensations do succeed in furnishing instinctive information about the relation of objects in the exterior world, albeit hazy and confused. However, as modifications of the mind, the sensible exercises a stronger attraction on it than the intelligible ideas which it perceives because of its link to God. Sense perceptions crowd out pure ideas from the understanding, and sensual pleasures lure the will away from its inclination toward God. Error stems from the intense hold the sensible can have on human liberty. The light of *évidence* informs the mind, but because it remains external, it leaves the freedom of the will intact:

> Because this light is outside us, it does not touch us or modify our soul; it does not push us toward the objects that it reveals to us; it only allows us to direct ourselves or to consent freely and reasonably to the inclination toward the good that God gives us.

> Car la lumière est hors de nous: elle ne touche, ou ne modifie point notre âme: elle ne nous pousse point vers les objets qu'elle nous découvre, elle fait seulement que nous nous portons nous-mêmes ou que nous consentons librement et par raison à l'impression que Dieu nous donne vers le bien. (5:131)

Bypassing the reason, sensual pleasure as a modification of the mind pushes us to act instinctively.

> Pleasure is in the soul; it touches and modifies it. Thus it diminishes our freedom; it makes us love the good through a love based on instinct and transport instead of through a

love based on reasoned choice; it carries us away, so to speak, toward objects that can be perceived by the senses.

Le plaisir est dans l'âme: il la touche et la modifie. Ainsi il diminue notre liberté; il nous fait aimer le bien plutôt par un amour d'instinct et d'emportement que par un amour de choix et de raison; il nous transporte, pour ainsi dire, vers les objets sensibles. (5:131)

Once Adam had opted for the sensible pleasure of the body instead of the light found in his duty to God he discovered that his union to his body and to God was irrevocably transformed. The senses and passions were no longer limited to providing an instinctual warning to the mind about the health of the body; they occupied the capacity of the mind with such intensity that it could no longer be properly attentive to God. Indeed, Adam lost the power to arrest them at will so that henceforth the body exercised a stronger attraction on the mind than its union with God. The loss of this ability to control the senses and passions and the consequent weakening of the freedom of the will constitute concupiscence according to Malebranche (3:36–37).

This disorder was at once manifested physiologically in the form of a flow of animal spirits aroused by the sensual pleasure of his sin that left an indelible imprint in his brain. This legacy of brain tracings is passed from parents to children and accounts for the physical transmission of original sin (1:247). It also explains how individuals are susceptible to the rhetoric of distraction in which the sensible diverts both the mind's faculties from the *évidence* of truth and love of moral order: "[T]he passions act on the imagination, and the corrupted imagination struggles against the will by continually representing things, not as they are in themselves . . . but as they are in relation to the passion at hand" ("[L]es passions agissent sur l'imagination, et l'imagination corrompue fait effort contre la raison, en lui représentant à toute heure les choses, non selon ce qu'elles sont en elles-mêmes . . . mais selon ce qu'elles sont par rapport à la passion présente" [2:234]). The mechanism by which the attention is distracted is inspired by Descartes, but the urgency of Malebranche's denunciation of false eloquence comes from his belief that this distraction prolongs the Fall.

Yet the seduction of the rhetoric of distraction is not irresistable. Malebranche protests that the senses and passions are not absolutely corrupted or deranged; we have merely lost control of them (1:76). Indeed, the Incarnation and grace allow for a restored human nature. In order to counteract the increased attraction of the sensible since the Fall, God provides the grace of sentiment. As the second Adam, Christ offers a remedy against the disorders that stem from the first Adam in the form of pleasures and pains directly opposed to those caused by concupiscence (5:96). This *holy concupiscence* operates according to the same psychological laws as the passions it counteracts (12–13:105). By providing sentiments that cancel out those of concupiscence, it restores freedom of choice and reestablishes an equilibrium in the mind that leaves the will truly free to choose.[14]

The Social Dimension: The Rhetoric of Imitation

Malebranche's analysis of the rhetoric of distraction in the individual suggests how rhetorical appeals to the imagination dazzle the understanding and how impassioned oratory deflects the will's inclination toward God. In both cases the mind's attention is the victim, and the body alone, the machine in Cartesian parlance, is persuaded.

Malebranche offers special insight into the social dynamics of this mechanical persuasion where humans communicate chiefly at the level of the body. Descartes had suggested in *L'Homme* that even a mindless body could be so disposed as to imitate other such machines, or even real men (1:461). Pascal had described a discourse of the machine based on custom and habit.[15] Malebranche elaborates Descartes' concept by picturing society as an assemblage of living machines, each setting the others in motion by a process of imitation: "Man is a machine that moves in the direction it is pushed. Chance more than reason guides him. All live by opinion. All act on the basis of imitation" ("L'homme est une machine qui va comme on la pousse. C'est plus le hasard que la Raison qui le conduit. Tous vivent d'opinion. Tous agissent par imitation" [12–13:128]). This communication is mechanical in that it takes place unconsciously at the level of the corporal machine. It propagates opinion rather than truth because it operates uncritically without the intervention of reason. Its physiological basis is a common disposition in the brain which humans share with animals that leads them to model their judgments and passions on one another (1:321). God has endowed humans with this instinctive mimetic tendency to facilitate the conservation of civil society in the same way that he has provided the senses and passions for the preservation of each individual's body. To the extent that this imitation can be reserved for the mutual protection of life, it is legitimate. However, the Fall has left this mimetic tendency of the body stronger than our union with God (11:145). The result too often is the false eloquence of imitation which operates horizontally from body to body as if humans were only mindless automatons, incapable of reflection. Malebranche considers this social intercourse a double original sin (4:109). The flow of animal spirits aroused by false eloquence reinforces the pattern of brain tracings inherited by children as a result of original sin, which in turn only prolongs the body's dominion over the mind.

Malebranche depicts this mimesis in a variety of situations which demonstrate its role as a social bond. The desire to please among friends of equal rank leads them to accept each other's opinions without reflection. Developing the mechanical analogy, he compares them to lutes so perfectly tuned that when a chord is struck on one, the other sounds automatically (11:205). The tendency to imitate one's superiors is even more irresistable since they are the natural object of respect. The success of English and German rulers in establishing national churches during the Reformation can be attributed to just this imitation of monarchs by their subjects (1:331–40).

The most remarkable instance of this mechanical persuasion, "the contagious communication of strong imaginations," demonstrates how this mimetic disposition of the brain that is essential to the conservation of civil society also makes possible false eloquence. The audience for such false eloquence is comprised of those who possess weak imaginations, that is, whose brains are disposed to receive mechanically the impression of the images that agitate them (1:329). Such weak imaginations are activated by strong ones, speakers whose brains can be filled with extremely deep and long lasting grooves which so fill the capacity of the mind that they are unable to attend to anything except the images corresponding to the grooves (1:323). The persuasive power of such speakers does not lie in an intellectual mastery of their subject. Indeed, the vivid images produced in their imagination by the grooves of the brain make them incapable of attention to pure ideas. The least intellectual of the five divisions of rhetoric—memory and delivery—will stand them in good stead for they have only to repeat with vigor ideas they have read somewhere, perhaps without any comprehension (4:164–65). Their power stems solely from their ability to transfer the intense sensible impressions produced by the agitation of animal spirits in their brain to those of their listeners. Thus for such a speaker, the rules of rhetoric are superfluous: "[A]lthough his rhetoric is often irregular, it does not fail to be most persuasive" ("[Q]uoique sa rhétorique soit souvent irrégulière, elle ne laisse pas d'être très persuasive" [1:329]).

In one of the most famous fragments of his *Pensées* Pascal had accumulated example after example of how the imagination, "this mistress of error and falsehood" ("cette maîtresse d'erreur et de fausseté"), allows kings, judges or doctors to persuade the credulous to submit to them.[16] Malebranche, on the other hand, gives a more balanced view of its mechanism, not just a catalog of its misdeeds, by situating his analysis of imaginative rhetoric within a comprehensive discussion of both the dangers and benefits of this faculty.

The Language of the Body

The rhetoric of imitation distracts the mind by perverting both language and the whole communication process. The ideal use of words, according to Malebranche, is to communicate the pure ideas of the mind. "Words have only been invented to express thoughts" ("Les mots ne sont inventés que pour exprimer les pensées" [11:95; cp. 11:136]). Sensations cannot be adequately represented by words.[17] While pure ideas are objective and perceived in a uniform manner by all because they are seen in God, the sensations are subjective and vary from individual to individual. They can only be experienced, not represented or described by an arbitrary sign like a word (1:145). Moreover, since by their nature the sentiments are a confused mode of thought, it is impossible to assign them labels with univocal meanings (2:222–23). If the terminology used to describe the passions is equivocal and conducive to misunderstandings, how much more so must be the figured language and images to which strong imaginations habitually have recourse to convey their passions?

Since words are inadequate to communicate a message that is primarily sensible, the speaker of strong imagination will have to look elsewhere for a medium. Indeed, according to Malebranche, the rhetoric of imitation depends more on delivery than speech to persuade. Gesture, animation, and tone of voice carry the principal burden. More effective than words alone, this body language Malebranche calls *l'air* forms a natural language of the passions understood by all humans. In *La Recherche* he gives an elaborate psychophysiological account of the difference between this body language and speech. The bases of the language of gesture are the links between the brain traces corresponding to the image of some passion and the idea of the passion—for example, between the image of a person suffering and the idea of suffering. Thus, each time we see a person grimace as if in pain, a psychophysiological process is set in motion that occasions in the mind the idea of suffering. This natural language of the passions has been established by God as a bond among humans to facilitate social life (1:217).

These impressions in the brain are not only uniform in all humans, but they are also deeper, and thus more lasting, than the weaker, arbitrary tracings that link the sound of words to their meanings, especially abstract ones (1:219–20). Facial expressions, body movements, and the like thus convey a universal meaning across cultural boundaries, while the sign and meaning of a word in any given language are joined together by convention.

> Certainly the spoken word alone is an equivocal, deceptive sign in the mouths of most men. Moreover, as it is an arbitrary construction, it does not vividly persuade the truths it expresses. . . . But air and manners are a natural language, one which makes itself understood without reflection, which persuades by a vivid impression and which pours, one might say, conviction in the mind.

> Certainement la parole toute seule est un signe équivoque
> et trompeur dans la bouche de la plupart des hommes. De
> plus comme elle est d'institution arbitraire, elle ne persuade
> pas vivement les vérités qu'elle exprime. . . . Mais l'air et les
> manières sont un langage naturel, et qui se fait entendre
> sans qu'on y pense, qui persuade par une vive impression,
> et qui répand pour ainsi dire la conviction dans les esprits.
> (11:255)

Body language is at once less equivocal and more vivid than
verbal communication, with the result that it persuades more
readily.

Malebranche discusses rhetorical figures in terms of the same
psychophysiology of brain tracings that he invokes to explain
why the natural language of gesture is more potent than the
arbitrary verbal one. Groups of tracings that were imprinted at
the same time are linked together so that when a flow of animal
spirits reactivates one, the others are as well. This "mutual connection of traces" ("liaison mutuelle des traces") accounts for all
rhetorical figures (1:222). While Malebranche does not assign
figures of speech to the rhetoric of imitation (in fact, as I show
below, he grants them a certain legitimacy), his comments certainly suggest how they can easily become an instrument of obfuscation. The examples he gives involve the metonymical substitu-
tion of one idea for another:

> If, for example, a man finds himself in some public ceremony
> and notes its circumstances and all the chief personages in
> attendance, the weather, the locale, the day, and other such
> details, it will suffice for him to remember the locale, or even
> some other less notable circumstance of the ceremony in or-
> der to represent to himself all the others. . . . And when one
> cannot find the true name of a person or when it is most conve-
> nient to designate him in some other manner, he can be la-
> beled as this face scarred by the pox, this handsome man, this
> little hunchback according to the inclinations one has for him,
> although it is wrong to use such scornful words.

> Si un homme par exemple se trouve dans quelque cérémonie
> publique, s'il en remarque toutes les circonstances, et toutes

les principales personnes qui y assistent, le temps, le lieu, le jour et toutes les autres particularités, il suffira qu'il se souvienne du lieu, ou même d'une autre circonstance moins remarquable de la cérémonie pour se représenter toutes les autres. . . . Et ne pouvant trouver le nom propre d'une personne, ou étant plus à propos de le désigner d'une autre manière, on le peut marquer par ce visage picoté de vérole, ce grand homme bien fait, ce petit bossu, selon les inclinations qu'on a pour lui, quoi qu'on ait tort de se servir des paroles de mépris. (1:222)

The mechanism Malebranche has in mind makes use of Arnauld and Nicole's distinction between principal and accessory ideas, which he refers to later in *La Recherche* when discussing the mutual linking of brain traces. Rhetorical figures thus involve allowing an accessory idea to replace the principal one—the pockmarked face for the preacher himself with all the connotations of disrespect associated with the term. Malebranche scores two points against ideas linked in this way and implies that such strategies are most appropriate in a rhetoric of distraction. First, the interplay of related principal and accessory ideas only increases the agitation of animal spirits, thereby making calm reflection more difficult (2:182). Second, the same principal ideas will not uniformly evoke the same accessory ones in all members of an audience (2:183), thereby making them unreliable instruments in any rhetoric, but especially in one that seeks to foster clear thinking.

Even in those cases in which the words of a strong imagination, rather than delivery alone, have persuasive force, the words do not function as signifiers of pure ideas. For a Cartesian like Malebranche, verbal language suffers from the dualism that permeates human nature: the sound and meaning of words are joined together arbitrarily, just as are the body and the mind. In the rhetoric of imitation the sensual component of language appeals directly to the sensual element in humans. This appeal to the senses is so forceful that even though Tertullian, Seneca, and Montaigne lack the advantage of oral delivery, their tainted words on the page have a hypnotic effect that is stronger than the reason of many of their readers: "They enter, they penetrate, they dominate in the soul in such an imperious manner that they make themselves obeyed without being understood" ("Elles entrent, elles pénètrent, elles dominent dans l'âme d'une manière si impérieuse, qu'elles se font obéir sans se faire entendre" [1:341]).

Malebranche's analysis of the style of these three authors points to some of the devices that allow them to sidetrack language from its ideal role as the signifier of pure ideas. Tertullian, for example, cultivates obscurity as one of the chief rules of his rhetoric (3:124); his hyperboles, figures of speech, and pompous descriptions are typical of his tendency to exaggerate (1:342). Among the charms of Seneca is the cadence of his prose whose rhythm, quite independently of the meaning of his words, gives the illusion of progress toward a reasoned conclusion: "He imagines that he advances greatly; but he resembles those who, when dancing, always return to the spot where they began" ("Il s'imagine qu'il avance beaucoup; mais il ressemble à ceux qui dansent, qui finissent toujours où ils ont commencé" [1:345]). Montaigne's style is a warning against the dangers of emotional persuasion. The affected negligence of his gallant air (1:359) is particularly insidious because it excites a pleasure that is grounded in concupiscence and that operates by entertaining and fortifying the passions, albeit in an almost imperceptible way: "[T]his author's manner of writing is only pleasant because it touches us and imperceptibly awakens our passions" ("[L]a manière d'écrire de cet auteur n'étant agréable, que parce qu'elle nous touche, et qu'elle réveille nos passions d'une manière imperceptible" [1:360]).

In the last analysis, Malebranche sees the force of all the levels of style as depending on their appeal to our fallen nature: "[A]ll the various styles are ordinarily only pleasing because of the secret corruption of our hearts" ("[T]ous les divers styles ne nous plaisent ordinairement, qu'à cause de la corruption secrète de notre coeur" [1:360]). Thus whether it is the sublime style which flatters our love of grandeur, or a delicate, effeminate one which appeals to our desire for sensual pleasure (1:360–61), the will is deflected by passion from its true goal.

This perversion of language is so extensive that in extreme cases the words convey no meaning, only the feeling of persuasion. "One submits to their orders without knowing them. One wishes to believe without knowing what one believes" ("On se rend à leurs ordres sans les savoir. On veut croire mais on ne sait que croire" [1:341]). The rhetoric of imitation produces conviction without content. It represents the ultimate example of the degradation of language as a medium for pure ideas prevalent in ordinary discourse. "Words, whose chief use should be to represent the pure ideas of the mind, only serve in common usage to express ideas keyed to the senses and the movements of the soul" ("Les paroles, dont le principal usage devrait être de représenter les idées pures de l'esprit, ne servent d'ordinaire qu'à exprimer des idées sensibles, et les mouvements de l'âme" [11:136]). Like Satan in the garden of Eden, these latter-day purveyors of false eloquence use language to bedazzle the understanding with the sensible and to deflect the will's natural inclination to God by using the passions to attract it to some ephemeral pleasure:

> They fancy themselves beautiful and rare geniuses because they know how to satisfy the ear with a pleasing harmony, flatter the passions with winning figures of speech and gestures, and entertain the imagination with vivid expressions appealing to the senses, although they leave the mind empty of ideas and without light or understanding.

> Ils s'imaginent être de beaux et de rares génies à cause qu'ils savent contenter l'oreille par une juste mesure, flatter les passions par des figures et des mouvements agréables, réjouir l'imagination par des expressions vives et sensibles, quoiqu'ils laissent l'esprit vide d'idées sans lumière et sans intelligence. (2:231)

The Rhetoric of Attention:
The Prompter/Interior Master Relationship

The temptation to resort to this mimetic rhetoric addressed to the body is so pervasive in fallen mankind that a rhetoric appealing to the mind might seem unlikely. Even Malebranche's own style, as André Robinet has noted, is at times more affective than cognitive.[18] The Oratorian was well aware of the danger. In the *Entretiens* Ariste makes the same observation when he wonders

out loud if Malebranche's spokesman Théodore is not guilty of
such misuse of language: "Your exhortation, Théodore, seems
to me to be most lively for a metaphysical discussion. It appears
to me that you are exciting emotions in me instead of causing
clear ideas to be born there" ("Votre exhortation, Théodore, me
paraît bien vive pour un entretien de Métaphysique. Il me semble
que vous excitez en moi des sentiments, au lieu d'y faire naître des
idées claires" [12–13:69]). Ariste fears the onset of the uncritical
feeling of persuasion produced by the rhetoric of imitation. The
first part of Théodore's defense seems to reject the possibility
of any communication between humans; no meaning is being
exchanged, only the empty noise of words bereft of signification:
"I relate to you what I see, and you do not see it. This is proof
that men do not instruct each other. . . . I speak to your ears.
Apparently, I am only making so much noise in them" ("Je vous
dis ce que je vois, et vous ne le voyez pas. C'est une preuve
que l'homme n'instruit pas l'homme. . . . Je parle à vos oreilles.
Apparemment, je n'y fais que trop de bruit" [12–13:69]). Yet
when Théodore goes on to explain that he is not Ariste's master
but his prompter or *moniteur*, it becomes clear that language can
be used to communicate above the level of the senses. If Ariste
is not yet convinced, it is because "our single Master is not yet
speaking clearly enough to your mind; or rather reason is constantly speaking to it most distinctly but for lack of attention,
you are not sufficiently distinguishing his replies to you" ("notre
unique Maître ne parle point encore assez clairement à votre
esprit: ou plutôt la Raison lui parle sans cesse fort nettement;
mais faute d'attention, vous n'entendez point assez ce qu'elle vous
répond" [12–13:69]. A rhetoric appealing to the mind may be
possible after all, if it takes into account the three elements cited
here: the role of attention, the prodding of the *moniteur*, and the
action of the *Maître intérieur* or Universal Reason.

If Descartes had been Malebranche's sole *moniteur*, it is unlikely
that he would ever have envisaged a reformed rhetoric along
these lines. The distinctive elements of the Oratorian's positive
views on persuasion are predicated on his theory of the mind's
union with God, a doctrine not found in Descartes. He found his
inspiration in Augustine, not so much the Augustine of rhetorical
treatises such as the fourth book of *De Doctrina christiana*, but in

philosophical extracts from works like *De Trinitate* or *De Magistro* which had been anthologized by his fellow Oratorian André Martin under the title *Philosophia christiana*.[19]

According to Malebranche's doctrine of vision in God, the understanding is united to the Divine Reason of God. This Universal Reason is the Eternal Wisdom of God, whom Malebranche identifies with the second person of the Trinity and in whom humans perceive all clear and distinct ideas. Such ideas include our concepts of moral order, the ideas of mathematical relationships, and what he calls intelligible extension, the archetype of extension which makes possible our knowledge of material objects. The superiority of pure ideas over sensible ones, which is at the heart of Malebranche's epistemological objections to the rhetoric of imitation, finds its ultimate guarantee in the fact that pure ideas are seen in God. While sensible perceptions are only modifications of our minds, pure ideas possess this extramental reality that confers their intelligibility. Humans can break out of the subjectivity of the sensible that the rhetoric of imitation exploits and communicate at the level of necessary, eternal truth because they are all united to the same Divine Reason. Authentic communication is possible only when one individual assumes the role of a *moniteur* who prompts others to consult the Divine Reason until all share the illumination of the ideas in God. The horizontal dynamics of the rhetoric of imitation are transformed into a vertical relationship of attention between each individual and the Divine Reason.

Malebranche on Attention

The notion of attention is at the nexus of Malebranche's system. Pierre Blanchard calls it "his original intuition. Attention is the whole of Malebranche's doctrine and method."[20] Malebranche retains Descartes' concept of attention as the intense application of the understanding directed by the will to the problem at hand, but when it enters the context of vision in God, attention takes on new and subtle complexities. Blanchard, whose analysis is the most exhaustive, singles out three somewhat overlapping aspects of attention.[21]

First, it is the occasional cause of knowledge. Malebranche, of course, reserves all efficient causality in the production of ideas, as in all other domains, to God alone. Nonetheless, God grants humans access to ideas on the basis of their attention (2:247). In fact, Malebranche repeatedly stresses a necessary correlation between the intensity of attention and success in attaining truth: "All those who apply themselves to the truth discover it in proportion to their application" ("Tous ceux qui s'appliquent à la vérité, la découvrent à proportion de leur application" [5:102]). Thus, strengthening the capacity for this mental effort that results in the light of *évidence* is one of his constant concerns.

Second, although the suggestions Malebranche offers for protecting and extending the range of attention resemble those of Descartes in many ways, attention for Malebranche is not merely the implementation of an intellectual method. It is an intimate consultation of the Interior Master, one person addressing another. The *Méditations chrétiennes,* a dialogue between a disciple and the "Eternal Word, the Word of the Father, Word which has always been uttered" ("Verbe éternel, Parole du Père, Parole qui a toujours été dite" [10:9]), illustrates this relationship perfectly. Malebranche demands a certain asceticism as a precondition for this dialogue since the clamor of the senses is louder than the voice of reason. Attention requires a continuing effort to impose silence on the body (10:7).

The third aspect of attention, as natural prayer—"the natural prayer by which we prevail on God to enlighten us" ("la prière naturelle par laquelle nous obtenons que Dieu nous éclaire" [5:102])—signals attention's entry into the system of nature and grace. Attention is natural in that it predates the establishment of the realm of the grace of sentiment made necessary by the Fall. Adam was capable of attention before sinning, and although concupiscence has much weakened human attentiveness, God continues to answer requests for light, even from sinners and unbelievers. Attention is responsible for all we know naturally and is unaided by revelation. Attention is also a prayer because, as a request for the light of *évidence*, it is analogous to the request for grace that the believer addresses to the Incarnated Word. The natural prayer of attention is directed to the Divine Reason as a request for light; the prayer of faith is directed to the same second person of the Trinity, but as the Redeemer who restores fallen nature with the grace of sentiment.

The need for this grace of sentiment to supplement the light of intelligibility is a sign of the frailty and limits of attention since the Fall. Malebranche pictures attention as a battle-ground—"this struggle of the mind against the impressions of the body" ("ce combat de l'esprit contre les impressions du corps" [12–13:32])—but since the mind's hold on the body has been weakened by concupiscence, it is a struggle the mind too often loses. Unable to sustain the intellectual concentration needed to reach *évidence*, the exhausted mind takes refuge in the probable (11:21). Moveover, due to the mind's limited capacity, reason is unable to discover certain truths such as the Trinity or the Eucharist, which nonetheless are crucial for salvation (1:395). Finally, the product of attention, the light of intelligibilty, cannot move the mind with the same intensity as sensible pleasure, especially since the Fall.

The Incarnation as Rhetoric

The Incarnation of the *Sagesse éternelle* carries within it a remedy for this rebellion of the body that weakens the attention. Because humanity in its fallen state could never attain all the truth it needed, much less act upon it, the Divine Reason became incarnate and instituted a realm of grace to restore nature. Faith supplies the understanding with the truths essential to salvation, which the natural prayer of attention cannot reach, and a grace of sentiment compensates for pleasure's attraction on the will. "Reason only became incarnate in order to lead men to reason through the senses" ("La Raison ne s'est incarnée que pour conduire par les sens les hommes à la Raison" [11:35]). The Word speaks in two manners: "As Universal Reason and intelligible light, I illuminate from within all minds by the evidence and clarity of my doctrine; as Wisdom incarnated and adjusted to their weakness, I instruct them by faith" ("Comme Raison universelle et lumière intelligible j'éclaire intérieurement tous les esprits par l'évidence et la clarté de ma Doctrine: comme Sagesse incarnée et proportionnée à leur faiblesse, je les instruis par la foi"

[10:27]). The *Conversations chrétiennes* cites Christ's use of miracles, parables, and everyday similes (4:112), but such instruction through the senses is not the most profound meaning of the Divine Wisdom's rhetoric. Malebranche repeatedly points to the Incarnation itself as a rhetorical act.[22] By entering the world of *res extensa* the Divine Reason becomes an instrument for drawing attention toward the intelligible. The Incarnation is at once the rationale and the model for authentic persuasion among fallen humans. The most striking presentation of this theme occurs, in fact, in the midst of a warning against false eloquence in *La Recherche:*

> The truth must be made known to others just as as the truth itself has made itself known. Since the sin of their first father, the vision of humans has been too weak to behold the truth in itself; thus this sovereign truth has made itself accessible to the senses by covering itself with our humanity so as to draw our gaze, to illuminate us, and to make itself worthy of love in our eyes. Following this example, we can cover the truths we want to understand and teach to others with something perceptible to the senses so as to fix the mind which loves sense perceptions and which is not easily caught by anything that does not flatter the senses.

> Il faut exposer aux autres la vérité, comme la vérité même s'est exposée. Les hommes depuis le péché de leur père, ayant la vue trop faible pour considérer la vérité en elle-même, cette souveraine vérité s'est rendue sensible en se couvrant de notre humanité, afin d'attirer nos regards, de nous éclairer, et de se rendre aimable à nos yeux. Ainsi on peut à son exemple couvrir de quelque chose de sensible les vérités que nous voulons comprendre et enseigner aux autres, afin d'arrêter l'esprit qui aime le sensible, et qui ne se prend aisément que par quelque chose qui flatte les sens. (2:260–61)

It was not unusual for seventeenth-century theorists to point to the Incarnation as a model for rhetoric. Bossuet, for example, in the *Panégyrique de l'apôtre Saint Paul* (1657) appeals to Christ's dual nature to justify stylistic simplicity.

He [Christ] is an incarnate wisdom, who, covering himself
voluntarily with the infirmity of the flesh, hid from the great
of the earth by means of the obscurity of this veil. . . . Do
not be astonished, he [Saint Paul] tells us, if preaching a
hidden wisdom, my discourse is not adorned with the lights
of eloquence.

Il [Christ] est une sagesse incarnée, qui, s'étant couverte
volontairement de l'infirmité de la chair, s'est cachée aux
grands de la terre par l'obscurité de ce voile. . . . Ne vous
étonnez pas, nous dit-il, si, prêchant une sagesse cachée,
mes discours ne sont point ornés des lumières de l'éloquence.[23]

However, while Bossuet uses the Incarnation to justify an absence
of rhetorical devices, Malebranche takes the opposite approach.
The fact God took on human flesh legitimizes recourse to techniques appealing to the sensual.

As a model for rhetoric, the Incarnation applies most directly
to persuasion dealing with the ethical and religious issues of
humanity's duty to God: "[T]he primary design of Jesus Christ
was not to teach us certain speculative truths which do not lead
in themselves to the knowledge and love of the sovereign Truth"
("[L]e principal dessein de Jésus-Christ n'a pas été de nous
instruire de certaines vérités spéculatives, qui ne conduisent
point par elles-mêmes à la connaissance et à l'amour de la souve-
raine Vérité" [4:160]). Christ's instruction through the Incarnation refers first of all to the path of faith based on authority
rather than the evidence of light achieved through attention
(10:27). Yet in Malebranche's system where grace and nature,
faith and *évidence,* serve each other, the Incarnation is the ultimate model whenever the senses are called upon to lead to the
intelligible, even in scientific and practical matters. Thus I center
my discussion of Malebranche's rhetoric of attention around
three points exemplified by the Incarnation. First, the Incarnation justifies taking into account the position and psychology of
the audience; second, it authorizes the use of the senses and
passions that had been so decried in the rhetoric of imitation; yet,
finally, the limits and dangers of the sensible are never forgotten.

The Incarnation as Audience Adaptation

Malebranche's conviction that there is only one Universal Reason speaking with a single voice to all who will listen does not prevent a keen appreciation of the need to adapt to each particular audience. Just as God accommodated himself to mankind by taking on a body, so proofs must be chosen which are acceptable to each audience:

> It is permissible in China to draw the proofs of our dogmas from Confucius, that country's philosopher. . . . In order to persuade people readily one must speak to them according to their ideas in a language that they understand well and that they listen to willingly.

> Il est permis à la Chine de tirer de Confucius Philosophe du Pays des preuves de la vérité de nos Dogmes. . . . Pour persuader promptement les gens, il faut nécessairement leur parler selon leurs idées, un langage qu'ils entendent bien, et qu'ils écoutent volontiers. (4:4; cp. 12–13:316)

Malebranche recommends as a first step familiarizing oneself with the audience: "Before speaking, try to assess the strength and capacity of those who listen to you" ("Avant que de parler tâche de connaître la force et la capacité de ceux qui t'écoutent" [10:204]). He offers a series of hints on psychological strategies to use with a variety of audiences: those disposed to truth (10:205); *esprits forts,* with whom equivocal terms should be avoided (11:39); and heretics, who must be taught to distrust their own judgment (1:396).

The dialogues themselves illustrate how to deal with an audience which manifests a great love of truth; with them one can expose one's thoughts directly, no matter how abstract the principles may be: "[T]heir love of the truth will give them attention, and attention will cause light to be born in them" ("[L]eur amour de la vérité leur donnera l'attention, et l'attention fera naître en eux la lumière" [10:205]). Yet persuasion is seldom this easy. In all three dialogues, once the willing learner has mastered the fundamentals of Malebranche's system, the discussion turns to

how to convert others. Different tactics are in order for those
who have only some love of the truth or who are even scoffers:

> Question, but as a disciple so that pride will renew and
> strengthen attention. Approve whatever is good in the re-
> plies you receive without paying attention at first to the rest.
> Uncover the truth in a way that they fancy that they have
> discovered it themselves; act so that everyone who deals with
> you is intelligent. Attribute to others any solid thoughts that
> they might only partially express and that they perhaps do
> not even have. If men are to love the truth, it must belong
> to them, and touch them. They must consider it a product
> of their minds.

> Interroge, mais en Disciple, afin que l'amour-propre renou-
> velle et fortifie l'attention. Approuve ce qu'il y a de bon dans
> les réponses qu'on te rend, sans faire d'abord attention au
> reste. Découvre la vérité de manière qu'on s'imagine soi-
> même la découvrir, fais en sorte qu'avec toi tout le monde
> ait de l'esprit. Attribue aux autres des pensées solides, qu'ils
> n'expriment qu'à demi, et qu'ils n'ont peut-être pas. Afin
> que l'homme aime la vérité, il faut qu'elle lui appartienne,
> et qu'elle le touche: il faut la regarder comme une produc-
> tion de son esprit. (10:205)

Malebranche acknowledges the element of manipulation here,
calling it elsewhere a charitable dissimulation (12–13:317). He
goes so far as to suggest playing the devil's advocate: "But when
you have recognized that truth is penetrating them, then combat
it without fear that they will abandon it. They will consider it to
be a possession that belongs to them" ("Mais lorsque vous aurez
reconnu que la vérité les pénètre, alors combattez-la sans craindre
qu'ils l'abondonnent. Ils la regarderont comme un bien qui leur
appartient" [12–13:317]). He shows no qualms about using *ad
hominem* arguments that he himself finds weak: "One can even
use a very weak argument in order to persuade an established
truth when those one wishes to instruct find it good, and it
is more convincing for them than another one that would be
conclusive if they could appreciate its force" ("On peut même,
pour persuader une vérité constante, se servir d'une preuve très

faible, lorsque ceux qu'on veut instruire, la trouvent bonne; et qu'elle est plus convaincante pour eux, qu'une autre serait démonstrative, s'ils pouvaient en comprendre la force" [16:155–56]). For example, the confused notion of providence held by the ignorant may be far from the clear understanding the enlightened have of this dogma, but even their inadequate concept contains a kernel of truth that should be exploited (12–13:315–16).

In such cases, audience adaptation is clearly not grounded in respect for the other's position. Instead it means accommodating oneself to a perceived weakness, and Malebranche justifies any deception by comparing himself to a doctor treating a self-indulgent patient: "When a sick person loves his illness, he must be tricked to be cured" ("Lorsque un malade aime son mal, il faut le tromper pour le guérir" [10:204]). Nevertheless, in the context of the theory of vision in God, the deception implied in a recommendation like "one must always instruct [others] so that they imagine that they are teaching us" ("il faut toujours . . . les [les autres] instruire en sorte qu'ils s'imaginent nous régenter" [4:58]) is less manipulative than it might seem. Neither participant is a true teacher for, as we have seen, "men do not instruct each other." They are not *maîtres* but *moniteurs*, who serve to prompt the attention to the true *Maître intérieur*, the sole source of truth. In fact, the very enterprise of audience adaptation is likely to be somewhat haphazard since Malebranche insists that we can know the souls of others only by conjecture (1:454). We have no certain knowledge of their intentions, for only God reads their hearts (11:203). Each individual must make a personal discovery of truth by focusing the attention on the common source of Divine Wisdom.

The Incarnation:
The Intelligible Made Sensible

The need to make abstract ideas accessible to persons of faltering attention is a recurring theme of Malebranche:

> The Order that must reform us is too abstract to serve as a model for base minds. . . . Let it therefore be given a body;

make it accessible to the senses; dress it in various manners
to make it lovable to the eyes of carnel men; let it be incarnated so to speak.

L'Ordre, qui doit nous réformer, est une forme trop ab-
straite pour servir de modèle aux esprits grossiers.... Qu'on
lui donne donc du corps, qu'on le rende sensible, qu'on le
revête en plusieurs manières pour le rendre aimable à des
hommes charnels: qu'on l'incarne pour ainsi dire. (11:33)

If the Incarnation is a rhetorical act using the senses to make
known the intelligible, the recourse to the sensible to strengthen
the attention and to fortify the will's resolve to do good gains
legitimacy. The specific examples Malebranche offers in the fifth
and sixth books of *La Recherche* to a great extent follow Descartes'
lead. The Oratorian discusses how passions like admiration can
buttress the attention (2:262–81). Much as Descartes had done,
Malebranche refers back to the laws governing the union of the
body and mind to suggest how the passions may be stimulated
(2:257). In addition, just as in Descartes, the recommendations
he gives in *La Recherche* are more concerned with the quest for
truth than its communication, with science more than rhetoric.
Nevertheless, even if Malebranche does not provide a detailed
list of strategies, the rationale for the rhetorical use of the imagination and the passions is implied.

Thus his comments on the imagination as an aid in geometry
and other physical sciences shed light on its use in rhetorical
images. The imagination is most helpful in disciplines based on
relations of extension such as geometry, astronomy, or mechanics
(2:274), but even there the diagrams and figures of the scientists
are incapable of providing the light of *évidence* without the intervention of reason. His ideal is a controlled imagination that sus-
tains attention and is tempered by reason: "[B]y the aid of geometry the mind controls the movement of the imagination; and the
controlled imagination supports the gaze and application of the
mind" ("[P]ar le secours de la Géométrie l'esprit règle le mouvement de l'imagination; et l'imagination réglée soutient la vue et
l'application de l'esprit" [2:278]). An unbridled imagination is
unable to enlighten the mind concerning even the extended

world represented in the drawings of geometers; only the pure ideas of intelligible extension perceived in God provide *évidence* to the mathematician.

If the imagination alone fails to represent the extended world, how much more inadequate is it in representing the world of unextended substance? Malebranche resorts to such comparisons to illustrate central points in this system. For example, he adopts Descartes' metaphor of the mind as a ball of wax to explain how ideas modify the mind, and he develops the image of rain falling on cultivated and uncultivated fields alike to illustrate the distribution of grace to the just and unjust. In such cases he is quick to point out that the analogy between the two substances is imperfect and presents them as rhetorical strategies rather than as heuristic devices: "[O]ne only compares these two things in order to make the mind more attentive and to make others feel what one wishes to say" ("[O]n ne compare ensemble ces deux choses, que pour rendre l'esprit plus attentif, et faire comme sentir aux autres ce que l'on veut dire" [1:41]). Such mundane comparisons might make abstract ideas more familiar and even more distinct (1:41), but rooted as they are in the sensible, they inevitably contain an element of confusion, and thus cannot provide the perfect clarity of *évidence* (12–13:125). The imagination's role as a rhetorical ornament is similarly limited. Malebranche does not deny the attraction of a beauty that appeals to the senses. However, the true basis of such pleasure is found in the proportions and harmony the mind perceives behind the senses, that is, in an intellectual beauty which the mind seldom fully appreciates, so powerful is the attraction of the senses (10:42–43).

Malebranche's treatment of the passions follows the pattern set by Descartes. His explanation of how the commotion of animal spirits aroused by the passions can impart the strength and courage needed to maintain attention (2:254) is rooted in Cartesian psychophysiology. Likewise, just as Descartes had recommended the most intellectual of the passions, admiration, Malebranche counsels passions that stem from the love of truth itself—the desire to rid oneself of error and prejudice, and the desire to acquire knowledge to conduct oneself well in practical affairs (2:256). Other passions such as ambition, the quest for fame, or pride may second the attention with more force in fallen humanity than the reasonable ones, but as a Christian moralist he warns against them as aids in the quest for truth (2:254–55), just as he denounced the appeal to vanity in the eloquence of Seneca and Montaigne.

Like Arnauld and Nicole in the *Logique de Port-Royal*, Malebranche defends figures of speech through which the passions are expressed in language when the emotional reaction is appropriate to the speaker's idea. In the ninth *Eclaircissement* (1678) he notes that Tertullian, for all his stylistic excess, was wise not to write like a geometer when treating religious and ethical questions:

> The figures of speech that express our thoughts and movements in regard to the truths that we expose to others are absolutely necessary. And I believe that especially in discourse about religion and morality one must use ornaments that secure for the truth all the respect due it as well as the movements that stir the soul and lead it to virtuous actions.
>
> Les figures qui expriment nos sentiments et nos mouvements à l'égard des vérités que nous exposons aux autres, sont absolument nécessaires. Et je crois que principalement dans les discours de Religion et de Morale, l'on doit se servir d'ornements qui fassent rendre à la vérité tout le respect qui lui est dû, et de mouvements qui agitent l'âme et la portent à des actions vertueuses. (3:126)

The Port-Royal authors had invoked their distinction between principal and accessory ideas to argue that religious truth must be proposed not just to be known speculatively, but must also be loved, revered, and adored, and they had contrasted favorably the figured style of the church fathers to the arid language of the scholastics. Malebranche stresses, like Quintilian, that speakers must experience the emotional reaction to their ideas which they hope to excite in others: "Excite, therefore, first of all in yourself the movements that the truth must give rise to and then expose your feelings without constraining yourself. You must be penetrated to touch others" ("Excite donc d'abord en toi-même les mouvements que la vérité y doit faire naître, et expose ensuite tes sentiments sans te contraindre. Il faut que tu sois pénétré pour toucher les autres" [10:205]). The emotional proof tends to merge with the ethical one that displays the sincerity of the speaker. Such zeal for truth animated by Christian charity in Malebranche is the counterpart of the *générosité* that is basis of the Cartesian ethical proof.

However, while the emotions that human eloquence can arouse may be a sufficient aid to attention in matters that do not concern salvation, they are never enough to reunite fallen mankind with God. As the Word of the *Méditations chrétiennes* says, "Without my help, one cannot seriously think of being converted" ("Sans mon secours, on ne peut penser sérieusement à se convertir" [10:145]). Only the grace of the Redeemer can counteract the sensible pleasure of concupiscence, and, although this grace of sentiment operates in the mind according to the same psychological laws as the human pleasures and passions it opposes, it is a pure gift of God and not attributable to human efforts. Christian orators can expose the truth to their audience, they can excite their passions, but in so doing they only prepare the way for the efficacious grace of sentiment.

> When a preacher who has great natural talents undertakes to demonstrate a very simple truth and convince others of it, one must admit that he can persuade his listeners and even stir up their consciences, give them fear and hope, and excite passions in them that can render them less resistant to the efficacy of the grace of Jesus Christ.

> Lorsqu'un Prédicateur, qui a de grands talents naturels, entreprend de démontrer une vérité très simple, et d'en convaincre les autres; il faut demeurer d'accord qu'il peut en persuader ses auditeurs, et même remuer leur conscience, leur donner de la crainte et de l'espérance, et exciter en eux quelques passions, qui les mettent en état de moins résister à l'efficace de la Grâce de Jesus Christ. (5:103)

This is fitting in Malebranche's system where nature and grace complement each other: grace presupposes nature, and it is only appropriate that nature should serve grace (10:148). Thus the emotion aroused naturally by the preacher paves the way for the grace of sentiment, and this grace in turn fortifies the natural attention of the listener.

The Incarnation as the Priority of the Intelligible

Finally, the Incarnation delineates the boundaries of emotional and imaginative persuasion by establishing the true function of the sensible:

> It is permissible to incarnate the truth in order to accommodate it to our natural weakness and to support the mind's attention which finds no grasp in things without corporal substance. But it is always necessary for the sensible to lead us to the intelligible, for the flesh to direct us to Reason, and for the truth to appear as it is without any disguise.

> Il est permis d'incarner la vérité pour l'accommoder à notre faiblesse naturelle, et pour soutenir l'attention de l'esprit, qui ne trouve point de prise à ce qui n'a point de corps. Mais il faut toujours que le sensible nous mène à l'intelligible, que la chair nous conduise à la Raison, et que la vérité paraisse telle qu'elle est sans aucun déguisement. (12–13:225)

Christian rhetoric must be an *imitatio Christi*. If Christ took on a body it was only to sacrifice it through his death: "The Eternal Wisdom . . . became perceptible to the senses in order to condemn and sacrifice in his person all that pertains to the senses" ("La Sagesse éternelle . . . s'est rendue sensible pour condamner et sacrifier en sa personne toutes les choses sensibles" [2:261]). Just as the Christian must mortify the body, human eloquence should eventually sacrifice whatever use it makes of the sensible through images or appeals to the emotions: "We must employ something sensible that we can disperse, destroy, and sacrifice with pleasure upon sighting the truth toward which it has led us" ("Nous devons nous servir de quelque chose de sensible, que nous puissions dissiper, anéantir, sacrifier avec plaisir à la vue de la vérité vers laquelle elle nous aura conduits" [2:261]). In addition, just as Christ avoided all facile brilliance, all *éclat*, so eloquence should be muted lest higher truth be forgotten. Had Christ appeared in splendor as a king instead of as a carpenter, the dream of worldly success might have attracted his disciples instead of spiritual promise. "The Eternal Wisdom appeared outside of us in a form accessible to the senses, not to detain us externally, but to make us withdraw into ourselves" ("La Sagesse éternelle s'est présentée hors de nous d'une manière sensible, non pour nous arrêter hors de nous, mais afin de nous faire rentrer dans nous-mêmes" [2:261]). Thus almost every passage in which Malebranche counsels the passions or senses as aids to attention serves as a preface to a warning not to allow oneself to be carried away by them. For example, despite its approval of the use of rhetorical figures of speech, the ninth *Eclaircissement* ends with a double warning to both speaker and audience: "One must not convince or allow oneself to be convinced without knowing with *évidence*, distinctly, and precisely what one is convincing or being convinced of" ("Il ne faut pas convaincre ni se laisser convaincre sans savoir évidemment, distinctement, précisément de quoi on convainc, ou de quoi on est convaincu" [3:126]). Malebranche consistently recommends the least addictive of these remedies to the attention. He suggests the imagination because, as the perception of absent objects, it does not engage the understanding as deeply as direct sense perception (2:262), and admiration because it affects the will the least of all the passions (2:204). In fact, the Oratorian's distrust of the body is so much greater than Descartes' that the chapter of *La Recherche* "Concerning the use one can make of the passions and senses to hold the attention of the mind" ("De l'usage qu'on peut faire des passions et des sens pour conserver l'attention de l'esprit" [2:254]) represents less an attempt to increase the number of aids to attention than a warning against their dangers.

Language and Silence

Given the model of the Incarnation, it is not surprising that the sensual element of language, which dominates in the rhetoric of imitation, no longer is the chief agent of persuasion. Since a word's sound is only an arbitrary sign for Malebranche even in the rhetoric of attention, it can lead to truth only in so far as it serves as a *moniteur* which directs the attention to the Interior Master:

However exact your language when you speak to me and I consult Reason, there occurs at the same time an indistinct sound of two different replies, one directed at the senses the other at the intelligence. . . . You need time to pronounce your words; but all the replies of Reason are eternal and immutable. They have always been uttered, or rather they are always being spoken without any succession of time.

Car quelque justes que soient vos expressions, quand vous me parlez et que je consulte la Raison, il se fait en même temps un bruit confus de deux réponses différentes, l'une sensible, et l'autre intelligible. . . . Car il vous faut du temps pour prononcer vos paroles; mais toutes les réponses de la Raison sont éternelles et immuables. Elles ont toujours été dites, ou plutôt elle se disent toujours sans aucune succession de temps. (12–13:89)

First, human language involves the senses, while the consultation of the Universal Reason is an affair of the understanding alone. Second, although verbal dialogue consisting of utterances that begin and end is bound by time, the ideas seen in God are available eternally and thus always accessible when the Interior Master is consulted. Finally, the replies of the Universal Reason are immutable, while human language changes over time and varies from culture to culture. So imperfect is verbal communication in comparison with the wordless consultation of the Interior Master that Malebranche suggests that in the world to come after death humans may be able to communicate without signs, although he is not willing to speculate openly on the question (1:415–16).

For those who know how to consult this inner voice there is no need to articulate every argument word for word: "Those who withdraw deeply into themselves to listen to interior truth and to study its eternal laws glimpse things that appear incomprehensible to other men" ("Ceux qui rentrent dans eux-mêmes pour y écouter la vérité intérieure, et pour étudier les lois éternelles, comprennent à demi mot des choses qui paraissent incompréhensibles aux autres hommes" [17:1.413]). At the point where *évidence* is finally achieved language becomes irrevelant. As André Robinet insists, "There the role of language is, so to speak, annulled. The presence of the idea is the coextension of the soul with truth."[24] The attention by which certainty is obtained is only a first step, according to Pierre Blanchard, "a first contact with the truth, a contact that is always precarious and fragile, and which becomes interiorized upon reflection."[25] This *évidence* must be further internalized by reflection and meditation where language plays an even more reduced role. In the dialogues, Ariste does not profess to be persuaded immediately upon hearing Théodore's arguments, but only after having a full day to reflect on them and consult the *Maître intérieur*.

The Rhetoric of the Incarnation as a Rhetoric of Praise

The need for an eloquence of the senses and passions or for a grace of sentiment only offers additional confirmation of the superiority of the intelligible over the sensible in Malebranche's eyes. Love freely chosen based on the light of *évidence* remains his ideal. The certainty of *évidence* is preferable to the certainty of faith; attention unaided by the grace of sentiment is more meritorious than attention that requires grace. The divine incursion into the sensible, the Incarnation, in no way mitigates Malebranche's distrust of the body.

However, while the Incarnation is a rhetorical act for Malebranche that uses the sensible to reveal the intelligible to fallen man's attention, it is much more. To view the Incarnation as God addressing humanity through the Word made flesh is to adopt the human perspective; from the theocentric standpoint Malebranche strives to reach, the Incarnation is an act through which God glorifies himself (5:58–59; 12–13:348). Had Adam never sinned and the Redemption not been necessary, the Incarnation still would have occurred (12–13:204). Its primary goal is to glorify the Father by uniting the Son with creation to build the eternal temple of the Church at the end of time (12–13:206).

After death, as building blocks of this eternal temple, the saved will have no need of a rhetoric of attention: "[T]he slightest mental attention represents to them clearly both ideas and their relationships" ("[L]a moindre attention de l'esprit leur représente clairement les idées et leurs rapports" [11:20]). Their glorified and uncorruptible bodies will be submissive to their minds (12–13:432). United to Christ they will form a perfect society modeled on the harmony among the persons of the Trinity and animated by light and charity that will give continuous glory to God, "a single choir of praises" ("un même choeur de louanges" [12–13:427]).

Malebranche refuses to go beyond the details given by Scripture on the human condition after death (12–13:435). However, it is only in light of this perfect society, the heavenly Jerusalem, where the only possible rhetoric will be one of praise and adoration, that the two rhetorics that Malebranche does describe in some detail take on their full meaning—the rhetoric of imitation that functions in unredeemed society, and the rhetoric of attention whose privileged arena is the Church on earth.

False eloquence operates at the level of the body, as if humans were destined only for a society concerned with material wants, "a society animated by the passions, subsisting in a communion of private, perishable goods whose end [is] the comfort and conservation of the life of the body" ("une société animée par les passions, subsistante dans une communion de biens particuliers et périssables, et dont la fin [est] la commodité et la conservation de la vie du corps" [11:193]). The mechanical persuasion it produces is the result of the operation of the laws of the union of mind and of body impaired by original sin, and it ignores the mind's more perfect union with God. It is a rhetoric of distraction, a rhetoric that prolongs the separation from God caused by the Fall. Witness in this regard, the vain Stoicism of Seneca or the Pyrrhonism of Montaigne.

The forum for the rhetoric of attention modeled on the Incarnation is the visible Church, "a society ordered by Reason, sustained by faith, subsisting in the communion of true goods, whose end [is] a blessed life for eternity" ("une société réglée par la Raison, soutenue par la foi, subsistante dans la communion des vrais biens, et dont la fin [est] une vie bienheureuse pour l'éternité" [11:193]). In most domains of human knowledge, this rhetoric that fortifies the natural power of attention by using the senses, the imagination, and the passions can communicate truth. However, to assure complete union with God, a grace of sentiment is also required.

Malebranche surrounds this rhetoric with caveats, even though the Incarnation is its model, because it is but a pale shadow of the rhetoric of praise which will characterize the heavenly Jerusalem. It belongs to the Church on earth, which only prepares the way for the eternal temple. In that perfect society there will be no need for a grace of sentiment, for there will be no concupiscence, no need to employ the sensible because the light of *évidence* will suffice. The Incarnation as a supplement to attention will give way to its primary mission as an act of glorification. The rhetoric of attention will be replaced by a rhetoric of eternal praise to the glory of God.

6

Lamy's Science of Persuasion

Vivacity and the Inclinations

> There is nothing that cannot be per-
> suaded when one knows how to use
> men's inclinations properly.
>
> Il n'y a rien qu'on ne puisse per-
> suader quand on sait bien se servir
> des inclinations des hommes.
>
> Lamy, *L'Art de parler*

Rhetorical theory is not the center of interest for any of the thinkers considered so far. However, in Bernard Lamy we find a writer with a considerable reputation as a Cartesian militant whose most famous work, the *Art de parler*, is an attempt to recast the whole range of questions normally treated by rhetoricians in light of the new philosophy.[1] Indeed, his teaching career was interrupted by charges that he had introduced Descartes' teachings into his classes, and he was considered a friend and disciple of his fellow Oratorian two years his senior, Malebranche, who is reported to have read Lamy's text in manuscript form and encouraged its publication.[2] The first editions of his rhetoric appeared in late 1675, at approximately the same time that Malebranche was publishing the second part of *La Recherche*.

In spite of Malebranche's *imprimatur*,[3] some of the most insightful commentators on Lamy have found in his rhetoric just the opposite of the values Malebranche is considered to represent. Michel Charles declares Lamy's work "a rhetoric of passion" where emotion is the "final and essential instrument of persuasion."[4] Ulrich Ricken describes Lamy's defense of the passions and imagination in eloquence as "a reply to objections of the sort raised by Malebranche."[5] Citing a passage in which Lamy seems more than pleased that the knowledgeable orator has greater power over his listeners than the most skillful mechanic over his machines, Jean-Paul Sermain points to "the assimilation of discourse to a machine on which B. Lamy founded the essential part of his art of speaking."[6] Not only does Lamy acknowledge the potency of the mechanical persuasion that Malebranche had analyzed only to condemn, it would seem that he consents to its use.

To be sure, passages in the first edition that were never modified through successive editions suggest that appeals to the heart can replace the *évidence* of truth. However, to consider such statements as the core of Lamy's view of persuasion is to overlook its central thrust. His deepest impulse is not to allow the passions to supplant reason in persuasion but to insist that rhetoric must be invoked to add affective proofs to the force of truth. "Reason alone is not enough; craftiness is necessary" ("La raison seule ne suffit pas; l'adresse est nécessaire").[7] That reason alone may not suffice does not mean that it may be dispensed with; rather it is to be supplemented by the indirect methods furnished by rhetoric. In fact, much of Lamy's agenda revolves around various strategies for enhancing attention. "The greatest secret of eloquence is to hold minds attentive and to prevent them from losing sight of the goal to which they must be led" ("Le plus grand secret de l'éloquence est de tenir les esprits attentifs, et d'empêcher qu'ils ne perdent de vue le but où il faut les conduire" [1676:257]).

Lamy's rhetoric is comprised of two arts, the art of persuasion concerned with *res*, and the domain of *verba*, or art of speaking. Reversing Lamy's own order of exposition, after a brief summary of his career as it relates to rhetoric, I first examine the psychology that grounds his *art de persuader* before showing how this exchange is effected in vivid language, that is, his *art de parler*, which provides the title for the entire treatise. I then show that attention to the image of the orator's ideas and emotions presented with vivacity is at the heart of his system, particularly after the crucial 1688 revisions of his text.

A Cartesian Educator

Just as Malebranche's views on communication stem from his desire to make Descartes' philosophy serve the Church's mission, Lamy's experience as an educator in the schools and seminaries of the Oratory marks his combination of rhetoric and Cartesianism. He received his education in various Oratorian institutions, first in their college in his birthplace, Le Mans, where he studied rhetoric under Jules Mascaron, and then at Paris. Especially decisive were his two years of philosophy at Saumur (1659–61) where the Augustinian currents that proved so receptive to Descartes were strong and where he might have met Malebranche. Then followed seven fruitful years as humanities instructor in colleges in Vendôme and Juilly (1661–68) when he laid the foundation for a number of his future works. François Girbal notes that the *Art de parler* took its impetus from the rhetoric lectures Lamy dictated in 1667 to his class at the royal academy of Juilly where he taught grammar, Latin, Greek, history, geography, and rhetoric from 1663 to 1668.[8]

His concurrent interest in mathematical and scientific questions developed while he was officially charged with teaching the humanities. During these years Lamy was undergoing what Girbal calls his Cartesian novitiate.[9] Girbal speculates that Lamy's initial interest, like that of Malebranche, was awakened by scientific treatises such as the *Géométrie*, the *Dioptrique*, or the *Traité de l'homme*.

The years immediately preceding the publication of the *Art de parler* in 1675 were spent at Saumur where he studied theology and at Angers where he taught philosophy. At Saumur he had the opportunity to meet Arnauld and Nicole.[10] He was thereafter to remain on cordial terms with Nicole, and he used Arnauld's *Nouveaux Eléments* as the basis on his own 1685 *Eléments de géométrie*, which extends Arnauld's text by adding a section on solids.[11] Lamy's title, *L'Art de parler*, suggests that he wishes to present it as the rhetorical companion to Arnauld and Nicole's *Art de penser*.

At Angers, Lamy's adhesion to Cartesianism became a matter of public scandal. The official policy of the Oratory, as dictated by royal edict, was to remain faithful in philosophy classes to the

Aristotelianism of Saint Thomas and to avoid any hint of the new doctrines. Orders were given requiring suspected Cartesians like Lamy to submit their lecture notes for examination by doctors of the Sorbonne. Propositions considered injurious to the state were found in which Lamy supposedly preferred democratic government to hereditary monarchy. A *lettre de cachet* exiled Lamy to a monastery near Grenoble and forbade him to teach or to preach. This affair came to a climax in late 1675, precisely as the *Art de parler* was appearing.

By the middle of the following year Lamy was allowed to return to an active life, teaching in the seminary of Grenoble for eleven years (1676–86) before returning to the Oratory's seminary in Paris for three years of research (1686–89). He spent the remaining years of his life in Rouen as a teacher and a scholar. In these post-Angers years he published most of his many textbooks, and during this period his affinities with Malebranche became more pronounced, as seen in his 1688 *Morale chrétienne* and in the additions to the 1694 edition of the *Entretiens*.

The *Art de parler,* a Functional Art: *Verba* in the Service of *Res*

Lamy revised the *Art de parler* frequently until just before his death, making it necessary to take into account the successive editions which often incorporate substantial changes. Geneviève Rodis-Lewis has studied the copies held in the Bibliothèque Nationale and concluded that five major states of the text can be distinguished.[12] The first two states were published under the title *L'Art de parler*: (1) 1675, 1676 and (2) 1678, 1679, 1685. The pivotal revision of 1688, when, among other changes, four new chapters dealing with the inclinations and attention were added, increased the work's size by about a third, and the last three states, incorporating these and later, less extensive changes were published under the expanded title of *La Rhétorique ou l'art de parler*: (3) 1688, 1699; (4) 1701, 1712; and (5) 1715. The last edition was registered on 19 December 1714, about a month before Lamy's death on 29 January 1715.[13]

In the first two states, rhetoric as the art of persuasion occupies an appendix of sorts to the dominant art concerned with *verba*.

Indeed, the work is divided until 1688 into two *discours* of unequal length. The first discourse of 275 pages composed of four parts that successively treat language as a reflection of thought, the function of tropes and figures, phonology and euphony, and levels of style, is labeled *l'art de parler*, and lends its name to the entire work. The second discourse of only 60 pages, entitled *l'art de persuader*, stands apart and treats chiefly rhetorical invention and disposition. Only in the pivotal 1688 edition was the division into two disproportionate discourses dropped. The second discourse on persuasion joined the four parts of the first discourse as the fifth "book" of an expanded work under the new, more inclusive title

These changes are symptomatic of Lamy's determination to free the art of speaking from the allegation that it is an art of ornamentation, independent of function. The *Art de parler*'s first states note that common usage tends to distinguish between the *ars bene dicendi* and the *ars persuadendi* (1676:276). However, Lamy makes clear that such a distinction is artificial and regrettable, "because one is not much good without the other" ("car l'un ne sert pas de grand'chose sans l'autre" [1676:313]). The resources of eloquence are not destined to display the virtuosity of orators, but to win over the audience to their opinions.

At the same time, Lamy takes pains to stress that persuasion is an omnipresent enterprise. Not limited to the pulpit, the law courts, or negotiations—the traditional areas of *la grande éloquence*—persuasion takes place in all areas of life, whenever we seek to bring others around to our views. "[I]n a word, the goal that we have in social relations is to persuade those with whom we deal and to make them come around to our views" ("[E]n un mot, le but que nous avons dans le commerce de la vie est de persuader ceux avec qui nous traitons, et de les faire tomber dans nos sentiments" [1676:280]). The preface of the 1688 version, whose new title seems to equate rhetoric not with both arts mentioned in 1675, but with the art of speaking alone, in reality, gives more prominence to this broad notion of persuasion. The *ars bene dicendi* is not the ability to produce showy eloquence, but to persuade: "We only speak to make those who listen to us enter into our opinions" ("Nous ne parlons que pour faire entrer dans nos sentiments ceux qui nous écoutent" [1699: preface]). Once this functional goal is firmly acknowledged as the end of all speech, labeling rhetoric as the art of speaking suffices: "That is why when one says 'the art of speaking,' one means that the goal of this art is to persuade since this is the intention of all who apply themselves to speaking well" ("C'est pourquoi quand on dit *l'Art de parler*, on fait connaître que la fin de cet Art est de Persuader, puisque c'est l'intention qu'ont tous ceux qui s'appliquent à bien parler" [1699: preface]). Figured speech is an instrument of persuasion, not an end in itself. *Verba* and *res* are reunited but not as equals; *elocutio* is subordinate to *inventio*.

Orator, Message, and Audience in 1675

The 1688 preface, in keeping with the new title, seems to equate speaking with persuasion. However, the 1675 edition had defined persuasion more narrowly, stressing the elements of challenge and difficulty inherent in it. Those who are skillful persuaders know "the secret of winning over the heart and of attracting to their views those who are far removed from them" ("le secret de gagner les coeurs, et d'attirer à leurs sentiments ceux qui en sont éloignés" [1676:276]). He reserves it for those occasions when a considerable gap separates speaker and listener, as suggested by "éloignés." Reducing this distance by drawing the listener to the position of the speaker requires skills not available to all ("le secret") and the ability to engage the emotions and the will ("les coeurs").

Lamy's concept becomes clearer if we examine his notion of persuasion in terms of the relation between orator, message, and audience—an issue he treats in 1688 as well as in the early states. It is useful to contrast the situation of the orator and the geometer, taking into account their respective subject matter and its relation to their public. In 1675 he notes that mathematicians deal with topics that depend on a small number of self-evident principles (1676:239–40), while the topics of orators are obscure, depending on a multitude of independent circumstances whose interrelation is not immediately evident. We have seen that in the preface to the *Nouveaux Eléments de géométrie* Nicole pointed to just such topics, without assigning them to rhetoric:

They do not depend on a certain number of elemental and certain principles such as those of mathematics, but on a large number of proofs and circumstances that the mind must see all at once and which, although not convincing separately, do not fail to persuade rightly when they are joined and united together.

Elles ne dépendent pas d'un certain nombre de principes grossiers et certains, comme les vérités mathématiques; mais d'un grand nombre de preuves et de circonstances, qu'il faut que l'esprit voie tout d'un coup, et qui n'étant pas convaincantes séparément, ne laissent pas de persuader avec raison, lorsqu'elles sont jointes et unies ensemble.[14]

Lamy summarizes this description in his evocation of the orator's subject matter:

The truths that are demonstrated in courtroom orations and in speeches are not of the nature of mathematical truths. The latter only depend on a small number of certain and infallible principles; the former depend on a multitude of circumstances which, when separated, lack compelling force and which can only convince when they are gathered and united together. One cannot gather them together without art, and it is here that the craftiness of ingenious orators appears.

Les vérités qui se démontrent dans les Plaidoyers, et dans les Harangues, ne sont pas de la nature des vérités mathématiques: Ces dernières ne dépendent que d'un petit nombre de principes certains et infaillibles: Les premières dépendent d'une multitude de circonstances qui séparées n'ont pas de force, et qui ne peuvent convaincre que lorsqu'elles sont ramassées et unies ensemble. On ne peut les ramasser sans art, et c'est où paraît l'adresse des Orateurs subtils. (1676:239–40)[15]

Lamy thus goes beyond Nicole by assigning such convergent proofs to eloquence and making them a legitimate form of reasoning alongside mathematical demonstrations.

However, the orator's chief challenge lies in the stance of the audience vis-à-vis the subject. While the geometer can usually take for granted an audience with no stake in the theorem being propounded, the orator deals with contested issues (1676:238).

> When it is only a matter of proving that the three angles of a triangle are equal to two right angles it is not necessary to predispose the mind to receive this truth. . . . But when one proposes things contrary to the inclinations of those to whom one speaks, craftiness is necessary.

> Lorsqu'il n'est question que de prouver que les trois angles d'un triangle sont égaux à deux angles droits, il n'est point nécessaire de disposer les esprits à recevoir cette vérité. . . . Mais lorsque l'on propose des choses contraires aux inclinations de ceux à qui on parle, l'adresse est nécessaire. (1676:299–300)

The detached, impersonal discussion that characterizes geometry is impossible when an audience's own desires are at issue. Moreover, as the preceding example illustrates, Lamy envisages the difficulty in terms of the moral rather than intellectual fraility of the orator's audience. The speaker's message is not opposed in good faith, but because it is contrary to the desires of the listeners. The art of convincing based on logical demonstrations fails because audiences hate unwelcome truths (1676:113, 291). Thus, the orator must fall back on rhetorical means, "catch men by their weak point" ("prendre les hommes par leur faible" [1676:336]), either by indirect methods of stealth and insinuation, or by open appeals to the emotions. Indeed, the model implicit in the orator-audience relation that dominates his discussion of rhetoric in the 1675 edition is that of a preacher proclaiming the truths of the Christian religion to a fallen flock. Their ignorance is compounded by the fact that acceptance of the preacher's message will entail considerable sacrifice.

Orator, Message, and Audience in 1688

The 1688 additions develop this contrast between orator and geometer but without assuming that the orator's audience suffers from moral infirmity. In the new first chapter of Book 2 dealing with the figures, Lamy presents the gap that separates speaker and listener as a simple difference of perspective that does not imply the moral superiority of the orator. The figured language of eloquence would not be necessary if everyone thought in the same manner. Geometers, who share the same perception of clear mathematical principles, are able to shun such imaged speech in favor of a simple language common to all. "Almost all geometers speak the same language . . . they use the same expressions because nature induces us to speak as we think and because when people think in the same way, they speak the same language" ("Les Géomètres tiennent presque tous le même langage . . . ils se servent des mêmes expressions; parce que la nature nous détermine à parler comme nous pensons, et que quand on pense de la même manière, on tient le même langage" [1699:85]). On most other topics individuals are separated by a personal judgment that marks their own subjective relation to the issue. "The same thing never appears the same to all men. It is worthy of love for some; others can only view it with aversion" ("La même chose ne paraît jamais la même à tous les hommes. Elle est aimable aux uns, les autres ne la peuvent regarder qu'avec des sentiments d'aversion" [1699:86]). Because each person's will judges differently, each individual registers a different perspective on each issue, a unique manner of viewing it. Persuasion involves closing this gap: to persuade is to communicate one's perceptions and accompanying movements to an audience that cannot be counted on to share this point of view.

Lamy's instrument for bridging this gap generalizes the vivacity stressed by Arnauld and Nicole in their description of perfect religious eloquence as the vivid image of the speaker's ideas and emotions[16] and extends it to all rhetoric. The 1688 text declares:

> The entire secret of rhetoric (whose end is persuasion) consists in making things appear as they appear to us; because if one creates a vivid image resembling the one we have in our minds, without a doubt, those who see it will have the same ideas that we have; they will conceive the same movements in regard to them and will enter into all our views.

> Tout le secret de la Rhétorique dont la fin est de persuader,
> consiste à faire paraître les choses telles qu'elles nous parais-
> sent; car si on en fait une vive image semblable à celle que
> nous avons dans l'esprit, sans doute que ceux qui la verront,
> auront les mêmes idées que nous; qu'ils concevront pour
> elles les mêmes mouvements, et qu'ils entreront dans tous
> nos sentiments. (1699:88)

Human individuality is thus the source of both the universality of the rhetorical enterprise and its inherent difficulty. Even in the most ideal situation some minimal gap exists between speaker and listener due to their personal points of view. This distance between individuals becomes formidable when their wills tug in opposing directions. Rhetoric is especially reserved for bridging such wide gaps when a wayward heart compounds the separation.

Lamy returns to this point in a new chapter dealing with persuasion in Book 5 where the contrast between orator and geometer is transmuted into one between orator and philosopher, and Descartes' contrast between *assensio* and *persuasio* becomes a contrast between *convaincre* and *persuader*. "How is it that the philosopher can convince and almost never persuade, while an excellent orator does not fail to do both?" ("D'où vient que le Philosophe peut convaincre et qu'il ne persuade presque jamais, au lieu qu'un excellent orateur ne manque point de faire l'un et l'autre?" [1699:326–27]). Both persuasion and conviction result from exposure to the truth: "only the truth can convince and persuade" ("il n'y a que la vérité qui puisse convaincre et persuader" [1699:327]). Yet it is not enough merely to propose the truth in a general way in order to persuade, no matter how systematically and thoroughly, as if the same form of proof were suitable for all audiences. The geometer or philosopher assume an audience of disciples, uniformly receptive to their message, with the result that they often convince without persuading.

Persuasion, as Lamy describes it, can be seen as carrying the process through to a successful conclusion because it takes into account the individuality of the persons involved. First, persuasion requires adapting the proof to the point of view of the listeners, that is, to any particular prejudices or opinions they might hold: "It is not enough to propose the truth if one does not find the ways of making it apparent and if at the same time one does not remove the preconceptions that stand as an obstacle to it" ("Ce n'est pas assez de la [la vérité] proposer si on ne trouve les manières de la faire apercevoir et si en même temps l'on n'ôte les préventions qui lui sont un obstacle" [1699:327]). This recalls Descartes' notion of *persuasio* as a psychological satisfaction due to overcoming the obstacles presented by prolonged childhood. Furthermore, persuasion involves engaging the listener's will in regard to the truth to be persuaded, a step that is taken for granted by the philosopher or geometer: "The orator does not permit indifference" ("L'Orateur ne souffre point d'indiffé- rence" [1699:328]). This too requires an effort to individualize the speaker's presentation since no two persons react in the same way to the same idea. Thus, the intensity that persuasion adds to conviction finds its ultimate source in its personalized dynamics. Persuasion activates an individual's natural inclination toward the truth by taking into account that person's unique viewpoint and desires.

The Pre-1688 Art of Persuasion

Since it is difficult to perceive the configuration of Lamy's system of invention in the first states of the text, there is little wonder that commentators have almost exclusively stressed his treatment of the passions. As I show below, only in 1688 when the psychology underlying his approach becomes explicit, does his discussion adequately take into account the whole range of traditional modes of proof.

To be sure, the earliest editions acknowledge the tripartite division of intellectual, emotional, and ethical proofs dating back to Aristotle—"les arguments ou les preuves, les moeurs et les passions" (1676:278)—and he devoted substantial sections to each mode of proof. However, he clearly felt that the last two, which both involve some measure of craftiness (*adresse*), are the special province of rhetoric, and it is here that the new philosophy can make the most valuable contribution (1676:293).

This is not to say that Lamy distains intellectual persuasion. Indeed, he grounds it in the irresistable clarity of *évidence*, and he introduces his discussion of the intellectual proofs with a testimonial to its power. "Clarity is the character of truth; one cannot doubt a clear truth. When its evidence is at its highest point the most stubborn are obliged to abandon their arms and submit" ("La clarté est le caractère de la vérité, l'on ne peut douter d'une vérité claire; et lorsque son évidence est dans le dernier degré, les plus opiniâtres sont obligés de quitter les armes, et de s'y soumettre" [1676:278]. Moreover, he implies that the philosophy of *évidence* has stripped traditional rhetoric of its usefulness to the intellectual proofs. Thus, he perfunctorily summarizes in two chapters the system of topical invention before dismissing it as at best a method of amplification, noting that knowledge of subject matter is paramount (1676:289–90).

Lamy finds justification for the ethical and emotional proofs in the mind's difficulty in maintaining its attention. Descartes defined clarity in the *Principes* in terms of its attraction for the attentive mind, an *assensio* that is effective only as long as the mind attends to this *évidence*. The truth may be irresistible, but only when gazed upon, and Lamy notes how easily we can be distracted, or even worse, voluntarily turn our back to it. "If men loved the truth, proposing it in a vivid and sensible way would suffice to persuade them; but they hate it because it rarely matches their interests" ("Si les hommes aimaient la vérité, il suffirait de la leur proposer d'une manière vive et sensible pour les persuader; mais ils la haissent; parce qu'elle ne s'accorde que rarement à leurs intérêts" [1676:113]. Hence the necessity of the two remaining modes of persuasion involving *adresse*, whose secrets Lamy prides himself on revealing, is apparent.

Critics have ignored his treatment of the ethical proof as a strategy of insinuation and concentrated instead on his much more dramatic presentation of the emotional ones. This affective persuasion seems reserved for the most obdurate refusals to attend to *évidence*, and its almost invincible force is the glory of the rhetor's art. "Eloquence would thus not be the mistress of hearts and it would meet strong resistance if it did not attack them with other arms than those of truth" ("L'éloquence ne serait donc pas la maîtresse des coeurs, et elle y trouverait une forte résistance, si elle ne les attaquait par d'autres armes que celles de la vérité" [1676:113]). In its most extreme form Lamy allows for emotional persuasion to act apart from *évidence*. Mastery of an audience's passions makes the orator the equal of the operator of a machine that can be made to advance or retreat on command (1676:114). The skillful lawyer summons up a flood of emotions "to make the judges move where he wishes to lead them" ("pour faire aller les Juges où l'on veut les mener" [1676:115]), and Lamy seems thus to propose that the orator move listeners to action without the intervention of their reason: "exciting in the minds of his listeners the passions that will make them lean in the direction he wishes to bring them" ("exciter dans l'esprit de ses Auditeurs, les passions qui les feront pencher du côté où il les veut porter" [1676:308–9]).

However, having allowed for this affective persuasion that commentators have often taken as the core of his system of invention, Lamy devotes his analysis to emotions that seem ill suited to mechanical persuasion. Instead of treating violent ones like fear, love, or hate that are usually most effective in such overt appeals, he claims to furnish a particularly exact discussion of admiration, the primary Cartesian passion, along with derivatives such as esteem and scorn (1676:314–17). Thus Lamy's 1675 treatment of invention is unsatisfactory on several scores. It is incomplete, with its most notable gap in the area of the intellectual proofs due to the absence of a replacement for the topics. Moreover, Lamy felt himself open to attack for his acceptance of insinuation and his open reliance on emotional appeals. Lamy was troubled enough by such objections to include chapters defending his treatment of both the ethical and emotional proofs on moral grounds (1676:305–12).

Lamy's Science of Insinuation and Pascal's *Art d'agréer*

Lamy's efforts in the early editions to legitimize these ethical and emotional proofs are enhanced when read in the context of the 1688 revisions. The four new chapters stressing the mind's inclination toward truth and goodness and the role of attention that he inserted at the end of his discussion of the intellectual proofs in Book 5 make explicit the rationale behind his theory of rhetorical invention.[17]

Given the fact that Lamy tends to equate rhetoric with *adresse* and insinuation, a comparison with Pascal's art of pleasing described in *De l'Art de persuader* offers illuminating parallels.[18] Pascal had noted that approval could be secured for a proposition through either the will or the understanding. When the desires of the will and the principles accepted by the understanding are in harmony, an art of convincing can address rigorous arguments to the understanding. This corresponds in Lamy's system to persuasion based on the clarity of *évidence* provided by logic. But as often as not, especially in questions of ethics, the two are in conflict. Original sin has left the appeal of pleasure on the will stronger than the truth's attraction to the understanding, and because the balance leans toward the corrupted will, an *art d'agréer* addressed to that faculty is the most effective method.

Lamy's method of insinuation is likewise concerned with winning over the fallen will, but he is more confident than Pascal about the possibility of formulating its rules. Pascal's skepticism stems from his doubts as to whether the motor forces that drive the will—pleasure and desire—can be known sufficiently either in individuals or in humans in general to permit formulating any consistent system: "The principles of pleasure are not firm and stable. They are diverse in all men and vary in each individual with such diversity that there is no man more different from another man than from himself at various times" ("Les principes du plaisir ne sont pas fermes et stables. Ils sont divers en tous les hommes, et variables dans chaque particulier avec une telle diversité, qu'il n'y a point d'homme plus différent d'un autre que de soi-même dans les divers temps").[19]

Pascal deems an adequate treatment of the *art d'agréer* a difficult, if not impossible, task: "I do not know if it is possible to give firm rules for matching speeches with the inconstancy of our caprices" ("Je ne sais s'il y a moyen de donner des règles fermes pour accorder les discours à l'inconstance de nos caprices").[20] Lamy, on the other hand, acknowledges the difficulty of formulating his *art d'insinuer*, but professes from the first that it is not beyond the reach of an experienced moral philosopher. "It is acquired by sublime speculations, by reflections on the nature of our mind, the inclinations, and the movements of our wills" ("Elle s'acquiert par de sublimes spéculations, par des réflexions sur la nature de notre esprit, sur les inclinations, sur les mouvements de notre volonté" [1676:293–94]). Lamy claims for his enterprise the status of a science based on knowledge of human nature, "the science of winning over the heart" ("la science de gagner les coeurs" [1676:293]).

Lamy's assurance finds its source in his conception of the inclinations. Pascal had referred to "certain natural desires common to all men such as the desire to be happy" ("certains désirs naturels et communs à tous les hommes, comme le désir d'être heureux")[21] which might furnish universally valid premises to an *art d'agréer*, if only they were not negated by the subjective vagaries characteristic of the attraction of pleasure. The equivalent for Lamy of these "désirs naturels" is the will's inclinations which he discusses in more detail in the 1688 additions. Lamy notes that the mind is drawn to truth in two fashions: to know it through the understanding (which Lamy most often calls *l'esprit*) and to love or desire it through the will (which he often refers to as *le coeur*). The understanding is drawn irresistably to clarity, the mark of the truth, just as pleasure attracts the will to love the good. These attractions are natural inclinations placed in mankind by God, who is the final guarantor of truth and goodness (1699:318–19,321). "All the truly natural inclinations are thus good, and we cannot go astray if we follow them" ("Toutes les inclinations vraiment naturelles sont donc bonnes, et nous ne pouvons manquer en les suivant" [1699:318]). In fact, Lamy claims in the 1678 *Nouvelles réflexions sur l'art poétique* that these inclinations toward truth and goodness are really an attraction to God.[22]

This analysis of the will as a general tendency toward God allows Lamy to view the particular manifestations of the inclinations in individuals in a more favorable light.[23] For Pascal they are the product of caprice and thus unpredictable; furthermore, such individual desires tend to be pernicious. However, for Lamy, the individual's personal inclinations, no matter how debased, can be understood as a deflection of the general impulse toward the good shared by all humans and instilled by God. Error results when the appearance of truth (*vraisemblance*) is accepted for truth itself (1699:319); moral evil stems from forgetting that pleasure is only a means to a higher good or from taking some erroneous judgment for a good worthy of pursuit. In addition, since each individual's inclinations fit into a wholesome overall pattern and form part of a general movement toward God, they cannot be dismissed as entirely evil. For Pascal, no general rules seem possible in the *art d'agréer*, and thus a new rhetoric must be invented for each audience. By distinguishing general patterns within human inclinations and desires, Lamy is able to ground traditional rhetorical strategies on broad psychological principles.

Lamy insists from the outset in his 1675 preface that the unique character of his rhetoric is to be found in his analysis of the mechanism of eloquence. Rejecting the *je ne sais quoi* of the Jesuit Dominique Bouhours, Lamy promises to lay out in scientific fashion the sources of the pleasure provided by eloquence: "When the author speaks of what pleases in speech, he does not attribute it to a *je ne sais quoi* which has no name; he names it and proceeding to the source of this pleasure, he reveals the principles behind the rules that make them pleasing" ("Lorsque l'Auteur parle de ce qui plaît dans le discours, il ne dit pas que c'est *un je ne sais quoi,* qui n'a point de nom, il le nomme; et conduisant jusques à la source de ce plaisir, il fait apercevoir les principes des règles qui suivent ceux qui sont agréables." [1676: preface]). Indeed, his confidence increases markedly from edition to edition. The 1676 "It is difficult to determine what pleases and the nature of the *je ne sais quoi*" ("Il est difficile de déterminer ce qui plaît; et en quoi consiste le *je ne sais quoi*" [1676:252]), becomes in 1678 "It is not difficult to determine. . . " ("Il n'est pas difficile de déterminer . . ." [1678:227])! His constant probing of every aspect of this pleasure gives the ultimate shape to his rhetorical theory.

Lamy does not underestimate the perversion of the inclinations. The need for craftiness (*adresse*) stems from the fact that the inclination toward truth is often in conflict with self-interest (1676:291). Although Lamy does not explicitly explain it as such, this *intérêt* is a deformation of the legitimate inclination toward self-love. Rhetorical *adresse* involves taking advantage of whatever element of truth can be salvaged in the audience's position while playing one inclination off against another. Insinuation takes into account deformed inclinations such as *intérêt* as a first step in redirecting the listener toward a more worthy goal. "One must fight their inclinations by means of their inclinations and use the inclinations to draw them toward the opinions that one wants them to adopt, just as sailors use the opposing winds to arrive in the port from which the wind drives them away" ("On doit combattre leurs inclinations par leurs inclinations, et s'en servir pour les attirer dans les sentiments qu'on leur veut faire prendre, comme les matelots se servent du vent contraire pour arriver dans le port d'où le vent les éloignent" [1676:300]).[24]

The Intellectual Proofs:
The Return of the *Vraisemblable*

Paradoxically, the mind's inclination toward the clarity of *évidence* becomes in 1688 the basis for appeals to *vraisemblance*. As already noted, Lamy summarized the system of the *loci* in the first edition, but closed his presentation by describing them as an ineffective method of invention. Lamy applies to the commonplaces Descartes' condemnation of Raymond Lulle's system in the *Discours de la méthode*. At best a method of amplification that multiplies arguments, in Lamy's eyes the recourse to commonplaces guarantees that the single solid proof needed to win an argument will be lost amid a field of weak ones (1676:290–91). The topics most often serve to disperse the attention that is indispensible in discovering convincing arguments.

Two of the new chapters which he inserted following this rejection of the topics replace them with a method designed to accomplish just the opposite by reviving a traditional rhetorical method which Descartes had disparaged—appeals to verisimilitudes. Here orators are not so much concerned with finding arguments that will overcome the distraction of their listeners, as with weaning them away from their prior erroneous beliefs. Lamy assumes in this section not so much an inattentive audience as one in error.

When Descartes had recommended in his first rule of the *Discours* separating all that is evident from error or the merely probable, it was to reject the probable along with error. When Lamy, on the other hand, urges the orator to apply the same technique to the arguments of opponents in order to distinguish what is valuable in them, he has in mind making use of whatever is *vrai* in the *vraisemblable*:

> It is always, as we have said, the appearance of truth that deceives. Thus the effort of an orator must be to examine what might have been misleading, that is, from what principles the conclusions have been drawn. . . . Nothing persuades people better whose opinions one opposes than to sort out the things about which they are right from the ones about which they are mistaken: to grant them what is true and make them see what led them into error.

> C'est toujours, comme nous l'avons dit, l'apparence de la vérité qui trompe. Ainsi l'application d'un Orateur doit être d'examiner ce qui a pu tromper, c'est-à-dire, de quels principes on a tiré les conséquences. . . . Il n'y a rien qui persuade mieux ceux dont on combat les sentiments que de démêler les choses où ils ont raison, d'avec celles où ils se trompent: de leur accorder ce qui est vrai, et de leur faire voir ce qui les a trompés. (1699:323)

By focusing the audience's attention on the positive elements in their position, even if this involves at first more of the *vraisemblable* than the truth itself, the orator can gradually bring the listeners to rectify their stance. As he had already pointed out in 1675, "Without offending the truth one can focus attention first of all on what is true in the opinion one wishes to combat, and praise it to the extent that it is truthful and merits praise" ("On peut sans blesser la vérité s'attacher d'abord à ce qui en est vrai dans l'opinion que l'on veut combattre, et la louer en ce qu'elle a de véritable, et qui mérite de louanges" [1676:302]). Ordinary people may settle for the appearance of truth more often than truth itself: "It is for this reason that the orator sometimes adduces proofs that are weak in themselves but which are strong in the eyes of those to whom he speaks because they conform to their prejudices" ("C'est pour cela qu'il [l'Orateur] allègue quelquefois des raisons faibles en elles-mêmes mais qui sont fortes par rapport à ceux à qui il parle, parce qu'elles s'accommodent avec leurs préjugés" [1699:320]). Yet, for Lamy, this persuasion by the *vraisemblable* only underlines the attraction exerted by the true.

The Cartesians' reflection on Descartes' provision for moral certitude in the realm of action culminates here in Lamy's recuperation of the *vraisemblable* for rhetoric. Besides the Port-Royalists' comments that I have already discussed, Malebranche pointed Lamy in this direction by noting in *La Recherche* that verisimilitudes deserve at least conditional acceptance because they bear the image of the truth, even if we must not accord them full consent (1:57). Furthermore, Malebranche contrasts immutable, necessary truths depending on the will of God, and contingent ones based on the changing wills of humans, where *vraisemblance* is at least temporarily acceptable (1:63). Among the practical endeavors he cites as belonging to this second category, law, politics, and ethics all belong to the traditional space staked out by rhetoricians for their art. Lamy reclaims *vraisemblance* for rhetoric by making the connection explicit, while conveniently omitting Malebranche's warnings that *vraisemblance* must be accepted only provisionally.

The Ethical Proofs

The section on ethical proofs in the first edition adapts the conventional recommendations of rhetoricians to Lamy's *science d'insinuer*. His concern is to show why suggestions that the orator display such qualities as prudence and integrity, authority, good will, and modesty are effective in terms of his strategy of insinuation. Instead of being an obstacle to truth, *intérêt* can serve its cause if the orator seems animated by a concern for the audience—"a sincere zeal for their interest" ("un zèle sincère pour leur intérêt" [1676:294]).

For example, although no one wants to be deceived (1676:296), the task of winnowing truth from falsehood is arduous. Thus an aura of authority inspiring confidence can persuade an audience to entrust the search for truth to the orator (1676:296). Such authority is more powerful when based on a reputation for moral integrity and prudence than on one for expertise (1676:295). Marks of friendship on the part of the orator can bolster the attraction of truth and thus should precede any that might be interpreted as unfavorable (1676:297). Similarly, a modest demeanor can eliminate much of the interference to the reception of truth caused by self-interest (1676:297).

However, Lamy felt it necessary in 1675 to devote an entire section to a defense of his use of such strategies of insinuation against the charge that they are unworthy means that only flatter the audience's appetite for pleasure. The 1688 additions strengthen this defense by situating them in the context of the inclinations. When such strategies are seen as underpinned by the univeral inclination toward the truth, it becomes clearer why he had labeled them in 1675 as "natural," "good," and "right in themselves" ("naturels," "bons," and "justes d'eux-mêmes" [1676:306]). Likewise, the 1688 revisions affirm that pleasure in itself is not be condemned; it is a mark of the good, just as clarity is a sign of the truth (1699:318). Thus there is some measure of good in all pleasures just as there is some portion of truth in every verisimilitude, and orators are not flatterers if they appeal in their initial approach to these worthy elements. Disarming the audience with a pleasing air of moderation is legitimate as long as there is hope that the audience will see the errors of its ways (1676:307). Insinuation only becomes flattery when it no longer prods listeners to realign their false beliefs or unworthy pleasures on the divine truth and goodness that is the ultimate goal of the inclinations.

The Emotional Proofs

The 1688 emphasis on these inclinations makes it clear as well that, even in the first edition, the emotional proofs do not operate entirely independently of reason. Commentators who have argued for the ultimate primacy of emotion in Lamy have ignored the set of emotions he chooses to treat in detail in the 1675 section on invention. Lamy singles out admiration—the most fundamental of the six Cartesian passions—along with several of its derivatives in Descartes' scheme—esteem, scorn, and laughter.

The significance of admiration, the most intellectual among the passions, is only made explicit in the 1688 edition. The third additional 1688 chapter entitled "Attention is necessary to know the truth. How one can make a listener attentive" ("L'attention est nécessaire pour connaître la vérité. Comment on peut rendre attentif un Auditeur" [1699:324])—a chapter whose length was doubled in 1701—shows how the mind's inclination to truth can be reinforced when it falters by the use of traditional rhetorical strategies such as the figures of speech.

Like Malebranche, Lamy attributes distraction to the effects of original sin (1699:324), and notes with Descartes that the ability to maintain attention is the factor that distinguishes superior intellects from the mediocre (1699:325). Lamy provides the geneology of attention, showing that the discovery of *évidence* requires attentiveness, which in turn is grounded in the fundamental inclination toward truth. When excited by novelty or the unusual this curiosity transforms itself into attention:

> Since the soul is created for truth, which it has an ardent desire to know, as soon as it perceives something that it has not seen and that strikes it in an extraordinary way, it becomes curious; it wants to know it. Thus, in order to make the soul attentive, that is to say, to give it curiosity, it is only a matter of finding ingenious twists that give an extraordinary air to what one wants to have considered.
>
> Comme l'âme est faite pour la vérité, qu'elle a un désir ardent de savoir, aussitôt qu'elle aperçoit quelque chose qu'elle n'a point vu et qui la frappe d'une manière extraordinaire, elle a de la curiosité, elle la veut connaître. Ainsi pour rendre l'âme attentive, c'est-à-dire pour lui donner de la curiosité, il n'est question que de trouver des tours ingénieux qui donnent un air extraordinaire à ce qu'on veut faire considérer. (1699:325–26)

The geometer who takes for granted a docile audience may have no need to supplement logic with various devices to strengthen the mind's curiosity. However, orators facing a less attentive public must do all in their power to take advantage of its natural disposition to truth. In fact, this is the arena in which they can demonstrate their *adresse* (1699:326).

In the 1675 text Lamy insists on the need for application, that is, attention. "The truth persuades, but for that to happen it must be known; now for it to be known, the persons to whom it is proclaimed must apply themselves to knowing it" ("La vérité persuade, mais il faut pour cela qu'elle soit connue; or afin qu'elle soit connue, il faut que celui à qui on la déclare s'applique à la connaître" [1676:314–15]). By definition, admiration is the emotion that reinforces this application: "admiration is a movement in the soul that turns it toward the object presenting itself in an extraordinary way and that directs it to consider whether this object is good or bad so that the soul may pursue or avoid it" ("l'admiration est un mouvement dans l'âme qui la tourne vers un objet qui se présente à elle extraordinairement, et qui l'applique à considérer si cet objet est bon ou mauvais, afin qu'elle le suive, ou qu'elle l'évite" (1676:314). Novelty or surprise awakened by the extraordinary excites this wonder that aids the mind in maintaining its gaze. In itself, admiration is the purest and most intellectual emotion because it focuses the mind on its object rather than on the object's relation to the self, as in the case of love or fear.

However, as Lamy's definition of admiration shows, this intellectual vision is usually the prelude to a judgment concerning the worth of the object. His 1688 comments on pleasure as a mark of the good help buttress his explanation of how the derivatives of admiration further reinforce this attention. For example, scorn is the product of just such a judgment (1676:316), and it is pleasurable because it appeals to a natural inclination toward grandeur (1676:316–17). This pleasant feeling of superiority allows the mind to relax, all the while maintaining its attention. Thus the normally laborious task of applying one's mind is transformed into a delightful experience:

> Other passions are exhausting and affect health, but this one contributes to it; and one might say that admiration is more a repose than a movement for the soul, which finds relaxation in this passion, while with the other ones the soul labors with strain. . . . When it is only a matter of laughter and amusement, the listener applies himself willingly, and this application relaxes him.

> Les autres passions épuisent, et intéressent la santé; mais celle-là lui est utile, et on peut dire qu'elle est plutôt un repos

qu'un mouvement de l'âme, qui se délasse dans cette passion, au lieu que dans les autres elle travaille avec contention. . . . Lorsqu'il n'est question que de rire, et de se divertir, cet auditeur s'applique volontiers, et cette application lui donne du divertissement. (1676:317–18)

In this fashion the will's attraction to pleasure reinforces the understanding's attraction to truth, and pleasure becomes a source of attention.

Lamy considers the passions legitimate even when they serve more to move the will than to focus attention. For Lamy, the passions are the motor force of the soul, ("le ressort de l'âme" [1676:311]). Without them, there is no action: "Men can only be made to act through the movement of the passions" ("L'on ne peut faire agir les hommes que par le mouvement des passions" [1676:310]). They give impetus to the fundamental attraction toward the good (1676:309). As a reaction to some object as desirable or to be avoided, the passions are good in themselves. They become dangerous, in his view, only if the object that arouses them is unworthy, since this object largely defines their content (1676:309). Erroneous ideas and false judgments breed passions that are as dangerous as their source; one *dérèglement*, to use Lamy's term, gives birth to another.

Thus, Lamy has no hesitation about recommending passions inspired by worthy objects, but his real interest is in strategies for redirecting "unruly passions" ("les passions déréglées"), a skill crucial to rhetorical *adresse*. Although in 1676 Lamy had pointed out this rationale for exploiting whatever worthy elements can be identified in the object of the passion, this approach becomes more explicit after the 1688 additions when the detailed discussion of a similar process involving *vraisemblance* is introduced. Just as there is always some element of truth in a verisimilitude, there is always some worthy element in a passion (1676:310). The secret is to change its object. "The passions may change their target, but unless divine grace changes the heart, they always remain the same. Now this transfer of targets is not difficult" ("A moins que la grâce divine ne change le coeur, les passions peuvent changer d'objet; mais elles demeurent toujours les mêmes. Or ce changement d'objet n'est pas difficile" [1676:301]). Lamy conceives of the passion as a constant force whose general direction comes from an underlying inclination. Thus, in the case of a passion for beauty directed toward some unworthy object, Lamy proposes to reorient the affective movement toward a more authentic form of the beautiful:

> Is it not a good thing to love what is beautiful, what is great, what is noble? . . . [O]ne can without scruple awaken in the hearts this movement by proposing the beauty and grandeur of the thing to which one directs them, since I assume that one only undertakes to make them love what is beautiful with true beauty and possesses true grandeur.

> N'est-ce pas une bonne chose d'aimer ce qui est bien fait, ce qui est grand, ce qui est noble? . . . [O]n peut sans scrupule réveiller dans leur coeur ce mouvement, en proposant la beauté, et la grandeur de la chose vers laquelle on les porte, puisque je suppose qu'on n'entreprend de faire aimer que ce qui est beau d'une véritable beauté, et possède une grandeur réelle. (1676:310)

His view of the aberrant passions as a deflection in individuals of a universal inclination toward the good authorizes orators to accommodate themselves to the particular passion of a given audience while maintaining their position as enlightened moral guides. This audience adaptation can take surprising turns, explicitly using *ad hominem* arguments, as when a director of conscience detaches a lady of fashion from a love of cosmetics, not by appealing immediately to the love of God, but through the intermediate step of an appeal to her vanity (1676:312).

Thus, the 1688 additional chapters reunite all rhetorical invention under the aegis of insinuation. The *science d'insinuer* that had been reserved for the ethical and emotional proofs in 1675 expands into the intellectual ones with the rehabilitation of appeals to *vraisemblance* in 1688 to replace the outmoded system of the commonplaces. *Adresse* is as necessary in redirecting an audience's opinions as in aligning the image of the orator's character on their expectations or as in changing the object of their passions.

The Primacy of Truth

The 1688 additions also strengthen the suggestion that even the most overt assault of the passions is, in the final analysis, a form of the indirect approach that characterizes his notion of rhetorical proof. This had not been as clear in the first editions where the emotions were seen, in part, as a weapon of last resort available when an audience willfully refused to attend to the truth.[25] However, he does not view emotional persuasion as an affective substitute for *évidence,* but as an oblique method of achieving it; the belief that an intellectual judgment must eventually ratify or reject the passions is implicit. When dealing with listeners hostile to truth, "one must propose the truths of which they must be persuaded with such craftiness that they [the truths] be mistress of their hearts before they have perceived them" ("il faut proposer les vérités dont il est nécessaire qu'ils soient persuadés, avec cette adresse qu'elles soient maîtresses de leur coeur avant qu'ils les aient apperçues" [1676:292]). The head is not forgotten; in such cases one simply wins over the will before proceeding to the understanding.

Rhetoric in his eyes is a neutral art (cp. 1699:87). It is a weapon that can either be used for legitimate self-defense or for aggression (1676:103–8). He recognizes that elocutionists can exploit its techniques independently of truth, especially with popular audiences unable to maintain the attention required to achieve *évidence.* Echoing Malebranche's fear of mechanical persuasion, he notes that emotion, delivery, or *vraisemblance* can carry the day (1699:320).

However, Lamy's assumption that the heart is only being won over prior to the head explains his confidence that this emotional persuasion will not long be misused. Even when a sophist uses appeals to the passions on behalf of falsehood, eventually the audience will be disabused. "The elocutionists with whom this failing is widespread never deceive twice" ("Les Déclamateurs à qui ce défaut est ordinaire ne trompent jamais deux fois" [1676:116]). In 1688 Lamy applied the same argument to those who use half-truths to persuade: "One rarely allows oneself to be deceived twice" ("On ne se laisse guère tromper deux fois de suite" [1699:321]). This perhaps naive faith that the passions and prejudice are at best only a temporarily effective means of manipulating persuasion is rooted in his belief in an innate inclination toward truth. "A sophist is only esteemed for a short while; as soon as the art he used is discovered, he is scorned. . . . Only the truth persuades forever" ("Un sophiste n'est estimé que peu de temps: aussitôt que l'on a découvert l'Art dont il s'est servi, on le méprise. . . . [I]l n'y a que la vérité qui persuade pour toujours" [1699:321]).

We should remember that Lamy conceives of persuasion, in its most general sense, as communicating the orator's ideas and their accompanying affects as vividly as possible to an audience that cannot be counted on to share the same perception. Under ideal conditions, exciting the audience's attention while displaying the orator's own emotional involvement should be enough. However, in extreme forms of emotional persuasion, there is a temporary disjunction of the intellectual and emotional components of the message. Instead of conveying them simultaneously with equal force, the orator represents the emotional response more intensely than the underlying intellectual conviction.

Lamy's supposition, however, is that eventually both components must be reunited. The audience, having first accepted the orator's affective response, will later come to share his intellectual perception of the truth. Lamy was so convinced of the importance of the rational basis of the emotional proofs that the third state's final paragraph affirms this priority: "[I]n order to touch reasonably, what one says must be reasonable, and the movements that one wishes to inspire must be born naturally out of knowledge of the truth that one has set forth; otherwise, one only touches for a moment" ("[P]our toucher raisonnablement, il faut que ce que l'on dit soit raisonnable; et que les mouvements qu'on veut inspirer, naissent naturellement de la connaissance de la vérité qu'on a exposée, autrement on ne touche que pour un moment" [1699:374]). To be acceptable emotions must be reasonable, that is, they must second truth. Passions born of error will only persuade in the short run for they run counter to the mind's fundamental inclination.

Much of the difficulty stems from the fact that Lamy seems to conflate the corporal passions caused by a commotion of animal spirits with the will's deep-seated inclinations that the passions are meant to second. Neither Descartes nor Malebranche would disagree with Lamy when he writes, "The passions are good in themselves" ("Les passions sont bonnes en elles-mêmes" [1699:343]). However, both would insist that this goodness be judged in light of the finality of the passions, the conservation of the body. Descartes had also recognized purely intellectual emotions which depend exclusively on the will, but Lamy gives no indication of invoking them. In fact, he identifies the passions, which Descartes and Malebranche would see as legitimate when directed to the welfare of the body, with the mind's fundamental attraction toward God. Moreover, even though the passions are linked to concupiscence, Lamy does not keep them at arm's length, as do Arnauld and Nicole, or Malebranche. From their more austere perspective, the passions must be used reluctantly, if at all, because the emotions have become part of the mechanism of the will's attraction to self-love since the Fall.

This perhaps explains the tactical divergence between Lamy and Malebranche on the advisability of separating, even temporarily, emotional and intellectual proof. One has difficulty reconciling Malebranche's categoric demand in the ninth *Eclaircissement* that "one must not allow oneself to be convinced without knowing with evidence, distinctly, precisely . . . what one is convinced of" ("il ne faut pas . . . se laisser convaincre sans savoir évidemment, distinctement, précisément . . . de quoi on est convaincu" [3:126]) with Lamy's temporary dissociation of the two proofs.

However, the four interpolated 1688 chapters explicitly confirm the priority of intellectual persuasion for Lamy. These chapters conclude with a paragraph serving as a preface to the chapters on the ethical and emotional proofs, which remained all but unchanged throughout the many revisions of the work. This paragraph stands as a testimonial to the invincibility of the truth—the orator's task being to reveal this truth in full light so that it may be acknowledged.

> Thus the orator who has the talent for putting the truth in
> broad daylight must enchant since there is nothing more

enchanting than truth, and it must triumph over the resistance opposed to it since to be victorious the truth has indeed only to make itself known. We will speak of these manners that are special to orators.

Ainsi l'Orateur qui a le talent de mettre la vérité dans un beau jour doit charmer, puisqu'il n'y a rien de plus charmant que la vérité, et elle doit triompher de la résistance qu'on lui faisait, puisqu'effectivement pour être victorieuse elle n'a qu'à se faire connaître. Nous allons parler de ces manières qui sont particulières aux Orateurs. (1699:328)

These "manners that are special to orators" are the ethical and emotional proofs which commentators have tried to dissociate from the intellectual ones, but which are, Lamy affirms here, ultimately a means of making the truth known.

If Lamy had restricted eloquence to these ethical and emotional *manières,* rhetoric would have remained on the margins of logic, much as it had for Arnauld and Nicole. Only the mathematical method would provide valid demonstrations. However, Lamy's comparison of the orator and geometer makes clear that eloquence has its own method of intellectual proof appropriate to the circumstantial nature of the moral contingencies with which it so often deals. Indirect means of emotional and ethical insinuation complement the cumulative force of appeals to *vraisemblance* and probabilities legitimized in the 1688 additions. The broad 1688 notion of persuasion as reducing the gap between orator and audience due to their unique personal perspectives subsumes the narrower 1675 one that stressed overcoming the refusal to attend to unpleasant truths. The vivacity of thought and feeling Arnauld and Nicole had recommended to preachers becomes the universal instrument of persuasion.

Lamy's Rhetoric of Presence: The Vivid Language of Eloquence

The effectiveness of all language, including eloquence, must be measured against its task of conveying a faithful representation of the life of the mind. "The end and perfection of the art of speaking consists in representing with discernment this image that one has formed in the mind" ("La fin et la perfection de l'art de parler consistent à représenter avec jugement ce tableau qu'on a formé dans l'esprit" [1699:8]). Eloquence, however, requires more than a linguistic fit between the ideas and the words used to represent them. All language labors under the burden of using a physical medium to transmit a mental state from one mind to another. Moreover, since persuasion is usually reserved for occasions when obstacles stand in the way of the listeners' reception of the speaker's message—whether distraction, prejudice, or self-interest—eloquent language must be vivid if it is to be an efficient vehicle of communication.

Eloquence requires both a capacity for striking thought and the ability to transmit this mental activity with vivacity through language without losing any of the original force. It addresses itself to the listeners' resistance by riveting their attention on a representation of mental experience so powerful that they are forced to consider the speaker's message.

> It is no mean art to know how to express oneself with so much clarity and sharpness that the persons to whom one speaks seem to see before their eyes a painting appealing to the senses of what is described to them, and they only see what they should see without being distracted from it by the sight of useless objects. . . . An eloquent person strikes the mind so vividly and turns it toward him so completely that he obliges them to see what he proposes.

> Ce n'est pas un art méprisable de savoir s'exprimer avec tant de clarté et de netteté, que ceux à qui on parle semblent voir devant leurs yeux une peinture sensible de ce qu'on leur dit, et qu'ils ne voient que ce qu'ils doivent voir sans en être détournés par la vue de choses inutiles. . . . Il [un homme éloquent] frappe l'esprit si vivement et le tourne de son côté si entièrement, qu'il l'oblige de voir ce qu'il lui propose.[26]

Eloquence succeeds to the extent that the words dissolve, leaving the audience in direct presence of the orator's thought. The speaker's vivid image or "painting appealing to the senses" becomes the message it signifies. "The eloquent man enchants his listeners so that they do not notice that, so to speak, they are listening to words, but the image formed in their mind is so vivid that they imagine that they see what he says to them" ("Celui-là est éloquent qui enchante ses Auditeurs, de sorte qu'ils ne s'aperçoivent pas, pour ainsi dire, qu'ils écoutent des paroles, mais qu'ils s'imaginent voir ce qu'il leur dit, tant l'image qui se forme dans leur esprit est vive").[27] Lamy's ideal is to persuade by placing the listener in immediate contact with the speaker's message, so that the mind fastens itself through attention to the vivid presence of the ideas before it.

Figured Speech:
Attention and Pleasure

Does language have the resources to convey such vivid mental experience? Following Port-Royal, Lamy recognizes that speech is but a sensible sign of a spiritual, that is, a mental reality; its physical component has no resemblance to the idea in the mind it represents (1676:4). However, rather than dwell on any incompatibility, he stresses how well language conveys ideas: "The sounds formed by the organs of the voice have no resemblance in themselves to these ideas yet do not fail to signify them" ("Les sons que forment les Organes de la Voix, et qui n'ayant rien de semblable en eux-mêmes à ces idées, ne laissent pas de les signifier" [1676:4]). Indeed, he is fundamentally optimistic about the potential of language to represent the full range of the mind's activities, including the operations of both the will and understanding.

Lamy's analysis of figured discourse confirms this confidence. Ordinary speech may not provide a lexicon rich enough to supply a term for each nuance of the orator's thought and feeling (1676:57), but figured speech, "these extraordinary manners of speaking" ("ces manières de parler qui sont extraordinaires" [1699:43]), makes possible the communication of the most vivid ideas, judgments, or passions that would otherwise go unexpressed. Lamy defines figured speech in terms of a departure from ordinary usage; in some cases this norm might be accepted grammatical or semantic practice, but in others, it involves the absence of strong emotion (1676:28).

Although Lamy mentions a number of classifications of figures—rhetorical, grammatical, theatrical ("figures de rhétorique," "figures de grammaire" [1676:28], and "figures de théâtres" [1676:119])—his most fundamental divisions are organized around their mode of operation and the ratio of pleasure to utility within them. In terms of their operation, he divides the figures into two broad categories: the tropes, such as metonomy, metaphor, or irony, which involve shifts in meaning of words and communicate chiefly ideas and the relation between ideas; and the figures proper, such as exclamation, repetition, and questions, which involve shifts in syntax or in the order of words and represent the passions and movements of the will. However, Lamy is supple enough to acknowledge that the frontier between these two categories is extremely porous. Metaphor and other devices usually categorized as tropes can serve as figures and convey an emotional charge; for while tropes may be primarily addressed to the understanding, and the figures to the will, any single example of figured speech contains elements appealing to both faculties.

Because it addresses simultaneously the will and the understanding, figured speech pleases as well as instructs (1676:254). The pleasure results from engaging the senses and emotions; the utility stems from reinforcing attention.

> The tropes and figures are the flowers of style. The tropes allow the most abstract thoughts to be conceived in a way that appeals to the senses; they produce a pleasing picture of what one wishes to make known. The figures awaken attention; they inflame; they animate readers, which is pleasing.

> Les tropes et les figures sont les fleurs du style. Les tropes font concevoir sensiblement les pensées les plus abstraites; ils font une peinture agréable de ce que l'on voulait signifier. Les figures réveillent l'attention, elles échauffent, elles animent les lecteurs, ce qui est agréable. (1676:236)

Pleasure reinforces utility, and Lamy labels a "natural ornament" any pleasing use of language that is necessary to this goal of making known the truth (1678:227).

At the other extreme, when the component of pleasure dominates, figured speech is exemplified by the embellishments of poets whose primary goal is to please (1676:249), and who rarely hesitate to pervert the reader's inclinations.[28] Such figures may be legitimate in poetry if used with prudence, but become "false ornaments" (1678:233) if introduced into eloquence where the delight of figured speech must serve the orator's message.

Lamy is willing to concede an intermediate category of "artificial ornaments," embellishments which add grace and charm but which could be removed without harming the speech's essential persuasive force (1676:261). In fact, only when these figures detract from the message by calling attention to themselves do they become false (1676:257–58). When used with discretion, the incidental relaxation and pleasure they provide prepares the mind to concentrate more intensely because their beauty contributes at least indirectly to the task of maintaining attention: "They are only placed there as embellishment, and they have no other use than arresting the reader's mind by means of the pleasure that it receives from reading and making it apply itself more willingly" ("Elles n'y sont placées que pour l'embellissement; et elles n'ont point d'autre utilité que celle d'arrêter l'esprit du Lecteur par le plaisir qu'il reçoit de sa lecture, et de faire qu'il s'applique plus volontiers" [1676:261]). Such devices as emblems, figured speech, allusions and citations, and harmonious wording are mentioned in this category (1678:231). The source of pleasure they procure is the mind's inclination toward grandeur in the form of all that is rare and extraordinary. Such devices can give some degree of pleasure, but only God's grandeur is ultimately satisfying, hence the five pages of caveats he presents regarding their deployment (1676:261–66). In the best eloquence, the natural ornaments please inasmuch as they adequately convey the message in the speaker's mind: "[T]he pleasure one receives in a well made speech is only caused by the resemblance that exists between the image that the words form in the mind and the things they depict" ("[L]e plaisir que l'on prend dans un discours bien fait n'est causé que par cette ressemblance, qui se trouve entre l'image que les paroles forment dans l'esprit, et les choses dont elles font la peinture" [1676:253]). Such figures combine utility and delight to produce a beauty that is "the flower of health" ("la fleur de la santé" [1676:252]), echoing a traditional metaphor Descartes had used to describe the purity of Balzac's style.

The authentic eloquence that Lamy proposes results from the proper application of the pleasures of language to the pleasures of the mind. First, Lamy acknowledges the primacy of the pleasure stemming from knowledge of the truth. The most solid pleasures, those to be preferred over any afforded by language, obtain from truth (1676:266). In the 1688 additions Lamy defines truth as the fit between an idea and its referent, "[A]ll evident knowledge conforms to the thing known, and consequently . . . is true" ("[T]oute connaissance évidente est conforme à la chose qui est connue, et par conséquent . . . est vraie" [1699:318]). The most fundamental pleasure that language can afford parallels this fit; just as *la clarté* signals a fit between idea and referent, *la justesse* is a perfect accord between the ideas and words used to represent them, that is, when language conveys the mental activity of the speaker with precision (1699:9). This linguistic fit provides an intense pleasure grounded in the inclination toward order (cp. 1699:8). Especially intense is the pleasure of language that conveys the truth, for it incorporates the double conformity of words with ideas and ideas with reality. "The truth pleases because the truth of a discourse is nothing but the conformity of the words which comprise it with the subject matter" ("C'est la vérité qui plaît, car la vérité d'un discours n'est autre chose que la conformité des paroles qui le composent avec les choses" [1699:289]).

The Tropes

If eloquence depends on the ability to communicate thoughts with precision and vivacity (1699:90), it seems crucial that the orator have available a rich lexicon stocked with the exact term to convey each nuance of meaning. However, no such provision of words exists. The capacity to envisage issues from a multitude of perspectives far surpasses the limited vocabulary languages supply. "Ordinary words are not always precise; they are too strong or too weak. They do not convey the precise idea one wishes to give" ("Les mots ordinaires ne sont pas toujours justes,

ils sont ou trop forts ou trop faibles. Ils n'en donnent pas la juste
idée qu'on en veut donner" [1699:90]).

Fortunately, the tropes overcome this lexical sterility. The exact term to convey a particular idea may be absent, but this hardly
precludes its representation. By applying a related term, the
referent can be indirectly evoked; metonymy, in fact, is the basic
trope for Lamy (1676:59). Lamy condemns exaggerated transpo-
sitions in the name of fidelity to the referent. The transfer of
meaning must be clear, that is, it must be comprehensible to the
audience (1676:67), just as there must be a reasonable proportion
between the terms of the analogy on which it is based (1676:72).
Lamy does not require exact precision of the trope, but he does
reject any transposition so hermetic that it calls more attention
to itself than to the referent. Such extravagant tropes would
belong to his category of false ornaments (1676:255).

The paradox is that this indirect mode of representation neces-
sitated by the poverty of language becomes for Lamy an asset.
No mere extenders that dilute the lexicon, the tropes are instead
its wealth (1676:67). Even if the exact term to express a referent
is lacking, the trope carries with it a vividness that conveys more
intense presence than a precise word might carry. Moreover, by
heightening the mind's attention, this vivacity compensates for
any absence of precision that might have constituted an obstacle
to the understanding.

The three uses of the tropes that Lamy treats are related
to this vivacity whose objective is to foster attentiveness. Most
important is the appeal to the senses that is almost always part of a
trope's creation, since the usual process is to apply some concrete
image to the referent. The trope is a "picture appealing to the
senses" ("peinture sensible" [1676:74]), using one phenomenon
available to the senses to suggest another one or to suggest some
abstract notion. Lamy repeatedly stresses the aid that metaphors
and similes furnish the attention in focusing the mind on spiritual
ideas (cp. 1676:74, 248), citing as authoritative examples the style
of Scripture: "When the prophets speak of God, they continually
use metaphors drawn from things subject to our senses; they give
God arms, hands, eyes" ("Lorsque les Prophètes parlent de Dieu,
ils se servent continuellement de Métaphores tirées de choses
sujettes à nos sens: ils donnent à Dieu des bras, des mains, des

yeux" [1676:75]). Two other uses of the tropes likewise can be seen as making use of their vivacity to strengthen attention. The tropes promote a lively style by offering a multitude of ways to express the same subject (1676:75). This variety alleviates the boredom of repetition, but even more so, by displaying the many facets of the orator's thesis (1699:325), makes it more likely that each individual member of the audience will be reached. Finally, the concision fostered by the use of tropes reduces monotony and stimulates attention (1676:75).

The Figures of Sensation

While the tropes extend the potential of language for expressing subtle nuances of thought, the figures increase the range of techniques by which the passions are inscribed in discourse. The tropes depart from ordinary usage by relying on one term to suggest a referent to which it is not normally applied; the figures involve syntactic changes that depart from normal word order. They give presence to the speaker's emotional life, to the movements of esteem, scorn, hate, and love that mark our relation to various ideas (1699:89). The tropes make it possible to express the unique ways in which an idea registers in a slightly different fashion in each person's understanding, while the figures convey the will's subjective movements that vary from individual to individual and that stem from the fact that no object of thought is valued in exactly the same way by everyone (1699:86).

As Lamy considers an extensive list of figures, he takes pains to show in each case how some passion deflects the normal flow of speech to create a figure. He places exclamation at the head of his list as the most elemental irruption of the passions into discourse. According to his psychophysiological explanation, the agitation in the mind caused by the passions creates a flow of animal spirits that contracts the muscles of the mouth and throat so that the voice becomes more rapid and forceful (1676:83). His subsequent discussion of individual figures rarely invokes the animal spirits, but the principle has been established that the commotion of spirits that characterizes the passions provokes some irregularity in speech, thus rendering their presence manifest.

In order to transmit the orator's passions to the audience he recommends all the figures that contribute to creating a vivid painting of the object of the emotion. Figures such as repetition, antithesis, description, and hypotyposis add emotional overtones to this vivid portrait, and thus I label them figures of sensation. Others, for example, exclamation, apostrophe, and prosopopeia, display the speaker's reaction to the portrait and, in turn, guide the listeners' affective response (1676:115).

In applying Cartesian psychophysiology to demonstrate how the figures make present the emotions, Lamy simply transposes into the rhetorical terminology of the figures Descartes' discussion in the *Passions de l'âme* concerning the manner in which the imagination can summon up the emotions. As Lamy puts it, "Therefore, in order to kindle the passions in the heart of man, one must present him with their objects, and the figures are extremely useful to this end" ("Pour donc allumer les passions dans le coeur de l'homme, il faut lui en présenter les objets, et c'est à quoi servent merveilleusement les Figures" [1676:114]). No wonder he recommends above all hypotyposis, "a kind of enthusiasm that causes one to imagine that one sees what is not present" ("une espèce d'enthousiasme qui fait qu'on imagine voir ce qui n'est point présent" [1699:122]). The more vivid the portrait presented by the imagination, the more intense the emotional response.[29]

The Figures of Attention

Of course, the irony in the preceding example is that Cartesian psychophysiology is invoked to explain how listeners, whose perverted inclinations blind them to a direct exposition of the truth, can be moved to action through appeals to their emotions. Lamy's treatment of the passions, however, includes a more Cartesian turn that goes well beyond the suggestion of his predecessors. Malebranche had pointed to the support the emotions can give to attention, although he did not examine the consequence for rhetoric. Even in the first edition, Lamy devotes a chapter in Book 2 to how the vivid presence of emotion generated by the figures can render the mind more attentive: "The figures elucidate obscure truths and make the mind attentive" ("Les figures éclaircissent les vérités obscures, et rendent l'esprit attentif" [1676:109–13]). The new 1688 chapter on attention in Book 5 reinforces it by declaring that "all the rhetorical figures are only used for that end" ("toutes les figures de rhétorique ne s'emploient que pour cela" [1699:325]).

He insists that the figures can assist at all stages of attention, whether the task is the initial capture, the maintaining of an attentive stance, or the refocusing of faltering attention. The precise function that he attributes to various figures differs somewhat from list to list, but three major tasks can be distinguished. Verbs such as *awaken, strike, oblige, imprint strongly* (*réveiller, frapper, obliger, imprimer fortement*) point to the capacity of figures to seize attention. *Place a proposition in broad daylight, develop, expand* (*mettre une proposition dans son jour, développer, étendre*) indicate their use as a method of amplification, a function closely related to a third use in elucidating and clarifying notions, indicated by verbs such as *elucidate* and *explain* (*éclaircir* and *expliquer*).

Among the figures that attract initial attention he cites apostrophe, interrogation, suspension, and exclamation. Interrogation, for example, is "marvelously useful for applying the listeners to what one wishes they to hear" ("merveilleusement utile pour appliquer les Auditeurs à ce qu'on veut qu'ils entendent" [1676:96]). Suspension excites attention by playing on the listener's expectation of something marvelous to come (1676:93). Exclamation, interrogation, and apostrophes can likewise be used to revive languishing attention, reawakening listeners from their somnolence (1676:105). All of these figures function by infusing the discourse with the urgency of a speaker's own emotional reaction to the subject.

The two other functions ascribed to the figures are more closely related to the task that Lamy assigns to the tropes. In fact, when he discusses the ability of certain figures to clarify and amplify an idea, a function which involves an appeal to the understanding similiar to that of the tropes, he often includes tropes such as simile and metaphor among the figures (1676:111; 1699:325). Treating them as figures highlights their ability to convey an additional emotional charge as well as a cognitive element. Lamy stresses this affective element in his presentation of such "true figures" ("véritables figures" [1676:110]) as syllogism, enthymemes, and dilemmas, which are commonly thought to belong more to logic than to rhetoric. Descartes had ejected the syllogism from logic and labeled it a device more suitable for the demonstration of truth than its discovery; Lamy makes its rhetorical function even clearer by showing how such figures represent the intrusion of passion into the thought process. These figures are extraordinary manners of reasoning that are called upon only in the ardor of persuasion (1676:110). "The heat of passion does not permit one to submit entirely to the rules that logic presents for formulating exact syllogisms" ("La chaleur de la passion ne permet pas que l'on s'assujettisse entièrement aux règles que la Logique présente pour faire des syllogismes exacts" [1678:106]).

There is likewise an emotional element involved in these groups of figures that heighten attention by clarifying or amplifying ideas, such as repetition, synonym, description, enumeration, antithesis, and similitude (1676:110–11). He argues that such techniques of amplification as antithesis should not be labeled vain ornaments. Rather, they contribute to elucidating the subject by giving the listener a second chance to grasp the issue at hand when restated in a slightly different way. Like Descartes' zeal for the truth, they convey the speaker's intense desire to communicate his message: "When the ardor one has to make oneself understood gives one reason to fear that one has not explained oneself sufficiently, one expands on the subject matter even more" ("Quand l'ardeur que l'on a de se faire entendre donne un juste sujet de craindre qu'on ne se soit pas assez expliqué, on étend les choses encore davantage" [1676:110]). Moreover, when such figures describe the object arousing our passion, they transmit both the animation that the passion evokes and a vivid and exact representation of the object (1676:89–91), so that again emotion contributes to the task of attention.

The Force of Concision

The yoking of *vivid* and *exact* is no accident. Diffuse, inaccurate language dissipates energy instead of heightening presence. Indeed, the force of figured language, which allows it to address the understanding by focusing attention while simultaneously communicating emotional power, stems from its concentrated form. Lamy sees economy as the preference of language in general and the characteristic of effective eloquence in particular. In an oration, it is essential that the expressions be so intertwined "that they gather together and express all at once the ideas we want to make known" ("qu'ils ramassent et expriment tout d'un coup la pensée que nous voulons signifier" [1701:64]). Figured speech permits language to express an infinite combination of ideas and emotional states with a finite lexicon. The Port-Royal distinction between principal and accessory ideas, which Lamy invokes as a model, underscores the power of figures to allow ideas and emotions to overlap and reinforce each other. The tropes, primarily based on an analogy between two objects, permit the second object to be evoked by only mentioning the first. In addition, the relation between the two terms expressed by the trope is more often than not the product of some emotional reaction that inscribes itself within the analogy (cp. 1676:73). Likewise, the figures concentrate in a single expression both an idea conveyed by the words along with an emotional charge conveyed by the departure from normal word order. The vivacity that figured speech contributes to an eloquence of attention proceeds from the striking ideas and passions they represent and from the condensed form used to express them. Ulrich Ricken has pointed out that, while in the early states Lamy takes for granted a natural word order based on the temporal succession of subject, verb, and object in the mind, by 1701 he envisages thought as a complex of ideas that the mind seizes in a single glance (1701:64).[30] Thanks to the natural vivacity of the mind, ideas are conceived simultaneously rather than consecutively (1701:68). As the portrait of the mind, language has the duty to convey this fecundity and intensity of mental activity; the concentrated mode of figured speech allows eloquence to fulfill this requirement in a way that is at once faithful to the mind's natural vivacity and eminently forceful.

This concision is most apparent at the microlevel of the figured locution, but it is also applicable to the entire discourse. Lamy acknowledges in his brief discussion of *dispositio* (1676:323–36) that the circumstantial nature of an orator's typical subject matter precludes the direct simplicity of geometers who are content to propose their proofs and then rest their case (1676:332). The orator, on the other hand, may be obliged to cite a web of circumstances that cannot be unraveled (1676:331). This does not authorize the shotgun attack of a welter of unrelated arguments in the hope that one will find its mark. Rather the orator must identify a single, solid proof and link it to all the other arguments to form a chain binding the listener to the truth (1676:333).

> Those who know the secret of eloquence never waste time relating a batch and crowd of proofs; they choose one good one and treat it in this way. They solidly establish the principle of their argument; they expose its clarity with scope; they show the connection between this principle and the conclusion that they draw from it and that they wish to demonstrate. . . . They repeat this proof so many times that one cannot avoid it; they display it from so many angles that one cannot be ignorant of it, and they use so much craftiness to make it enter the listeners' minds that finally it becomes their mistress.

> Ceux qui savent le secret de l'éloquence ne s'amusent jamais à rapporter un tas et une foule de raisons: ils en choisissent une bonne, et la traitent de cette manière. Ils établissent solidement le principe de leur raisonnement, ils en font voir la clarté avec étendue: Ils montrent la liaison de ce principe avec la conséquence qu'ils en tirent, et qu'ils voulaient démontrer. . . . Ils répètent cette raison tant de fois qu'on ne peut pas en éviter le coup: Ils la font paraître sous tant de faces, qu'on ne peut pas l'ignorer, et ils la font entrer avec tant d'adresse dans les esprits, qu'enfin elle en devient la Maîtresse. (1676:332–33)

Mathematical brevity may not be compatible with eloquence, but arguments must be arranged to eliminate all extraneous material and to hammer home the single thesis chosen as the object of the audience's attention.

Vivacity versus Self-Evidence

Although persuasion is an ever-present concern of Descartes, Arnauld and Nicole, and Malebranche, none had much use for traditional rhetorical theory. When they did not see it as irrelevant to the communication of their message, they feared that the rhetorician's art encouraged dangerous habits of discourse and allowed error to enjoy the same persuasion that truth alone should generate.

Lamy, on the other hand, seeks to formulate a science of persuasion by applying Cartesian psychophysiology to many of the issues dealt with in the *ars bene dicendi* and the *ars persuadendi*. By equating the two arts, persuasion became a much more pervasive activity than it was for Descartes, who was chiefly concerned with the psychological assurance that should accompany *évidence*. Lamy treats persuasion as a universal human enterprise. It is the substance of everyday transactions, since seldom do two individuals see things exactly the same way. Moreover, language for Lamy is not a regrettable necessity imposed by the mind's union with a body. Eloquence, the highest form of persuasive language, transmits a vivid image of mental experience, both intellectual and affective.

However, in this prominent position, Lamy's rhetoric inevitably strains its Cartesian moorings, as interpreted by the Port-Royalists and Malebranche. Indeed, Lamy makes adjustments in most of the areas where traditional rhetoric seemed at odds with Descartes' philosophy of *évidence*. While Lamy rejects the topics as a tool of invention and the extravagant use of figures, he allows for *vraisemblance*, does not disparage the imagination, and accepts a disjunction of emotional and intellectual proofs.

Lamy's tendency is to stretch to their limits fundamental Cartesian positions in order to allow for traditional rhetorical practices. He pays homage to *évidence* and the linear chains of proof exemplified by geometry, yet he also makes room alongside them for a rhetoric that deals with contested issues where certainty comes from an accumulation of interlocking arguments, much as Descartes had allowed for moral certainty rather than self-evidence in the realm of action. When *évidence* cannot be reached, or when an audience refuses to attend to it, rhetorical stealth must be invoked. His stress on the vivacity of the orator's thoughts and affects assumes the framework of the Cartesian psychophysiology of the understanding and will, but he expands the permissible emotional charge beyond Descartes' generous zeal for truth or Arnauld and Nicole's veneration for religious doctrine.

Lamy's treatment of vivacity reflects in many ways this ambiguity, for there is a potential conflict between the rhetorical vivacity he prizes and Descartes' stress on the clarity of *évidence*. Indeed, Malebranche had been suspicious of eloquence because it relies on a dubious form of clarity, the vivid appeal of sense impressions rather than the clarity that proceeds from distinct ideas. Lamy's ideal of a vivid and exact representation incorporates both forms of clarity.

It should be pointed out that Lamy brings to the issue a rich rhetorical heritage. As far back as Dionysius of Halicarnassus and Quintilian, the requirement for a lively, vivid presentation was canonized under the heading of figures such as *enargeia* and *evidentia*.[31] In fact, Dennis Bormann has suggested that Descartes' demand for clear and distinct ideas in philosophy was shaped by this rhetorical tradition.[32] *Evidentia* is vivid narration that places events before the audience's eyes.[33] Its equivalent in Lamy is hypotyposis, along with the two figures he relates to it, description and distribution.[34] These are examples of what I call the figures of sensation, whose clarity is the vivacity of sense impressions. Their appeal is ultimately to the passions through the imagination, rather than the clarity of distinction. Lamy finds it necessary to invoke such sensual vivacity because he accounts for action by appealing to the passions, but in so doing, he risks appearing to shift the motor force of action from the will to the automatic mechanism of the animal spirits. Lamy is saved by the fact that, for him, the passions are the source of action only to the extent that they activate the inclinations.

A second form of vivacity stressing linguistic accuracy is a closer stylistic equivalent to Descartes' distinct ideas. Just as distinct ideas are necessarily clear according to Descartes, for Lamy the choice of terms that accurately convey the orator's thoughts produces a luminous clarity. Vivacity, he states in the *Entretiens*, depends on omitting none of the orator's ideas nor adding superfluous ones; when language is exact, elocution is the sun of eloquence.[35] There is less danger here that sensual appeal will masquerade as *évidence*, but the accurate transmission of the orator's ideas through the precise use of language is itself no guarantee that they are self-evident. The intense attention to the image of the orator's thoughts and emotions generated by rhetorical vivacity that characterizes eloquence always runs the risk of interfering with attention to *évidence*.

As a rhetorician, Lamy is concerned with the expression of ideas and emotions, that is, with their linguistic representation. Vivacity facilitates this efficient transmission. To be sure, ideas that are themselves clear and distinct lend themselves to such vivid expression, but in any case, once the representation has been effected, the ideas must still be judged according to the standards of self-evidence.

Lamy in no way repudiates Malebranche, but at the same time his rhetoric in the *Art de parler* is not animated by as extreme a distrust of the body as characterizes the Port-Royalists or his fellow Oratorian. He acknowledges the distinction between pure and sensible ideas, but does not devalue all that is corporal in order to privilege the truth of *évidence*. Instead, Lamy's guiding principle seems to be human nature's inclination toward God. Sin may weaken the will's movement toward God and shake its resolve to gaze upon *évidence*, but he has no hesitation about calling the senses and emotions into play; even in their weakened state, their finality remains divine. His science of persuasion, where vivacity is an agent along with *évidence*, is grounded in his confidence in the inclinations' essential goodness.

7

Conclusion

Attention and Cartesian Rhetoric

Two controversies in the 1690s helped solidify a narrow view that still persists of Cartesian rhetoric. In 1687 Charles Perrault brought the smoldering quarrel of the ancients and moderns into the open with his poem *Le Siècle de Louis le Grand,* which celebrates the artistic superiority of the Sun King's reign. The third dialogue (1690) of his *Parallèle des anciens et des modernes* is devoted to the demonstration of his contemporaries' excellence in eloquence. He establishes proper method leading to clarity as the essential quality of fine eloquence, whether the goal is to instruct, to please, or to persuade.[1] The true method, imperfectly known to the Romans and Greeks, but exemplified in the theory and practice of Descartes, assures the moderns' triumph.[2] Perrault's heirs were to include Fontenelle and the poet Antoine Houdar de La Motte. According to Fontenelle,

> The geometric spirit is not so linked to geometry that it cannot be extracted and transported to other fields of knowledge. A work of ethics, politics, criticism, and perhaps even eloquence, will be more beautiful, all things being equal, if it is drawn with the hand of a geometer.
>
> L'esprit géométrique n'est pas si attaché à la géométrie, qu'il n'en puisse être tiré, et transporté à d'autres connaissances. Un ouvrage de morale, de politique, de critique, peut-être même d'éloquence, en sera plus beau, toutes choses d'ailleurs égales, s'il est fait de main de géomètre.[3]

La Motte, in turn, sought to extend geometry to poetry and theater because he saw method as a universal requirement in all genres: "I believe . . . that method is necessary in all kinds of works" ("Je crois . . . qu'il faut de la méthode dans toutes sortes d'ouvrages").[4]

The second quarrel turned entirely on rhetoric. In his preface to a translation of Augustine's sermons in 1694, Goibaud Dubois invoked the authority of the author of *De doctrina christiana* for his recommendation that preachers limit their use of the imagination and senses.[5] His subsequent arguments based on psychological principles have a Malebranchian ring.[6] He denounces the imagination for paralyzing the intelligence, thus making attention to pure ideas impossible.[7] The essential religious truths that bring lasting conversion to sinners are perceived only by the pure intelligence; if appeals to the senses, whether affective or imaginative, are to be allowed at all, they are permissible only after the intelligence has been won over: "The entire man must be stirred; and one may do it without danger provided that one begins with the intellect . . . after having filled the intellect and convinced it of the truths one preaches, they can be communicated to the imagination." ("Il faut remuer l'homme tout entier; et on peut le faire sans danger pourvu qu'on commence par l'intelligence . . . après l'avoir remplie et convaincue des vérités que l'on prêche, on peut . . . les imprimer à l'imagination.")[8] Thus he recommends a geometric order in order to communicate truth more fully to the intelligence and advises a sparing use of stylistic ornament.[9] Accounts like those of Perrault or Dubois of an eloquence that is centered around method fixed the received notion of Cartesian rhetoric: a requirement that all rational proofs conform to the clarity of self-evidence, provision for the emotions only if they follow intellectual conviction, the use of impersonal geometry as a model for disposition, and the reduction of style to neutral mathematical notation.

However, a more positive reading of the rhetorical theory generated from Descartes' notion of persuasion and the psychology that underpins it is possible. In spite of Descartes' professed disinterest in the rules of eloquence, not only does he exploit its stratagems, but a space that might be labeled rhetorical emerges within his system. Despite claims to the contrary in the *Discours*, his replies to the *Sixièmes Objections* point to the fact that clear and distinct ideas are not always sufficient to persuade, at least when opposed by the relentless prejudices accumulated in childhood.

At the least, a rhetoric of philosophical discourse is authorized. Furthermore, he acknowledges that in the most urgent affairs of life, suspending judgment until self-evidence can be reached is impractical. Descartes left to his successors the task of resolving the triple problematic I alluded to in the introduction: circumscribing and identifying this rhetorical space, describing the psychological processes by which persuasion takes place within it (while taking into account the effects of the Fall), and analyzing the linguistic means of representing it.

These tasks were made all the more difficult by lacunae in Descartes' thought that undercut nascent Cartesian rhetorical theory. In spite of his admiration for eloquence, he never thought it worthwhile to analyze how this talent functions. Even more serious are both the sketchy state of his views on language and the fact that his increasing preoccupation with ethical issues in his later years never resulted in a definitive treatise on moral action. Thus, when critics extrapolate his rhetorical theory, given these gaps in his system, it is not surprising that the product is often a constricted view of the discipline, such as those of Perrault or Dubois, that serves best as a foil for more robust visions of rhetoric, whether Pascal's art of pleasing, Vico's defense of topical invention, or Perelman's new rhetoric of argumentation. Descartes has perhaps suffered unduly from comparisons in which critics exaggerate the narrowness of his rhetoric to provide a convenient stage for the canonization of their own favorite theorist.

Yet we have seen that Descartes and his successors came to an accomodation with rhetoric that was far richer than such a stereotype suggests. To be sure, even in the *Art de parler,* the Cartesians never embraced eloquence with the exuberance found in Balzac, but the grudging acceptance of an ill-defined rhetorical space of the *Logique de Port-Royal* is not their last word. In the course of my discussion of each theory, I have emphasized characteristic themes, such as Descartes' generosity or the centrality of the Incarnation for Malebranche. In concluding, I will point to the usefulness of the concept of attention in defining the scope and limits of Cartesian rhetoric.

Attention has never been ignored by rhetoricians, but since the nature of its assignment has varied, a comparison with both ancient and contemporary approaches provides a useful preliminary to Descartes' views. Attention is considered by the major treatises of antiquity, and Aristotle's rather brief discussion in Book 3 of the *Rhetoric* is typical (14.1415b).[10] He does not so much see attention as the active process it is for Descartes, as a prerequisite state of readiness that must exist before the orator's arguments can be profitably presented. Like later ancient theorists, he treats the topic in his discussion of the speech's introduction, where securing the audience's attention and benevolence is paramount, although he notes that such reminders to heed the orator's message are often better located later in the speech when concentration tends to lag. Thus, his concern is where in a speech to place specific calls for attention and how to motivate them. When Quintilian takes up Aristotle's recommendations, he too sees attention in terms of direct appeals for vigilance. He remarks that just as the exordium serves this purpose for the entire speech, calls to readiness can be inserted to preface new arguments at any point in a discourse and thus serve the same function as the exordium by renewing attention (*Institutio oratoria*, 4.1.75).

On the other hand, reflecting the interest in attention of psychologists since the late nineteenth century, American theories of persuasion have discussed attention in great detail. Attention was a central topic of investigation when modern academic psychology developed in the decades before the turn of the century. William James devoted a chapter to it in his 1890 *Principles of Psychology,* and researchers like E. B. Titchener at Cornell conducted elaborate experimental studies.[11] After an eclipse of interest between the two world wars due to the behaviorists' association of attention with introspection and the mentalistic approaches they disparaged, attention has reappeared on the agenda of cognitive psychologists. Such research has found its way into textbooks written by speech communications specialists who, much as Lamy did in the seventeenth century, have sought to reinvigorate rhetoric by applying current scientific data. However, in spite of the revival of interest today among psychologists, attention has not recovered the status it enjoyed in the first three decades of this century when handbooks on public speaking featured it most prominently. Thus, recent authors such as W.

L. Brembeck and W. S. Howell, devote a substantial chapter to attention, but describe it as a preliminary state of readiness much as did the ancient rhetoricians.[12] On the other hand, J. A. Winans' classic text on public address first published in 1916 made it central to his definition of persuasion as "the process of inducing others to give fair, favorable, or undivided attention to propositions."[13] It is crucial not only in gaining assent, but even in provoking action. Citing James' observation that "what holds attention determines action," Winans makes attention the key to moving the audience to act. To perform an action, is merely "to give it exclusive attention."[14]

When Descartes coupled the suspension of judgment with the need for attention and pointed to attention as the driving agent in the quest for self-evidence, he undoubtedly gave little thought to its implications for rhetoric. However, of the elements that lend a Cartesian orientation to the rhetorical theories of the writers I have treated—the primacy of *évidence*, mind/body dualism, the psychophysiology of the passions and imagination, and attention—attention alone constitutes the active force. Once the "pure and attentive intellect" ("mentis purae et attentae" [*Regulae*, A.-T., 10:368]) by which self-evidence is discovered moves to center stage, it assumes similar importance in persuasion.

Cartesian rhetoric at its best, thus, is a rhetoric of attention that allows the audience to reenact the orator's quest for *évidence*, a rhetoric that must be defined in terms of Descartes' notion of the mind's application. Unlike the ancients for whom attention is a initial state of alertness, Descartes envisages it as a dynamic process. He emphasizes its selective feature; attention is the mind's ability to focus itself ever more sharply in the quest for distinct ideas. However, unlike Winans, who extends attention's role beyond cognition to action, Descartes leaves its role as a motor force ill-defined. Indeed, Descartes never analyzes the resolve to act with the same detail he devotes to the process of assenting to truth. As Jean-Marc Gabaude has noted, "Descartes . . . scarcely took into account a phenomenology of volition in execution and performance."[15] The absence of a definitive treatment of ethics by Descartes leaves Cartesian rhetoric poorly equipped to account for action. Finally, unlike both ancient and contemporary notions of attention, Descartes' version aspires towards pure thought in which the corporal is reduced or eliminated. This orientation toward pure intellection makes Cartesian rhetoric ambivalent towards the imagination and passions.

The superiority of the pure understanding over the senses and imagination underlies the distrust of Cartesians towards rhetoric. Descartes' successors were obsessed with the perils of mechanical persuasion that never rises above the level of the body. Descartes himself had rather playfully alluded to such false eloquence in his rebuttal of Gassendi's *Cinquièmes Objections,* but the denunciation of this corporal eloquence took on a religious urgency when Arnauld and Nicole interpreted it in terms of their Augustinian preoccupation with concupiscence. The fallen mind prefers to apply itself to sensual images rather than maintain its attention on difficult truths. The Port-Royalists were the first to connect eloquence with the mind's application when they disparaged ostentatious discourse that never goes beyond the most accessible platitudes. The paroxysm of this criticism was reached in Malebranche's fulminations against the contagion of the eloquence of strong imaginations condemned as a rhetoric of distraction. Eloquent language contaminates, whether the body language of delivery, the pleasure of sonorous style, or the figures that activate the imagination and affects. Thus, the deepest impulse of Arnauld and Nicole, as well as Malebranche, was to reject any use of the passions or imagination in order to protect attention to pure ideas.

Yet, however great their temptation to bypass the body, the Port-Royalists and Malebranche knew well that the mind's union with it must be taken into account. Arnauld and Nicole led the way by recognizing that religious truths must not be only known by the understanding but also revered by the will. Movements of the will can legitimately be accompanied by corporal ones, that is, the passions. Malebranche echoed this argument in his 1678 ninth *Eclaircissement* in which he reminds his readers that the fathers of the church were wise not to write with the dryness of geometers. In addition, both the Port-Royalists and Malebranche recognized that the domain of contingencies, including practical conduct, escapes the regimentation of self-evidence and geometric method, thus opening a wider potential space for eloquence.

In the *Logique de Port-Royal,* thanks to the formulation of Arnauld and Nicole's concept of accessory ideas, the Cartesian psychology of the mind's two chief faculties and their union with the body leads to a stress on rhetorical vivacity. Figured speech is the instrument for transmitting a speaker's ideas and affects with intensity to an audience because the overlapping principal and secondary ideas engage at once the will and understanding, the senses and passions. But while the Port-Royalists make room for the rhetorical, they turn their back on formal rhetorical theory; they were chiefly concerned with demonstrating the deleterious effects of eloquence on attention rather than with studying how attention could be enhanced. In order to elaborate a more positive view of eloquence within a Cartesian framework, the focus must be on how attention imparts vitality both to Descartes' method and to the Cartesian rhetoric it informs.

It is no accident, for example, that attention is singularly absent from both Perrault and Dubois' descriptions of method. Perrault himself was by no means a thoroughgoing Cartesian, and Dubois' use of Cartesian psychophysiology was imprecise to say the least. Antoine Arnauld had little difficulty pointing out that Dubois' distinction between the intelligence and the imagination was as poorly drawn as his claim that his attack against the figures could be found in Augustine.[16]

Indeed, when the unique approach to attention in Descartes is properly appreciated, method is not necessarily to be equated with geometry, and the priority of rational conviction need not require that the emotions be aroused only after the intellect has been satisfied. Eliminating attention transforms Cartesian method into a lifeless scholasticism and risks the reductive superficiality of Perrault or Dubois. As Lamy describes method, "Almost all of it consists in paying attention to the topic one wishes to know" ("Tout consiste presque à faire attention à la chose qu'on veut connaître").[17] Descartes' rules of method are only suggestions to enhance the process by which the mind reaches *évidence,* whose clear and distinct ideas are defined in terms of attention. Clarity is a radiance that grips the attention; distinction results from the mind focusing its gaze to eliminate all that is extraneous from an idea, and since ideas become clearer as they become more distinct, the procedure reinforces itself. In contrast, sense perceptions, even though confused, have a clarity that overwhelms the attention.

Thus, this attention to clear and distinct ideas at times requires an almost heroic application of the will; the attention is less attracted to self-evidence than to sense impressions that are more intense, even if they are not distinct. However, although the senses lie in constant ambush for attention, Descartes and Malebranche show how they can be trained as its auxiliaries: properly dosed, the imagination and emotions strengthen the mind's faltering ability to arrive at truth.

Attention for Malebranche includes a dynamic missing in Descartes. For the Oratorian, attention involves not merely the interaction of the will and the understanding, and of the mind and the body; given the mind's union with God, to attend to truth is to interrogate the Divine Word. Hence the need to still the passions and to go beyond the imagination to pure ideas seen in God. To be sure, by placing the Incarnation at the center of his philosophy, Malebranche grounds a limited use of the sensual as a means of reaching pure ideas in a divine model. His rhetoric of attention redeems the body, making it an instrument for attaining higher truth. However, given his conviction that the mind's union with God is more important than its union with the body, any recourse to the corporal is only an expedient for arriving at the divine. He shows no interest in formulating an explicit rhetoric of attention, as if that would give undue substance to an earthly eloquence that pales before the rhetoric of praise to come in the eternal Jerusalem.

In spite of Lamy's links to Malebranche and the fact that in his later works, such as the *Entretiens* (1683) or the *Morale chrétienne* (1688–1709), Malebranchian themes are pronounced, in the *Art de parler* neither attention as mental prayer nor the centrality of the Incarnation is operative. In fact, it is perhaps because Lamy does not venture into such speculative doctrines that he was able to mobilize Cartesian psychophysiology for rhetoric. While Lamy shares the fear of mechanical persuasion that pervades the Port-Royalists and Malebranche, his treatment of the figures of attention shows that on the whole he is more confident that eloquent speech can promote the mind's concentration. Indeed, he invokes attention at every stage in the rhetorical process. It must be considered during the invention of intellectual and emotional proofs. In his chapters on disposition, not only does he examine it in his discussion of the exordium, as was the practice of the ancient theorists, but also he demonstrates how each part of a speech must promote attention. Finally, it appears repeatedly in his discussion of style, whether it be the figures and tropes, or rhythm. Thus, it is no surprise that in 1701 he repeated his 1675 statement that attention counts among the greatest secrets of eloquence (1676:257; 1701:389).

Lamy's stress on attention at every moment of the persuasive process marks the convergence of Cartesian philosophy and the humanist rhetorical tradition. Attention for him is much more pervasive than the overt appeals to remain alert recommended by the ancient rhetoricians. Lamy's insistence that a heightened attention be maintained throughout a discourse, especially at the crucial points in the argumentation, parallels Descartes' and Malebranche's doctrine that attention is the act by which the mind makes its personal contact with *évidence*. Likewise, his reinterpretation of traditional rhetorical devices in terms of their potential contribution to attentiveness marks his effort to adapt the teachings of the ancient rhetoricians to the new epistemology.

To a certain extent, Lamy's notion of attention lacks the depth and subtlety of that of both Descartes and Malebranche, and his frank acceptance of a temporary dissociation of emotional and intellectual proofs strains their view of the passions. Attention for Lamy consists more of attending to the vivid representation of the orator's ideas and movements than Descartes' effort to remove all that is extraneous from a concept to arrive at distinct ideas or Malebranche's interrogation of the Interior Master. By treating rhetoric as an art of speaking, Lamy focuses primarily on the image of ideas and movements, leaving their evaluation to the logician or moralist. Nonetheless, this vivid linguistic representation is only a means to an end. In Lamy's version of ideal eloquence, the audience's attention is so riveted to the orator's message that the words dissolve, leaving the listener in the direct presence of their referents. When the referent is an idea, rhetorical attention to this vivid image presupposes subsequent attention to the concepts represented so that they may be judged in terms of the standards of self-evidence. However, when the referent is an event or object evoked through the imagination, the ultimate goal is to incite action. Rhetorical vivacity, including in this case a strong dose of sensual stimulation, ensures the sustained application of the will necessary for action by exciting the passions to energize the inclinations.

Thus, these Cartesians illustrate Chaïm Perelman's observation that rhetoric flourishes in inverse proportion to Descartes' ideal of self-evident knowledge.[18] For them, eloquence operates in the space where self-evidence is elusive, or where there is a refusal to attend to it. Its mode of operation resembles that of the accessory ideas described by the Port-Royalists. Just as attention should always be directed to the principal idea, so the trappings of eloquence should merely add energy to the primary one. They remain a manner, a means of gaining attention for some concept. The figures of speech that engage the imagination and emotions can reinforce this necessary attention needed to attain the principal idea, or can be used to arouse an appropriate accompanying movement of the passions. Furthermore, because accessory ideas function at the margins of consciousness, they are ideally suited to strategies of insinuation, for they allow the rhetor subtly to redirect the attention of the audience.

Descartes himself had been content to let the gift of eloquence remain unexamined like an accessory idea. However, the Port-Royalists and Malebranche, beginning with their analysis of false eloquence and even more so in their discussion of how rhetoric can serve religious truth, retrieve it gradually from this neglect. Lamy goes much further, extending the notion of persuasion beyond Descartes' own project of reuniting *assensio* and *persuasio* to include the realm of contingencies that eloquence had traditionally included. Furthermore, he readmits rhetoric to the status of an art, which Descartes had dropped from the traditional triad of talent, art, and practice required of the orator. Lamy combines Cartesian psychophysiology with an awareness of the consequences of the Fall to produce a science of the heart. His *ars persuadendi* does not result from replacing rhetorical art with geometric method, but from uniting a concern for fostering attention—the heart of Cartesian method—with traditional rhetorical strategies.

Seen in this light, the resilience of rhetoric among Cartesians is not a repudiation of Descartes so much as a reconsideration of eloquence in terms of his psychology. Because *évidence* must be seconded by the psychological assurance of persuasion and the realm of action escapes the immediate control of clear and distinct ideas, rhetoric is gradually recovered as an art that complements Descartes' philosophy of self-evidence.

Notes
References
Index

Notes to Chapter 1

1. Chaïm Perelman and L. Olbrechts-Tyteca, *La Nouvelle Rhétorique: Traité de l'Argumentation* (Paris: PUF, 1958).

2. For a survey of the issue strongly biased against Descartes, see Ernesto Grassi, *Rhetoric as Philosophy: The Humanist Tradition* (University Park: The Pennsylvania State University Press, 1980), 35–39. "The entire attitude can be summed up in a single thesis: If the problem of philosophy is identical with that of rational knowledge, if this knowledge in its turn consists of tracing back our assertions to a 'first truth,' then emotive elements and with them the influence of images, of fantasy, of rhetoric play no role whatsoever in this rational process. They even appear as elements which interfere with the rational process" (37). Similarly, Michael Mooney's *Vico in the Tradition of Rhetoric* (Princeton: Princeton University Press, 1985) opens by setting Vico's theory of eloquence in opposition to "the methodological totalitarianism that followed the success of Cartesian analytic geometry" (6).

3. See for example Ralph Flores' chapter, "Cartesian Striptease," in *The Rhetoric of Doubtful Authority: Deconstructive Readings of Self-Questioning Narratives, St. Augustine to Faulkner* (Ithaca: Cornell University Press, 1984), 66–87. For a pertinent discussion of the relation of deconstruction to traditional rhetoric, including Nietzsche's early works, see Dilip Parameshwar Gaonkar's "Deconstruction and Rhetorical Analysis: The Case of Paul de Man," *Quarterly Journal of Speech* 73 (1987):482–98.

4. Henri Gouhier, "La Communication de la philosophie" and "La Résistance au vrai dans une philosophie sans rhétorique" in *La Pensée métaphysique de Descartes* (Paris: Vrin, 1962), 63–112.

5. Peter France stresses the various strategies used by Descartes in his chapter "Descartes: la recherche de la vérité," in *Rhetoric and Truth in France* (Oxford: Clarendon Press, 1972), 40–67. Sylvie Romanowski uses a structuralist approach to show how illusion is the generating theme of both the form and the content of Descartes' system; her diachronic study of Cartesian *discours* is especially pertinent: *L'Illusion chez Descartes: la structure du discours cartésien* (Paris: Klincksieck, 1974). See Timothy J. Reiss' critique of her study, "Cartesian Discourse and Classical Ideology," *Diacritics* 6 (1976):19–27. He raises the issue of "how Descartes' discourse, for operational purposes, concealed the

fact that its formal premises *had* been put into . . . serious question" (26). Finally, John D. Lyons has written a number of articles analyzing the Cartesian *ethos* in the *Discours*. See, for example, "Rhétorique du discours cartésien," *Cahiers de littérature du XVIIe siècle* 8 (1986):125–47. Rémy Saisselin provides a judicious overview of criticism dealing with Descartes' influence on French literature in *The Rules of Reason and the Ruses of the Heart* (Cleveland: Case Western Reserve University Press, 1970), 243–53. Marc Fumaroli's "Ego scriptor: rhétorique et philosophie dans *Le Discours de la Méthode*, in *Problématique et réception du Discours de la méthode et des Essais*, ed. Henri Méchoulan (Paris: Vrin, 1988), 31–46 appeared too late for me to use.

6. According to Cahné, Descartes usually disguises the fact that the metaphor is above all a method of investigation, not just of proof or exposition. *Un Autre Descartes: le philosophe et son langage* (Paris: Vrin, 1980), 96.

7. Hugh M. Davidson, "The Decline of Rhetoric in Seventeenth-Century France," in *The History and Philosophy of Rhetoric and Political Discourse*, ed. Kenneth W. Thompson (Lanham, Md: The University Press of America, 1987), 1:56–82.

8. Quintilian *Institutio oratoria* 4.1.5.

Notes to Chapter 2

1. For surveys of rhetoric in the Renaissance see Hanna H. Gray, "Renaissance Humanism: The Pursuit of Eloquence," in *Renaissance Essays*, ed. P. O. Kristeller and P. P. Wiener (New York: Harper Torchbooks, 1968), 199–216; Paul O. Kristeller, *Renaissance Thought and Its Sources* (New York: Columbia University Press, 1979), 242–60; Jerrold E. Seigel, *Rhetoric and Philosophy in Renaissance Humanism* (Princeton: Princeton University Press, 1968). The best *état présent* focusing on the situation in France within a European context is Marc Fumaroli's "Rhétorique et littérature française de la Renaissance et de l'époque classique," *Actes du XIe Congrès de l'Association Guillaume Budé* (Paris: Les Belles Lettres, 1985), 1:128–56.

2. Marc Fumaroli, *L'Age de l'éloquence: Rhétorique et "res literaria" de la Renaissance au seuil de l'époque classique* (Geneva: Droz, 1980).

3. Among the works dealing with Balzac's notion of eloquence are E. B. O. Borgerhoff, *The Freedom of French Classicism* (Princeton: Princeton University Press, 1950); H. Frank Brooks, "Guez de Balzac, Eloquence, and the Life of the Spirit," *Esprit créateur* 15 (1975):59–78; Morris W. Croll, *Style, Rhetoric, and Rhythm* (Princeton: Princeton University Press,

1966); Gaston Guillaumie, *J.-L. Guez de Balzac et la prose française* (Paris: Auguste Picard, 1927); Jean Jehasse, *Guez de Balzac et le génie romain* (Saint-Etienne: Publications de l'Université de Saint-Etienne, 1977); Jean Jehasse's introduction to his reprint of François Ogier's *Apologie pour Monsieur de Balzac* (Saint-Etienne: Publications de l'Université de Saint-Etienne, 1977), 7–44; F. E. Sutcliffe, *Guez de Balzac et son temps— littérature et politique* (Paris: Nizet, 1959); Zobeidah Youssef, *Polémique et littérature chez Guez de Balzac* (Paris: Nizet, 1972).

4. Sainte-Beuve, *Port-Royal* (Paris: Gallimard, 1952), 1:544; Gustave Lanson, *L'Art de la prose* (Paris: Librairie des annales, 1908), 66; René Bray, *La Formation de la doctrine classique* (Paris: Payot, 1931), 8.

5. *Les Premières Lettres de Guez de Balzac*, ed. H. Bibas and K. T. Butler (Paris: Droz, 1933–34), 1:240. References to this edition will follow this form: (Bibas, 1:240). References to Balzac, other than to the Bibas-Butler edition of the letters, will be to the *OEuvres de J.-L. Guez Sieur de Balzac*, ed. L. Moreau, 2 vols. (Paris: Jacques Lecoffre, 1854). The title of the work, the volume of the Moreau edition, and the page number will be cited.

6. Fumaroli, *L'Age de l'éloquence*, 695–705.

7. Gustave Cohen situates the stays of both Balzac and Descartes in Holland within the context of Dutch intellectual life in *Ecrivains français en Hollande dans la première moitié du XVIIe siècle* (Paris: Champion, 1920).

8. References to Descartes' works, except for the correspondence, will be to Ferdinand Alquié's edition of the *OEuvres philosophiques*, 3 vols. (Paris: Garnier, 1963–73); volume and page number will be indicated in parentheses in the text. His letters will be cited from the *Correspondance*, ed. Charles Adam and G. Milhaud, 8 vols. (Paris: Alcan-PUF, 1936–56); date, volume, and page number will be given. This edition is more complete than the selection of letters supplied by Alquié and gives translations of the Latin letters. When a text appears in neither of these editions, it will be cited from the *OEuvres de Descartes*, ed. Charles Adam and Paul Tannery, 11 vols. (Paris; Léopold Cerf, 1897–1913). A.-T. will precede the volume and page number in these cases.

9. This point is developed by Gilbert Gadoffre in "*Le Discours de la méthode* et l'histoire littéraire," *French Studies* 2 (1948):308–14.

10. See Youssef for an account of the quarrel, 22–86.

11. For discussion of Descartes' letter see Emile Krantz, *Essai sur l'esthétique de Descartes* (Paris: Germier Baillière, 1882), 77–90; Croll, 38–39; Sutcliffe, 31–32; Youssef, 85–86.

12. Croll, 39.

13. Youssef, 411.

14. In Jean-Louis Guez de Balzac, *OEuvres de Monsieur de Balzac*, ed. Valentin Conrart (Paris: Louis Billaine, 1665; rpt. Geneva: Slatkine, 1971), 2:151.

15. "Dialectic, rhetoric, poetics and similar skills, like swordplay, are more dangerous than helpful while they are being learned; for they teach us to be ignorant of things which we would naturally do very well without hesitation" ("Dialectica, Rhetorica, Poetica & similes artes, sicut gladiatoria, dum addiscuntur, nocent potius quam prosunt; monent enim nos ea nescire, quae vi naturae, si non dubitaremus, optime faceremus" [A.-T., 11:650]). Geneviève Rodis-Lewis discusses this neglected passage in her article "Cartesius," *Revue philosophique de la France et de l'étranger* 161 (1971):209–20, where she notes that Descartes stresses the natural spontaneity of eloquence.

16. "As for the music of Bannius, I think that it differs from an air of Boësset as a chria of a schoolboy who wanted to practice all the rules of rhetoric differs from a speech of Cicero where it is difficult to recognize them. I told him the same thing and I think that he admits it now; but that does not prevent him from being a very good musician besides being a gentleman and my good friend, nor from rules being good in music as well as in rhetoric" ("Pour la Musique de M. Bannius, je crois qu'elle diffère de l'air de Boësset, comme la Chrie d'un écolier qui a voulu pratiquer toutes les règles de sa Rhétorique, diffère d'une Oraison de Cicéron, où il est malaisé de les reconnaître. Je lui en ai dit la même chose, et je crois qu'il l'avoue à présent; mais cela n'empêche pas qu'il ne soit très bon musicien, et d'ailleurs fort honnête homme et mon bon ami, ni aussi que les règles ne soient bonnes, aussi bien en Musique qu'en Rhétorique" [December 1640, 4:218–19]). Compare this letter of December 1637 to Mersenne: "[W]hat I provide in the second book [of Geometry] concerning the nature and properties of curved lines and the way of examining them is, it seems to me, as far beyond ordinary geometry as the rhetoric of Cicero is beyond the *abc*'s of children" ("[C]e que je donne au second livre [de la Géométrie] touchant la nature et les propriétés des lignes courbes et la façon de les examiner, est, ce me semble, autant au-delà de la géométrie ordinaire que la rhétorique de Cicéron est au delà de *a b c* des enfants" [2:66]).

17. A.-T., 10:202. In the early *Studium Bonae Mentis*, he relegated it to the third class of sciences behind the cardinal ones concerned with first principles and the experimental group which forms the second level.

18. Jehasse, 478.

Notes to Chapter 3

1. Ferdinand Alquié, in *La Découverte métaphysique de l'homme chez Descartes*, 2nd ed. (Paris: PUF, 1966), 64–65, points out that in his youth Descartes seems to have had a marked predilection for such debates, in which he excelled in exposing the weakness of his opponents.

2. For a succinct discussion of Descartes' use of this terminology see the footnote of Jacques Brunschwig who edited the *Regulae* for Alquié's edition (1:128–129). He remarks that in Aristotle, dialectical syllogisms were distinguished from analytic ones. The premises of dialectic derive from commonly received opinions, also called probable, while analytics is based on necessarily true premises and leads to scientific knowledge. The distinction is grounded in the subject matter of the syllogism, not its form. By the Middle Ages, however, dialectic was used by the scholastics to refer to the syllogism itself, that is, to formal logic. Brunschwig believes that it is because of the confusion between the two meanings of dialectic that Descartes speaks of the probable syllogisms of the scholastics.

In addition, it should be noted that Aristotle called rhetoric the counterpoint of dialectic. Both are arts that allow one to reason from commonly shared opinions on practical and ethical questions about which no absolute conclusions can be drawn, but while dialectic involves the give and take of dialogue or debate between individuals, rhetoric involves speaking before large audiences. For more extensive comments on Aristotle's position, see Larry Arnhart, *Aristotle on Political Reasoning: A Commentary on the "Rhetoric"* (Dekalb: Northern Illinois University Press, 1981).

3. Gouhier, *La Pensée métaphysique*, 91.

4. Gouhier, *La Pensée métaphysique*, 92.

5. Martial Gueroult makes this contrast between persuasion and conviction in *Descartes* (1953, rpt. Paris: Aubier, 1968), 1:120.

6. Gouhier, *La Pensée métaphysique*, 95.

7. For commentary on this point see Geneviève Rodis-Lewis, *Descartes: Textes et débats* (Paris: Livre de poche, 1984), 556.

8. Jean-Marc Gabaude shows that it is inaccurate to speak of a provisional ethics that will be valid only until replaced by a definitive one. "The moral code will always be provisional." *Liberté et raison: la liberté cartésienne et sa réfraction chez Spinoza et chez Leibniz* (Toulouse: Publications de la Faculté des Lettres et de Sciences humaines de Toulouse, 1970), 1:222.

9. In *The Method of Descartes* (Oxford: Clarendon Press, 1952), L. J. Beck points out that Descartes uses the term analysis loosely throughout

his works. Sometimes it signifies "the order followed in resolving complicated and involved problems into an intelligible combination of simple elements which are clearly seen and self-evidently known" as in the *Méditations* (157). Sometimes it refers "in a more restricted sense . . . to geometrical analysis, which is a particular application of the general analytic method of regression from the complex to the simple" (158). It can also refer to what we now call analytic geometry (158). Beck concludes that the distinction between analysis and synthesis is not tidy (158).

10. On attention see L. J. Beck on attention in the ninth rule of the *Regulae* in *The Method of Descartes*, 55–59; Jean Laporte, *Le Rationalisme de Descartes* (Paris: PUF, 1945), 35–36, 155, 429; and Geneviève Rodis-Lewis, *L'Individualité selon Descartes* (Paris: Vrin, 1950), 175–96. Finally see L. Prenant, "Le sentiment d'évidence," *Revue philosophique de la France et de l'étranger* (1951), 168–98, who offers a subtle analysis of this "active orientation of thought" (184).

11. Laporte, 430.

12. Gabaude, 1:29.

13. Gabaude, 1:207.

14. Rodis-Lewis, *L'Individualité*, 182.

15. For detailed commentary, see Alquié's notes in his edition of *L'Homme*, in vol. 1 of the *OEuvres philosophiques*. For more extensive discussion situating Descartes' physiology in terms of seventeenth-century medical works see *The Treatise of Man*, translation and commentary by Thomas S. Hall (Cambridge: Harvard University Press, 1972).

16. Henri Gouhier, "Le Refus du symbolisme dans l'humanisme cartésien," *Archivio di filosofia* (1958), 68. See also his *Les Premières pensées de Descartes—contribution à l'histoire de l'anti-renaissance* (Paris: Vrin, 1958), 90–103.

17. T. Spoerri stresses the fact that these images are similes, not metaphors in "La Puissance métaphorique de Descartes," in *Descartes* (Paris: Editions de Minuit, 1957), 273–301.

18. In *L'Individualité* (170–76) Rodis-Lewis analyzes the use of the imagination in detail. She concludes that "the imagination is sometimes an auxiliary, sometimes an obstacle for the mind. It offers repose or stabilizes the progress of thought. Its illegitimate use is the source of almost all the lack of comprehension that Descartes had to contend with in metaphysics. In mathematics, certain polemics were born as well from the fact that the opponent stopped to consider specific cases instead of using general solutions. And the very errors of Cartesian physics are due more to the abuses of abstract systematization than to recourse to figured representations to elucidate phenomena" (175).

19. Cahné, 96.

20. Quintilian *Institutio oratoria* 6.2.29–31.

21. On the intellectual emotions, see Rodis-Lewis, *L'Individualité*, 218–28, where all the key Cartesian texts treating this issue are discussed.

22. François Ogier, in Jean-Louis Guez de Balzac, *Oeuvres* 2:149.

Notes to Chapter 4

1. Antoine Arnauld and Pierre Nicole, *La Logique, ou l'art de penser*, ed. Pierre Clair and Fr. Girbal (Paris; PUF, 1965), 29. All references to the *Logique* are from this edition. The *Grammaire générale* by Antoine Arnauld and Claude Lancelot, is cited from Herbert E. Brekle's facsimile edition of the 1676 text (Stuttgart: Friedrich Frommann, 1966). Other references to Arnauld's works are from the *OEuvres de Messire Antoine Arnauld*, 43 vols. (Paris-Lausanne, 1779; rpt. Brussels: Culture et civilisation, 1967).

2. Hugh M. Davidson, *Audience, Words, and Art* (Columbus: Ohio State University Press, 1965), 57–108. Davidson confronts the narrow view of rhetoric of the Port-Royalists with more robust traditions represented by Aristotle, Cicero, and Quintilian.

3. Sara E. Melzer, *Discourses of the Fall* (Berkeley: University of California Press, 1986), 18–26.

4. Louis Marin, *La Critique du discours* (Paris: Editions de Minuit, 1975), 362.

5. On Arnauld, see Leonardo Varga, *Il pensiero filosofico e scientifico di Antoine Arnauld*, 2 vols. (Milan: Pubblicazioni della Università Cattolica del Sacro Cuore, 1972).

6. Fumaroli, *L'Age de l'éloquence*, 624.

7. On Nicole see E. D. James, *Pierre Nicole, Jansenist and Humanist* (The Hague: Nijhoff, 1972).

8. On Cartesian elements in the *Grammaire* and on the respective contribution of Arnauld and Lancelot, see Roland Donzé, *La Grammaire générale et raisonnée de Port-Royal*, 2nd ed. (Berne: Editions Francke, 1971), 25–34.

9. On the *Nouveaux Eléments de géométrie* see Varga, 1:246–75.

10. The best recent review of the question is found in Henri Gouhier's *Cartésianisme et augustinisme au XVIIe siècle* (Paris: Vrin, 1978), 123–33.

11. For an extensive treatment of the probable in relation to history in the wake of Descartes' rule of self-evidence see Carlo Borghero, *La Certezza e la Storia—Cartesianesimo, Pirronismo e Conoscenza storica* (Milan: Franco Angeli, 1983). On Arnauld, 100–24.

12. Ian Hacking, *The Emergence of Probability: A Philosophical Study of Early Ideas about Probability, Induction, and Statistical Inference* (Cambridge: Cambridge University Press, 1975), 25.

13. For example, see Hans Aarsleff, "The History of Linguistics and Professor Chomsky," *Language* 46 (1970):570–85.

14. W. Keith Percival, "On the Non-existence of Cartesian Linguistics," in *Cartesian Studies*, ed. R. J. Butler (Oxford: Blackwell, 1972), 144.

15. André Robinet, *Le Langage à l'âge classique* (Paris: Klincksieck, 1978), 79.

16. *La Grammaire*, 153.

17. Melzer, 2–12.

18. Hugh M. Davidson, *Blaise Pascal* (Boston: Twayne Publishers, 1983), 102.

19. The best comprehensive discussion of Pascal's psychological vocabulary taking into account previous criticism is Buford Norman's *Portraits of Thought: Knowledge, Methods, and Styles in Pascal* (Columbus: Ohio State University Press, 1988), 3–62.

20. Blaise Pascal, *OEuvres complètes*, ed. Louis Lafuma (Paris: Seuil, 1963), 349. When a quotation is taken from the *Pensées* I give Lafuma's number for the fragment, as well as the page on which it appears (e.g., Pascal, L. 821:604).

21. Jean Mesnard's article "Universalité de Pascal," in *Méthodes chez Pascal* (Paris: PUF, 1979), 335–56, is the most useful of many excellent discussions of the role of "principes" in Pascal's methods of demonstration.

22. Pascal, 355–56.

23. "The principles are palpable but removed from common usage so that one has difficulty turning the head in that direction for lack of practice: but once one turns toward them, one sees these principles fully; and one would have to have a mind that was completely false to reason poorly on principles so obvious that it is almost impossible for them to slip away" ("Les principes sont palpables mais éloignés de l'usage commun de sorte qu'on a peine à tourner la tête de ce côté-là, manque d'habitude: mais pour peu qu'on l'y tourne, on voit les principes à plein; et il faudrait avoir tout à fait l'esprit faux pour mal raisonner sur des principes si gros qu'il est presque impossible qu'ils échappent" [Pascal, L. 512:576]).

24. "The principles are in common usage and before the eyes of everyone. . . . [I]t is only a question of having good sight, but it must be good: because the principles are so subtle and in such great number that is almost impossible that some do not slip away" ("Les principes sont dans l'usage commun et devant les yeux de tout le monde. . . . [I]l

n'est question que d'avoir bonne vue, mais il faut l'avoir bonne: car les principes sont si déliés et en si grand nombre, qu'il est presque impossible qu'il n'en échappe" [Pascal, L. 512:576]).

25. Pascal, L. 512:576.

26. Pascal, L. 574:582.

27. Pascal, L. 93:511.

28. Pascal, L. 887:615.

29. Pascal, L. 298:539.

30. Pascal, 349.

31. On this point see Gilbert Chinard's "Pascal et l'Embrazement de Londres,'" in *En lisant Pascal* (Geneva: Droz, 1948), 29.

32. For a comparison of Descartes, Pascal, and Nicole on the role of reason in apologetics see James, 72–73. "Nicole's belief in the possibility of rational proofs of these fundamental dogmas does not merely reflect a more rationalistic turn of mind, it also manifests a greater faith in the universality of divine aid" (72).

33. On this point see Louis Cognet's discussion of the attitude of Arnauld and Nicole to Pascal in his "Le Jugement de Port-Royal sur Pascal," in *Blaise Pascal: l'homme et l'oeuvre* (Paris: Editions de Minuit, 1956), 11–45. Cognet speaks of their reticence and points both to their lack of interest in the *Pensées* at the time of Pascal's death and to the editorial changes they made for the Port-Royal edition.

34. Pierre Kuentz, "Le 'rhétorique' ou la mise à l'écart," *Communications* 16 (1970):146.

35. Nicole was later to deal with many of these issues in his *Essais de morale* (Paris, 1733–71; rpt. Geneva: Slatkine, 1971), which contains many references to rhetoric. See, for example, the "Traité des moyens de conserver la paix avec les hommes," "L'Education d'un prince," or "Des Moyens de profiter des mauvais sermons."

36. *La Grammaire*, 158–60.

Notes to Chapter 5

1. Nicolas Malebranche, *OEuvres complètes*, ed. André Robinet *et al* (Paris: Vrin, 1958–67), 1:320. All citations will be from this edition.

2. Bernard Tocanne, *L'Idée de nature en France dans la seconde moitié du XVIIe siècle* (Paris: Klincksieck, 1978), 436. Tocanne provides one of the best overviews of the quarrels concerning rhetoric at the end of the century. Peter France, 29.

The following articles deal with rhetorical issues in Malebranche: Jacques Roger, "L'expression littéraire chez Malebranche," in *Journées*

Malebranche: *l'homme et l'oeuvre* (Paris: Vrin, 1967), 39–73, treats his style more than his theory of persuasion, but comments in the discussion that followed Roger's talk by two of the most prominent Malebranche scholars are particularly insightful: for Martial Gueroult, "[T]he functioning of eloquence would be for Malebranche the implementation of certain corporal mechanisms by which God, while impressing a concept in the intellect of the listener by virtue of his attention, imposes it at the same time in the listener's soul on the occasion of certain modifications of his body provoked by the orator so that affective sentiments accompany the pure perceptions" (69); for André Robinet, "One finds there this ambiguity of speech which expresses itself at the same time in two ways in the theological and philosophical perspective of Malebranche himself: through the Incarnation on the one hand and through the Eternal Wisdom on the other to which Reason is directly linked. But as long as this relation is not active in the listener, it is evident that the only means of making it come to the speaker is to use persuasion and didactic means; when persuasion has played enough of its hand, at that moment, one can apply in some manner the *a priori* proofs" (67–68).

Jean-Louis Chrétien, "L'Obliquité humaine et l'obliquité divine dans les *Conversations chrétiennes* de Malebranche," *Etudes philosophiques* (1980): 399–413. Jacques Croizer, "Les Voies de son Maître, à propos des *Conversations chrétiennes* de Malebranche," *Communications* 30 (1979): 223–34. Finally, Pierre Blanchard's *L'Attention à Dieu selon Malebranche, méthode et doctrine* (Paris: Desclée de Brouwer, 1956) contains an excellent chapter on communication, "L'Attention aux autres," 123–39.

The best introduction in English to Malebranche is in Charles J. McCracken, *Malebranche and British Philosophy* (Oxford: Clarendon Press, 1983), whose introductory chapters explain Malebranche's epistemological system with admirable lucidity.

3. Quoted in the *OEuvres complètes* 18:46. For commentary on this episode see Henri Gouhier, *La Vocation de Malebranche* (Paris: Vrin, 1926), 55–74.

4. Ferdinand Alquié, *Le Cartésianisme de Malebranche* (Paris: Vrin, 1974), 487. On the scientific work of Malebranche see André Robinet, *Malebranche et l'Académie des sciences, l'oeuvre scientifique, 1674–1715* (Paris: Vrin, 1970).

5. See Gouhier, *La Vocation de Malebranche*, 56–62; for a more recent appraisal, see Gouhier's *Cartésianisme et augustinisme au XVIIe siècle*, 52–58.

6. André Robinet, "Malebranche," in *Histoire de la philosophie*, ed. Yvon Belaval (Paris: Gallimard, 1973), 2:515. This article summarizes Robinet's presentation of the evolution of Malebranche's thought found

in *Système et existence dans l'oeuvre de Malebranche* (Paris: Vrin, 1965). Robinet traces the development from an early period marked by the influence of Descartes and Arnauld ("under the sign of the hidden God") up to 1677, through the mature system of 1677–1695 ("God revealed in the Wisdom Order") to a post-1695 late philosophy ("blossoming of the order of justice"). My own presentation deals primarily with texts from the first two periods.

7. On the *Traité* as the keystone of the mature thought of Malebranche, see the introduction to Ginette Dreyfus' critical edition, *Le Traité de la nature et de la grâce*, (Paris: Vrin, 1958), 7–47.

8. See Gouhier's commentary on the text in the *Notae in programma quoddam* where Descartes distinguishes these three domains: one reserved for faith, one reserved for reason, and a mixed area, in *La Pensée religieuse de Descartes*, 2nd ed. (1924; rpt. Paris: Vrin, 1972), 213–33.

9. See Gouhier, *La Vocation*, 162.

10. Etienne Gilson, *Introduction à l'étude de saint Augustin*, 2nd ed. (Paris: Vrin, 1982), 318.

11. See Gouhier, *La Vocation*, 145.

12. Alquié, *Le Cartésianisme de Malebranche*, 429.

13. Gouhier, *La Vocation*, 163.

14. Malebranche distinguishes two kinds of grace, the grace of light and the grace of sentiment. Only the second is most properly the grace of Jesus Christ who merited it by his death in order to counteract the effects of the Fall. The grace of light is the grace of the Creator and existed before original sin. Nevertheless, since God owes mankind nothing after Adam's sin, even this light can be considered a form of grace, especially when it illuminates matters touching on salvation (5:104–5).

15. Pascal, L. 821:604.

16. Pascal, L. 44:504–5.

17. For discussions of Malebranche's theory of language, see Ginette Dreyfus, "Le fondement du langage dans la philosophie de Malebranche", in *Le Langage, Actes du XIIIᵉ Congrès des sociétés de philosophie de langue française* (Neuchâtel: A la baconnière, 1966), 137–42; and André Robinet, *Le Langage à l'âge classique*, 162–64.

18. Robinet in the discussion following Jacques Roger's talk in *Journées Malebranche*, 67.

19. In his *La Philosophie de Malebranche*, 2nd ed. (1926; rpt. Paris: Vrin, 1948), Henri Gouhier stresses Martin's role as an intermediary between Augustine and Malebranche (284). Readers of Martin's five slender volumes first published between 1653 and 1658 would find a convergence between the extracts of Augustine and Descartes' philosophy. However, Gouhier insists that such readers did not so much find

a "cartesianized Augustinianism" as "the author of a work where we see how Augustianism, because of its anti-Aristotlianism, meets and annexes certain theses of Cartesian philosophy," Gouhier, *Cartésianisme et augustinisme*, 98.

See Marcia L. Colish on "Functions of Redeemed Speech" in *The Mirror of Language: A Study in the Medieval Theory of Knowledge* (New Haven: Yale University Press, 1968), 45–67, for an analysis of Augustine's theory of words as signs in relation to his Incarnational theology.

20. Blanchard, 11–12.

21. Blanchard, 27–43. On attention, see also the notes in the edition by Dreyfus of the *Traité*, whose analysis is somewhat different. She perceives a conflict between the two notions of attention. The first, as natural prayer, reflects the point of view of God; the second, as a concentration of the understanding by the will, represents the human psychological perspective, 288–90. Geneviève Rodis-Lewis also treats this issue in *Nicolas Malebranche* (Paris: PUF, 1963), 238–42.

22. On the Incarnation as a rhetorical act, see also 3:146–47; 4:112; 12–13:121.

23. Jacques-Bénigne Bossuet, *OEuvres*, ed. B. Vélat and Yvonne Champailler (Paris: Gallimard, 1961), 355.

24. Robinet, *Le Langage à l'âge classique*, 165.

25. Blanchard, 27.

Notes to Chapter 6

1. Biographical information on Lamy is taken from François Girbal, *Bernard Lamy, Etude biographique et bibliographique* (Paris: PUF, 1964).

2. In *Bernard Lamy*, Girbal points to a letter of Mascaron published in the 1715 edition that indicates that Malebranche had read and approved a manuscript version of the text and passed it on to Mascaron, 22. André Robinet tentatively dates the letter to 1671 in vol. 18 of the *OEuvres complètes* of Malebranche, 60.

3. Malebranche is quoted by Desmolets as writing in a letter, "If you do not have the Art of Speaking, your library is defective; you lack a very choice book, an excellent one in every respect" ("Si tibi deest ars dicendi, manca est tua bibliotheca, deest tibi liber exquisitissimus omnibusque suis numeris absolutus" [*OEuvres complètes*, 18:61]).

4. Michel Charles, *Rhétorique de la lecture* (Paris: Seuil, 1977), 160–61. Charles' chapter on Lamy, "Une théorie du discours," 155–84, is an excellent overview stressing Lamy's failure to resolve the tensions within his theory.

5. Ulrich Ricken, *Grammaire et philosophie au siècle des lumières* (Lille: Publications de l'Université de Lille III, 1978), 60. Ricken ably links his principal topic, the controversies over "natural" word order, to important rhetorical issues like the role of the imagination and emotions and to the larger philosophical issues of rationalism and sensationalism.

6. Jean-Paul Sermain, *Rhétorique et roman au dix-huitième siècle*, Studies on Voltaire, no. 233 (Oxford: The Voltaire Foundation, 1985):16. Sermain provides a concise synthesis of rhetorical theory from Lamy to Diderot in which he alludes to almost every rhetorician of note, 5–33.

7. Bernard Lamy, *De l'Art de parler* (Paris: Pralard, 1676; British and Continental Rhetoric and Elocution, no. 123), 277.

I have consulted the editions that mark the transitions between states (1675, 1678, 1688, 1701, 1715). However, since within each of the five states the text seems to have remained substantially the same, I quote from 1676 and 1699 facsimile or microform editions that are widely accessible, instead of the 1675 and 1688 editions.

De l'Art de parler (Paris: Pralard, 1676; British and Continental Rhetoric and Elocution, no. 123). The 1676 text is also available in facsimile in *De l'Art de parler/Kunst zu reden*, ed. Rudolf Behrens (Munich: Wilhelm Fink Verlag, 1980).

De l'Art de parler (Paris: Pralard, 1678).

La Rhétorique ou l'art de parler (Amsterdam: Paul Marret, 1699; rpt. Brighton: Sussex Reprints, 1969).

La Rhétorique ou l'art de parler (Paris: Pépié, 1701).

La Rhétorique ou l'art de parler (Paris: Debats, 1715).

Because I stress the evolution of Lamy's thought, rather than cite exclusively from the definitive 1715 edition, I quote from an edition within the state in which a passage first appeared.

8. Girbal, 21.

9. Girbal, 21.

10. Girbal, 28.

11. Girbal, 66–67.

12. Geneviève Rodis-Lewis, "Un Théoricien du langage au XVIIe siècle: Bernard Lamy," *Le Français moderne* 36 (1968):23. For a more recent discussion of the various editions see Bernard Louis Crampé, "Pour une réédition de *L'Art de parler*," in his dissertation, "Linguistique et rhétorique cartésiennes. *L'Art de parler* de Bernard Lamy," (NYU, 1984), 191–95.

13. John T. Harwood reproduces the 1676 anonymous London translation in *The Rhetorics of Thomas Hobbes and Bernard Lamy* (Carbondale: Southern Illinois University Press, 1986). This 1676 translation was reprinted in 1696 and 1708. See Harwood, xiii.

Harwood's introduction provides the best introduction to date of Lamy in English. He rightly takes Wilbur Samuel Howell's *Eighteenth-Century British Logic and Rhetoric* (Princeton: Princeton University Press, 1971) to task for unnecessarily downplaying Lamy's originality at the expense of Howell's favorite, Fénelon (132). Harwood proceeds to demonstrate how Lamy synthesizes "both ancient and modern theories of communication" (133) with a particularly able account of the influence of classical rhetoricians, although he tends to neglect recent commentators like Charles or Ricken.

14. *OEuvres de Messire Antoine Arnauld,* 42:8. Compare Malebranche's similar comments in *La Recherche*: "one must not completely scorn probabilities because it often happens that several joined together have as much convincing force as very evident demonstrations. One finds an infinity of examples in physics and ethics" ("il ne faut pas mépriser absolument les vraisemblances, parce qu'il arrive ordinairement que plusieurs jointes ensemble, ont autant de force pour convaincre que des démonstrations très évidentes. Il s'en trouve une infinité d'exemples dans la Physique et dans la Morale" [1:64]).

15. Cp. "The truths of geometry depend on a small number of principles: those that orators undertake to prove can only be elucidated by a great number of circumstances that strengthen each other and which would not be convincing detached from each other" ("Les vérités de la Géométrie dépendent d'un petit nombre de principes: celles que les Orateurs entreprennent de prouver ne peuvent être éclaircies que par un grand nombre de circonstances qui se fortifient, et qui ne seraient pas capables de convaincre étant détachées les unes des autres" [1676:331]).

16. Here Lamy echoes Arnauld and Nicole's description of perfect eloquence in the *Logique de Port-Royal:* "The chief thing consists in conceiving energetically the subject and expressing it so that a vivid and luminous image is conveyed to the minds of the listeners which does not only present this topic completely naked but accompanied by the movements with which it was conceived" ("La principale consiste à concevoir fortement les choses, et à les exprimer en sorte qu'on en porte dans l'esprit des auditeurs une image vive et lumineuse, qui ne présente pas seulement ces choses toutes nues, mais aussi les mouvements avec lesquels on les conçoit" [276]).

17. The first three of these new chapters (6,7,8) provide in abridged form material that Lamy inserted under the title "L'Idée de la logique," in the 1694 edition of the *Entretiens sur les sciences*, ed. François Girbal and Pierre Clair (Paris: PUF, 1966). In chapters 1 and 2 of this text that Girbal and Clair call "a sort of Malebranchian introduction to the reading of *L'Art de penser*" (6), Lamy develops the ideas on attention, the divine

origin of the inclinations, and *vraisemblance* (including the same example of mistaken identity of the Roman Metius) that appear in the new chapters of *L'Art de parler*.

18. Davidson, *Blaise Pascal*, 355–359. Hugh M. Davidson offers an excellent discussion of Pascal on rhetoric in "Pascal's Art of Persuasion," *Renaissance Eloquence*, ed. James Murphy (Berkeley: University of California Press, 1983), 292–300. Kathleen M. Jamieson argues that the influence on Lamy of Pascal is stronger than that of Descartes in "Pascal vs. Descartes: A Clash over Rhetoric in the Seventeenth Century," *Communication Monographs* 43 (1976):44–50.

19. Pascal, 356.

20. Pascal, 356.

21. Pascal, 355.

22. Bernard Lamy, *Nouvelles réflexions sur l'art poétique* (Paris: Pralard, 1678; rpt. Geneva: Slatkine, 1973), 64–65.

23. Like Malebranche, who devoted the entire fourth book of *La Recherche* to the inclinations, Lamy sees them as aspects of the will's fundamental orientation toward God. However, Lamy's treatment of them does not merely apply Malebranche's analysis to rhetoric. For example, while Lamy mentions many of the specific inclinations that Malebranche discusses such as toward grandeur (1676: 256) or towards sociability (1678: 81), he does not make use of Malebranche's grouping of all inclinations under three headings directed toward the good in general, *amour-propre*, or friendship.

In the discussion following his paper, "Bernard Lamy et René Rapin: deux conceptions de la culture," Michel Le Guern stresses Lamy's independence: "As for Lamy, one must not speak of him as a simple popularizer of the thought of Descartes; in fact, he is responsible for advancing considerably this current of thought. He is not a popularizer of Malebranche either. Malebranche is not the master and Lamy the pupil. . . . If one examines the chronology of the editions, one can establish that when Malebranche revised *La Recherche*, he took into account the work of Lamy" [*De la mort de Colbert à la Révocation*, Actes du 16e Colloque du C.R.M.17, (Marseille, 1984), 87]. See also his "La Méthode dans *La Rhétorique ou l'art de parler* de Bernard Lamy," in *Grammaire et méthode au XVIIe siècle*, ed. Pierre Swiggers (Leuven: Peeters, 1984), 49–67.

24. Douglas Ehninger, in "Bernard Lamy's *L'Art de parler:* A Critical Analysis," *The Quarterly Journal of Speech* 32 (1946): 429–34, sees Lamy as allying "himself more closely with our modern theories of motivation than with Aristotle's treatment" of invention (434).

25. "Eloquence would not be mistress of the heart, and it would

encounter strong resistance if it did not attack the heart with other arms than those of truth. The passions are the motor force of the soul: they make it act" ("L'éloquence ne serait donc pas la maîtresse des coeurs, et elle y trouverait une forte résistance, si elle ne les attaquait par d'autres armes que celles de la vérité. Les passions sont les ressorts de l'âme: ce sont elles qui la font agir" [1676:113]).

26. Lamy, *Entretiens*, 133.

27. Lamy, *Entretiens*, 134.

28. Lamy, *Nouvelles réflexions*, 85–98.

29. Rudolf Behrens discusses this aspect of the figures in his substantial chapter on Lamy in *Problematische Rhetorik: Studien zur französischen Theoriebildung der Affektrhetorik zwischen Cartesianismus und Frühaufklärung* (Munich: Wilhelm Fink Verlag, 1982), 115–60.

30. Ricken, 62–66.

31. For a discussion of these terms in the Renaissance, see Terence Cave, "*Enargeia:* Erasmus and the Rhetoric of Presence in the Sixteenth Century," *Esprit Créateur* 16 (1976):5–19.

32. Dennis R. Bormann, "*Enargeia:* A Concept for All Seasons," *Transactions of the Nebraska Academy of Sciences* 4 (1977):155–59.

33. Quintilian *Institutio oratoria* 6.2.32.

34. Description is the portrayal of absent objects as absent, while hypotyposis portrays them as present; distribution is the enumeration of the parts of an object of the passions.

35. Lamy, *Entretiens*, 142–43.

Notes to Chapter 7

1. Charles Perrault, *Parallèle des anciens et des modernes en ce qui regarde les arts et les sciences,* ed. H. R. Jauss (Paris, 1688–97; rpt. Munich: Eidos Verlag, 1964), 197.

2. Perrault, 194.

3. Bernard Le Bovier de Fontenelle, "Préface sur l'utilité des mathématiques", in *OEuvres de Fontenelle* (Paris: Salmon, 1825), 1:54.

4. Antoine Houdar de la Motte, "Discours sur la poésie en général," in *OEuvres complètes* (Paris: 1754; rpt. Geneva: Slatkine, 1970) 1:31.

5. Goibaud Dubois, *Sermons de Saint Augustin* (Paris, 1694), xiii-xvii.

6. Although Dubois' attack on the sensible does echo a prominent theme of Malebranche, it is unlikely that he was following a Malebranchian line. None of Dubois' previous writings show any strong influence of Malebranche or even Descartes; that they seem Malebranchian is an indication of the extent to which such ideas had become associated with

Cartesianism at the end of the century. Nor is it likely that Arnauld's refuation of Dubois was a covert continuation of his polemic with Malebranche. Dubois, in fact, was a friend of Arnauld whom the Jansenist consulted regularly, and Arnauld was never one to shrink from calling to task even friends and collaborators who had fallen into error, as can be seen from his critiques of Nicole's system of general grace. However, François Lamy did renew Dubois' attack along more Cartesian lines. See Arnaldo Pizzorusso, *Theorie letterarie in Francia* (Pisa: Nistri-Lischi, 1968), 179–221.

7. Dubois, xxiii-xxiv.

8. Dubois, xlvii.

9. Dubois, xlii.

10. See for example, the *Rhetorica ad Alexandrum* 29.1436b; Cicero *De Inventione*, 1.16 22–23; *De Partitione oratoria* 8.28–30.

11. For a recent collection of approaches current among psychologists, see *Varieties of Attention*, ed. Raja Parasuraman and D. R. Davies, (New York: Academic Press, 1984).

12. Winston L. Brembeck and William S. Howell, *Persuasion: A Means of Social Influence*, 2nd ed. (Englewood Cliffs, New Jersey: Prentice Hall, 1976), 280.

13. James Albert Winans, *Public Speaking* (New York: Century, 1926), 194.

14. Winans, 192.

15. Gabaude, 1:219.

16. Arnauld, "Réflexions sur l'éloquence des prédicateurs," *OEuvres*, 42:373–75, 381.

17. Lamy, *Entretiens*, 102.

18. Chaïm Perelman, *L'Empire rhétorique* (Paris: Vrin, 1977), 175.

References

Primary Sources

Arnauld, Antoine. *OEuvres de Messire Antoine Arnauld.* 43 vols. Paris-Lausanne, 1779; Reprint. Brussels: Culture et civilisation, 1967.

Arnauld, Antoine and Claude Lancelot. *Grammaire générale.* Edited by Herbert E. Brekle. Stuttgart: Friedrich Frommann, 1966.

Arnauld, Antoine and Pierre Nicole. *La Logique, ou l'art de penser.* Edited by Pierre Clair and Fr. Girbal. Paris: PUF, 1965.

Balzac, Jean-Louis Guez de. *OEuvres de J.-L. Guez Sieur de Balzac.* Edited by L. Moreau. 2 vols. Paris: Jacques Lecoffre, 1854.

———. *OEuvres de Monsieur de Balzac.* Edited by Valentin Conrart. 2 vols. Paris: Louis Billaine, 1665; Reprint. Geneva: Slatkine, 1971.

———. *Les Premières Lettres de Guez de Balzac.* Edited by H. Bibas and K. T. Butler. 2 vols. Paris: Droz, 1933–34.

Bossuet, Jacques-Bénigne. *OEuvres.* Edited by B. Vélat and Yvonne Champailler. Paris: Gallimard, 1961.

Descartes, René. *Correspondance.* Edited by Charles Adam and G. Milhaud. 8 vols. Paris: Alcan-PUF, 1936–56.

———. *OEuvres de Descartes.* Edited by Charles Adam and Paul Tannery. 11 vols. Paris: Léopold Cerf, 1897–1913.

———. *OEuvres philosophiques.* Edited by Ferdinand Alquié. 3 vols. Paris: Garnier, 1963–73.

———. "Texte original et traduction française d'un inédit de Descartes: la *dédicace du placard de licence en droit soutenue par Descartes le 21 décembre 1616 à Poitiers*," Edited by Jean-Robert Armogathe and Vincent Carraud. *Bulletin cartésien* in *Archives de philosophie* 50 (1987):1–4.

———. *The Treatise of Man.* Edited and Translated by Thomas S. Hall. Cambridge: Harvard University Press, 1972.

Dubois, Goibaud. *Sermons de Saint Augustin.* Paris, 1694.

Fontenelle, Bernard Le Bovier de. *OEuvres de Fontenelle.* 5 vols. Paris: Salmon, 1825.

La Motte, Antoine Houdar de. *OEuvres complètes.* 2 vols. Paris: 1754; Reprint. Geneva: Slatkine, 1970.

Lamy, Bernard. *De l'Art de parler*. Paris: Pralard, 1676; British and Continental Rhetoric and Elocution, No. 123.

———. *De l'Art de parler/Kunst zu reden*. 1676; Reprint. Edited by Rudolf Behrens. Munich: Wilhelm Fink Verlag, 1980.

———. *De l'Art de parler*. Paris: Pralard, 1678.

———. *Entretiens sur les sciences*. Edited by François Girbal and Pierre Clair. Paris: PUF, 1966.

———. *Nouvelles réflexions sur l'art poétique*. Paris: Pralard, 1678; Reprint. Geneva: Slatkine, 1973.

———. *The Rhetorics of Thomas Hobbes and Bernard Lamy*. Edited by John T. Harwood. Carbondale: Southern Illinois University Press, 1986.

———. *La Rhétorique ou l'art de parler*. Amsterdam: Paul Marret, 1699; Reprint. Brighton: Sussex Reprints, 1969.

———. *La Rhétorique ou l'art de parler*. Paris: Pépié, 1701.

———. *La Rhétorique ou l'art de parler*. Paris: Debats, 1715.

Malebranche, Nicolas. *OEuvres complètes*. Edited by André Robinet *et al.* 20 vols. Paris: Vrin, 1958–67.

———. *Le Traité de la nature et de la grâce*. Edited by Ginette Dreyfus. Paris: Vrin, 1958.

Nicole, Pierre. *Essais de morale*. Paris, 1733–71; Reprint. Geneva: Slatkine, 1971.

Ogier, François. *Apologie pour Monsieur de Balzac*. Edited by Jean Jehasse. Saint-Etienne: Publications de l'Université de Saint-Etienne, 1977.

Pascal, Blaise. *OEuvres complètes*. Edited by Louis Lafuma. Paris: Seuil, 1963.

Perrault, Charles. *Parallèle des anciens et des modernes en ce qui regarde les arts et les sciences*. Edited by H. R. Jauss. Paris, 1688–97; Reprint. Munich: Eidos Verlag, 1964.

Secondary Sources

Aarsleff, Hans. "The History of Linguistics and Professor Chomsky." *Language* 46 (1970):570–85.

Alquié, Ferdinand. *Le Cartésianisme de Malebranche*. Paris: Vrin, 1974.

———. *La Découverte métaphysique de l'homme chez Descartes*. 2d ed. Paris: PUF, 1966.

Arnhart, Larry. *Aristotle on Political Reasoning: A Commentary on the "Rhetoric."* Dekalb: Northern Illinois University Press, 1981.

Beck, L. J. *The Method of Descartes.* Oxford: Clarendon Press, 1952.

Behrens, Rudolf. *Problematische Rhetorik: Studien zur französischen Theorie-bildung der Affektrhetorik zwischen Cartesianismus und Frühaufklärung.* Munichen: Wilhelm Fink Verlag, 1982.

Blanchard, Pierre. *L'Attention à Dieu selon Malebranche, méthode et doctrine.* Paris: Desclée de Brouwer, 1956.

Borgerhoff, E. B. O. *The Freedom of French Classicism.* Princeton: Princeton University Press, 1950.

Borghero, Carlo. *La Certezza e la Storia—Cartesianesimo, Pirronismo e Conoscenza storica.* Milan: Franco Angeli, 1983.

Bormann, Dennis R. "*Enargeia:* A Concept for All Seasons." *Transactions of the Nebraska Academy of Sciences* 4 (1977):155–59.

Bray, René. *La Formation de la doctrine classique.* Paris: Payot, 1931.

Brembeck, Winston L., and William S. Howell. *Persuasion: A Means of Social Influence.* 2d ed. Englewood Cliffs, New Jersey: Prentice Hall, 1976.

Brooks, H. Frank. "Guez de Balzac, Eloquence, and the Life of the Spirit." *Esprit créateur* 15 (1975):59–78.

Cahné, Pierre-Alain. *Un Autre Descartes: le philosophe et son langage.* Paris: Vrin, 1980.

Cave, Terence. "*Enargeia:* Erasmus and the Rhetoric of Presence in the Sixteenth Century." *Esprit Créateur* 16 (1976):5–19.

Charles, Michel. *Rhétorique de la lecture.* Paris: Seuil, 1977.

Chinard, Gilbert. *En lisant Pascal.* Geneva: Droz, 1948.

Chrétien, Jean-Louis. "L'Obliquité humaine et l'obliquité divine dans les *Conversations chrétiennes* de Malebranche." *Etudes philosophiques* (1980):399–413.

Cognet, Louis. "Le Jugement de Port-Royal sur Pascal." In *Blaise Pascal: l'homme et l'oeuvre,* 11–45. Paris: Editions de Minuit, 1959.

Cohen, Gustave. *Ecrivains français en Hollande dans la première moitié du XVIIe siècle.* Paris: Champion, 1920.

Colish, Marcia L. *The Mirror of Language: A Study in the Medieval Theory of Knowledge.* New Haven: Yale University Press, 1968.

Crampé, Bernard Louis. "Linguistique et rhétorique cartésiennes. *L'Art de parler* de Bernard Lamy." Dissertation, New York University, 1984.

Croizer, Jacques. "Les Voies de son Maître, à propos des *Conversations chrétiennes* de Malebranche." *Communications,* 30 (1979):223–34.

Croll, Morris W. *Style, Rhetoric, and Rhythm*. Princeton: Princeton University Press, 1966.

Davidson, Hugh M. *Audience, Words, and Art*. Columbus: Ohio State University Press, 1965.

———. *Blaise Pascal*. Boston: Twayne Publishers, 1983.

———. "The Decline of Rhetoric in Seventeenth-Century France." In *The History and Philosophy of Rhetoric and Political Discourse*, edited by Kenneth W. Thompson, 1:56–82. Lanham, Md: The University Press of America, 1987.

———. "Pascal's Art of Persuasion." In *Renaissance Eloquence* edited by James Murphy, 292–300. Berkeley: University of California Press, 1983.

Donzé, Roland. *La Grammaire générale et raisonnée de Port-Royal*. 2d ed. Berne: Editions Francke, 1971.

Dreyfus, Ginette. "Le fondement du langage dans la philosophie de Malebranche." In *Le Langage, Actes du XIIIᵉ Congrés des sociétés de philosophie de langue française*, 137–42. Neuchâtel: A la baconnière, 1966.

Ehninger, Douglas. "Bernard Lamy's *L'Art de parler:* A Critical Analysis." *The Quarterly Journal of Speech* 32 (1946):429–34.

Flores, Ralph. *The Rhetoric of Doubtful Authority: Deconstructive Readings of Self-Questioning Narratives, St. Augustine to Faulkner*. Ithaca: Cornell University Press, 1984.

France, Peter. *Rhetoric and Truth in France*. Oxford: Clarendon Press, 1972.

Fumaroli, Marc. *L'Age de l'éloquence: Rhétorique et "res literaria" de la Renaissance au seuil de l'époque classique*. Geneva: Droz, 1980.

———. "Ego Scriptor: rhétorique et philosophie dans le *Discours de la méthode*." In *Problématique et réception du Discours de la Méthode et des Essais*, edited by H. Méchoulan, 31–46. Paris: Vrin, 1988.

———. "Rhétorique et littérature française de la Renaissance et de l'époque classique." *Actes du XIe Congrès de l'Association Guillaume Budé*. 1:127–56. 2 vols. Paris: Belles Lettres, 1985.

Gabaude, Jean-Marc. *Liberté et raison: la liberté cartésienne et sa réfraction chez Spinoza et chez Leibniz*. 2 vols. Toulouse: Publications de la Faculté des Lettres et de Sciences humaines de Toulouse, 1970.

Gadoffre, Gilbert. "*Le Discours de la méthode* et l'histoire littéraire." *French Studies* 2 (1948):308–14.

Gaonkar, Dilip Parameshwar. "Deconstruction and Rhetorical Analysis: The Case of Paul de Man." *The Quarterly Journal of Speech* 73 (1987):482–98.

Gilson, Etienne. *Introduction à l'étude de saint Augustin.* 2d ed. Paris: Vrin, 1982.

Girbal, François. *Bernard Lamy, Etude biographique et bibliographique.* Paris: PUF, 1964.

Gouhier, Henri. *Cartésianisme et augustinisme au XVIIe siècle.* Paris: Vrin, 1978.

———. *La Pensée métaphysique de Descartes.* Paris: Vrin, 1962.

———. *La Pensée religieuse de Descartes.* 2d ed. 1924: Reprint. Paris: Vrin, 1972.

———. *La Philosophie de Malebranche.* 2d ed. 1926; Reprint. Paris: Vrin, 1948.

———. *Les Premières pensées de Descartes—contribution à⁻ l'histoire de l'anti-renaissance.* Paris: Vrin, 1958.

———. "Le Refus du symbolisme dans l'humanisme cartésien." *Archivio de filosofia* (1958), 68.

———. *La Vocation de Malebranche.* Paris: Vrin, 1926.

Grassi, Ernesto. *Rhetoric as Philosophy: The Humanist Tradition.* University Park: The Pennsylvania State University Press, 1980.

Gray, Hanna H. "Renaissance Humanism: The Pursuit of Eloquence." In *Renaissance Essays,* edited by P. O. Kristeller and P. P. Wiener, 199–216. New York: Harper Torchbooks, 1968.

Gueroult, Martial. *Descartes.* 2d ed. 2 vols. 1953; Reprint. Paris: Aubier, 1968.

Guillaumie, Gaston. *J.-L. Guez de Balzac et la prose française.* Paris: Auguste Picard, 1927.

Hacking, Ian. *The Emergence of Probability: A Philosophical Study of Early Ideas about Probability, Induction, and Statistical Inference.* Cambridge: Cambridge University Press, 1975.

Howell, Wilbur Samuel. *Eighteenth-Century British Logic and Rhetoric.* Princeton: Princeton University Press, 1971.

James, E. D. *Pierre Nicole, Jansenist and Humanist.* The Hague: Nijhoff, 1972.

Jamieson, Kathleen M. "Pascal vs. Descartes: A Clash over Rhetoric in the Seventeenth Century." *Communication Monographs* 43 (1976):44–50.

Jehasse, Jean. *Guez de Balzac et le génie romain.* Saint-Etienne: Publications de l'Université de Saint-Etienne, 1977.

Krantz, Emile. *Essai sur l'esthétique de Descartes.* Paris: Germier Baillière, 1882.

Kristeller, Paul O. *Renaissance Thought and Its Sources.* New York: Columbia University Press, 1979.

Kuentz, Pierre. "Le 'rhétorique' ou la mise à l'écart." *Communications* 16 (1970):143–57.

Lanson, Gustave. *L'Art de la prose.* Paris: Librairie des annales, 1908.

Laporte, Jean. *Le Rationalisme de Descartes.* Paris: PUF, 1945.

Le Guern, Michel. "Bernard Lamy et René Rapin: deux conceptions de la culture." In *De la mort de Colbert à la Révocation,* Actes du 16e Colloque du C.R.M. 17 Marseille, 1984, 72–88.

———. "La Méthode dans *La Rhétorique ou l'art de parler* de Bernard Lamy." In *Grammaire et Méthode au XVIIe siècle,* edited by Pierre Swiggers, 49–67. Leuven: Peeters, 1984.

Lyons, John D. "Rhétorique du discours cartésien." *Cahiers de littérature du XVIIe siècle* 8 (1986): 125–47.

Marin, Louis. *La Critique du discours.* Paris: Editions de Minuit, 1975.

McCracken, Charles J. *Malebranche and British Philosophy.* Oxford: Clarendon Press, 1983.

Melzer, Sara E. *Discourses of the Fall.* Berkeley: University of California Press, 1986.

Mesnard, Jean. "Universalité de Pascal." In *Méthodes chez Pascal,* 335–56. Paris: PUF, 1979.

Mooney, Michael. *Vico in the Tradition of Rhetoric.* Princeton: Princeton University Press, 1985.

Norman, Buford. *Portraits of Thought: Knowledge, Methods, and Styles in Pascal.* Columbus: Ohio State University Press, 1988.

Parasuraman, Raja, and D. R. Davies, eds. *Varieties of Attention.* New York: Academic Press, 1984.

Percival, W. Keith. "On the Non-existence of Cartesian Linguistics." In *Cartesian Studies,* edited by R. J. Butler 137–45. Oxford: Blackwell, 1972.

Perelman, Chaïm. *L'Empire rhétorique.* Paris: Vrin, 1977.

Perelman, Chaïm. and L. Olbrechts-Tyteca. *La Nouvelle Rhétorique: Traité de l'Argumentation.* Paris: PUF, 1958.

Pizzorusso, Arnaldo. *Teorie letterarie in Francia.* Pisa: Nistri-Lischi, 1968.

Prenant, L. "Le Sentiment d'évidence." *Revue philosophique de la France et de l'étranger* (1951).168–98.

Reiss, Timothy J. "Cartesian Discourse and Classical Ideology." *Diacritics* 6 (1976):19–27.

Ricken, Ulrich. *Grammaire et philosophie au siècle des lumières.* Lille: Publications de l'Université de Lille III, 1978.

Robinet, André. *Le Langage à l'âge classique.* Paris: Klincksieck, 1978.

―――. "Malebranche." In *Histoire de la philosophie.* edited by Yvon Belaval, 2:508–36. Paris: Gallimard, 1973.

―――. *Malebranche et l'Académie des sciences, l'oeuvre scientifique, 1674–1715.* Paris: Vrin, 1970.

―――. *Système et existence dans l'oeuvre de Malebranche.* Paris: Vrin, 1965.

Rodis-Lewis, Geneviève. "Cartesius." *Revue philosophique de la France et de l'étranger* 161 (1971): 209–20.

―――. *Descartes: Textes et débats.* Paris: Livre de poche, 1984.

―――. *L'Individualité selon Descartes.* Paris: Vrin, 1950.

―――. *Nicolas Malebranche.* Paris: PUF, 1963.

―――. "Un Théoricien du langage au XVIIe siècle: Bernard Lamy." *Le Français moderne* 36 (1968):19–50.

Roger, Jacques. "L'expression littéraire chez Malebranche." In *Journées Malebranche: L'Homme et l'oeuvre,* 39–73. Paris: Vrin, 1967.

Romanowski, Sylvie. *L'Illusion chez Descartes: la structure du discours cartésien.* Paris: Klincksieck, 1974.

Sainte-Beuve. *Port-Royal.* 3 vols. Paris: Gallimard, 1952.

Saisselin, Rémy. *The Rules of Reason and the Ruses of the Heart.* Cleveland: Case Western Reserve Univerity Press, 1970.

Seigel, Jerrold E. *Rhetoric and Philosophy in Renaissance Humanism.* Princeton: Princeton University Press, 1968.

Sermain, Jean-Paul. *Rhétorique et roman au dix-huitième siècle.* Studies on Voltaire, no. 233. Oxford: The Voltaire Foundation, 1985.

Spoerri, T. "La Puissance métaphorique de Descartes." In *Descartes,* 273–301. Paris: Editions de Minuit, 1957.

Sutcliffe, F. E. *Guez de Balzac et son temps—littérature et politique.* Paris: Nizet, 1959.

Tocanne, Bernard. *L'Idée de nature en France dans la seconde moitié du XVIIe siècle.* Paris: Klincksieck, 1978.

Varga, Leonardo. *Il pensiero filosofico e scientifico di Antoine Arnauld.* 2 vols. Milan: Pubblicazioni della Università Cattolica del Sacro Cuore, 1972.

Winans, James Albert. *Public Speaking.* New York: Century, 1926.

Youssef, Zobeidah. *Polémique et littérature chez Guez de Balzac.* Paris: Nizet, 1972.

Index

Thomas M. Carr, Jr., has been an Associate Professor since 1978 at the University of Nebraska-Lincoln, where he teaches French civilization and eighteenth-century literature

After receiving his B.A. in French from the Catholic University of America, he did graduate work at the University of Wisconsin-Madison, spending 1967–68 in Paris on a Fulbright Fellowship. He received his Ph.D. in 1972.

He has published articles on rhetorical issues in Voltaire's philosophic tragedies and *contes*, on Malebranche's theory of rhetoric, and on Marivaux. He has also written a series of articles treating the use of film and the visual arts in the teaching of French civilization.

He is currently preparing a critical edition and commentary of Antoine Arnauld's *Réflexions sur l'éloquence* (1695). The edition will also make avaliable other texts by Goibaud Dubois and François Lamy related to the quarrel over the proper balance between reason and the imagination in preaching.